# Study Guide

# FINANCIAL ACCOUNTING
## *THE IMPACT ON DECISION MAKERS*

## THIRD EDITION

# Study Guide

MARY NISBET
*University of California, Santa Barbara*

COBY HARMON
*University of California, Santa Barbara*

# FINANCIAL ACCOUNTING
## *THE IMPACT ON DECISION MAKERS*

## THIRD EDITION

## GARY A. PORTER
*The University of Montana*

## CURTIS L. NORTON
*Northern Illinois University*

**Harcourt College Publishers**

Fort Worth   Philadelphia   San Diego   New York   Orlando   Austin   San Antonio
Toronto   Montreal   London   Sydney   Tokyo

ISBN: 0-03-029352-9

Portions of this work were published in previous editions.

*Address for Domestic Orders*
Harcourt, Inc., 6277 Sea Harbor Drive, Orlando, FL 32887-6777
800-782-4479

*Address for International Orders*
International Customer Service
Harcourt, Inc., 6277 Sea Harbor Drive, Orlando, FL 32887-6777
407-345-3800
(fax) 407-345-4060
(e-mail) hbintl@harcourt.com

*Address for Editorial Correspondence*
Harcourt College Publishers, 301 Commerce Street, Suite 3700, Fort Worth, TX 76102

*Web Site Address*
http://www.harcourtcollege.com

Printed in the United States of America

0  1  2  3  4  5  6  7  8  9    202    9  8  7  6  5  4  3  2  1

# Contents

# Preface

This Study Guide is designed as a self-study aid for use with Gary Porter and Curtis Norton's text "Financial Accounting - The Impact on Decision Makers". The Study Guide will help you master the material in the text, since it expands the explanation and illustration of text material, and provides practice test questions and problems that you can use to test your understanding. For each chapter in the text, there is a corresponding chapter in the Study Guide containing each of the following components:

- An **introduction** that identifies the chapter's main focus, states the learning objectives of the chapter and highlights key text book exhibits.

- A **review of key concepts** that provides a comprehensive outline, keyed to learning objectives, of the material covered in the text chapter. As well as highlighting important material, the Study Guide illustrates particularly complex concepts with additional examples and exhibits. An innovation is the use of "Sixty Second Quiz!" boxes where you are encouraged to interpret and apply the preceding concepts.

- A **review of key terms** that gives a complete listing of new terms introduced in each chapter. Each term is defined and keyed to the relevant learning objective.

- **Practice test questions and problems** keyed to learning objective. These practice questions include 15 fill in the blanks questions, 15 true/false questions, 15 multiple choice questions and an average of four problems. Each chapter contains one problem that emphasizes critical thinking, and encourages you to apply what you have learned to a particular decision making situation.

- **Solutions** to test questions and problems that provide answers to all questions, explanations for all true/false questions and solutions to all problems.

The way you use the Study Guide will depend on your personal study habits and preferences. However, one possible approach is to first read the Study Guide's introduction. Then read each section of the text chapter followed by the corresponding section of the Study Guide's review of key concepts. The Study Guide will provide both a summary of what you have read in the text and additional explanatory problems and exhibits. You can reinforce your understanding of new words by using the review of key terms. The practice test questions and problems could then be tackled, using the answers and solutions provided to correct any mistakes and misunderstanding.

The Study Guide adopts the innovative approach of the Porter and Norton text by providing a conceptual introduction to financial accounting, while covering essential procedural material. This approach ensures that the needs of both accounting majors and non-majors are satisfied, since both a user focus and an adequate preparation for intermediate accounting are provided. Published financial statements are used throughout the Study Guide, particularly in problems highlighting decision making.

We must thank Jamie Yuen for her constructive, helpful and careful reviews. We must also thank our editor, Jennifer Yusin, who significantly improved the final product. Any remaining errors are, of course, our own.

Mary Nisbet, Coby Harmon
Santa Barbara
July 2000

# Getting Started in Business

This module provides you with a basic understanding of what business is, the types of organizations that engage in business, and the various activities they conduct. You will come to understand that business is the foundation on which accounting is based.

## Learning Objectives

**LO 1** Explain why financial information is important in making decisions.

**LO 2** Understand what business is about.

**LO 3** Distinguish among the forms of organization.

**LO 4** Describe the various types of business activity.

## Key Textbook Exhibits

**Exhibit GS-1** illustrates the various types of businesses and how they interact to provide goods and services. *Self-Test:* Does Walt Disney Company provide a product or service?

**Exhibit GS-2** illustrates the various forms of organization that exist in our economy. Note that the principal division is between those that are organized to earn a profit (business entities) and those that are not (nonbusiness entities). *Self-Test:* Who is the owner of the entities that are organized as a corporation?

**Exhibit GS-3** summarizes the key activities of a business. *Self-Test:* Are all three of these activities necessary for the success of a business?

## Review of Key Concepts

**LO 1** The financial implications of many decisions are critical. Both personal decisions (such as which school to attend, which job to accept, which apartment to rent) and business decisions (which products to sell, how and when to borrow money, whether to build a new factory) require financial information.

**LO 2** Business consists of all the activities necessary to provide the members of an economic system with goods and services. Some businesses produce or manufacture products, some distribute goods as wholesalers or retailers, and others engaged in activities that are service oriented.

**LO 3** **Business entities** are organized to make a profit. There are three main types:
- **Sole proprietorships** have a single owner, who often both owns and operates the business. The owner is ultimately responsible for any unpaid debts that the business incurs. Consequently, the business and its owner are not regarded as separate legal entities. However, financial statements are prepared for the business separate from its owner. The owner and the business are therefore separate accounting entities, but not

legal entities. This is an application of the **economic entity concept**, which requires that a single, identifiable unit of organization be accounted for in all situations.

• **Partnerships** are businesses owned by at least two people. The agreement between the partners is a statement of their financial rights in, and obligations to, the partnership. Again the partnership and the partners are separate accounting, but not legal, entities.

• **Corporations** are organizations that are distinctive because they are separate legal as well as accounting entities. A **share of stock** is a certificate that provides evidence of part ownership of the corporation. A **bond** is a certificate that provides evidence of a loan to the company. The advantages of corporations include the ability to raise large amounts of capital, easy transfer of ownership, since many stocks are traded on stock exchanges, and the limited liability of the stockholder.

## Sixty Second Quiz!

**Question:** Of the three types of business entity, which one provides the owner(s) with the greatest financial protection?

**Answer:** The corporation. Although the business is a separate accounting entity for all three types, in both partnerships and sole proprietorships the owners can be held responsible for the business's debts, and therefore could lose their personal assets. Stockholders in a corporation are normally liable only for the amount they have contributed to the corporation, so their personal assets are protected.

**LO 3**  **Nonbusiness entities** are organized for purposes other than to make a profit and do not normally have clearly defined owners. A special type of accounting called **fund accounting** is used for this type of entity.

**LO 4**  Business activities can be classified into three main types:

• **Financing activities** relate to raising the money (or capital) needed to start and operate a business. The principal financing activities of corporations relate to selling bonds and issuing stock. Bonds represent a liability of the company and are therefore a temporary form of financing; stock represents part ownership in the company and is therefore a permanent source of financing for the company.

• **Investing activities** are concerned with acquiring (and sometimes disposing of) the **assets** needed for the business. An asset represents the right to receive a future benefit, and can be long-term (for example, property, plant, and equipment), or short term (for example, inventory and cash).

• **Operating activities** are the activities that are necessary to achieve the purpose of the business. These could include manufacturing products, selling inventory, employing staff, and using utilities such as water and gas.

## Review of Key Terms

| | |
|---|---|
| **Asset** | A future economic benefit. |
| **Bond** | A certificate that represents a corporation's promise to repay a certain amount of money and interest in the future. |
| **Business** | All the activities necessary to provide the members of an economic system with goods and services. |
| **Business entity** | Organization operated to earn a profit. |
| **Capital stock** | A category on the balance sheet to indicate the owners' contributions to a corporation. |
| **Corporation** | A form of entity organized under the laws of a particular state; ownership is evidenced by shares of stock. |
| **Creditor** | Someone to whom the entity owes a debt. |
| **Economic entity concept** | The assumption that a single, identifiable unit must be accounted for in all situations. |
| **Expense** | An outflow of assets resulting from the sale of goods or services. |
| **Liability** | An obligation of a business. |
| **Nonbusiness entity** | An organization operated for some purpose other than to earn a profit. |
| **Partnership** | A business owned by two or more individuals; organization form often used by accounting firms and law firms. |
| **Revenue** | An inflow of assets resulting from the sale of goods or services. |
| **Share of stock** | A certificate that acts as ownership in a corporation. |
| **Sole proprietorship** | Form of organization with a single owner. |
| **Stockholder** | One of the owners of a corporation. |

## Practice Test
## Questions and Problems

### Circle the alternative that best answers the question:

**LO 3** 1. Which of the following is a feature of a sole proprietorship?
- a) An ability to raise large amounts of capital
- b) Easy transfer of ownership
- c) Limited liability of owners
- d) Management of the company normally carried out by owners

**LO 3** 2. Which certificate provides evidence of a long-term loan to the company?
- a) A bond
- b) A share of stock
- c) An invoice
- d) An account

LO 4    3.    Which of the following groups of activities would be classified as operating activities?
- a) Issue of stock, redemption of bonds, payment of dividends
- b) Sale of goods, purchase of inventory, payment of wages
- c) Purchase of plant, purchase of stock, sale of land

LO 4    4.    Which of the following groups of activities would be classified as financing activities?
- a) Issue of stock, redemption of bonds, payment of dividends
- b) Sale of goods, purchase of inventory, payment of wages
- c) Purchase of plant, purchase of stock, sale of land

## Indicate whether each of the following statements is true or false:

LO 3    5.    The form of organization that provides the greatest financial protection to its owners is the sole proprietorship.

LO 4    6.    Investing activities include both the sale and purchase of long-term assets.

## Complete each of the following statements:

LO 3    7.    Businesses owned by at least two people are known as _____.

LO 3    8.    Entities that are organized for reasons other than to make a profit are called _____.

LO 4    9.    Issuing stock and selling bonds are examples of the _____ activities of a business.

## Answer the following problem:

LO 3    10.    For each of the entities listed below, recommend the type of organization that suits it best and list at least three items, other than cash, that are likely to appear in the entities' financial statements.

1.    A law firm is owned and operated by two lawyers, who are all equally active in the practice.

2.    A hot dog stand is owned and operated by a student during the summer.

3.    A shipbuilding business, owned by a large group of people none of whom is actively involved in the day-to-day running of the business, employs managers to run the business on their behalf.

4.   A dental building is owned jointly by seven dentists, and they rent space for their individual practices from the building.

5.   An organization owns and operates a large number of fast food restaurants, including franchises. It was originally owned and operated by one man but is now a large multinational organization with the ownership and day-to-day management separated.

## Solutions

## Multiple Choice
1.   d
2.   a
3.   b
4.   c

## True/False

**COMMENT/EXPLANATION**

5.   False     Because stockholders have limited liability, the corporation provides the greatest protection to owners.

6.   True

## Fill in the Blanks
7.   partnerships
8.   nonbusiness entities
9.   financing

## Problem 46
1.   Partnership; fee revenue, professional subscriptions, office expenses.
2.   Sole proprietorship; cash sales, cost of sales, asset (hamburger stand).
3.   Corporation; ships in progress, wages expense, inventory (steel, etc.).
4.   Partnership; rental income, building maintenance expense, utilities expense.
5.   Corporation; income from foreign operations, franchise fees, advertising.

# Chapter 1

# Accounting as a form of Communication

**Accounting** provides organizations with one of the most important ways of identifying, measuring, and communicating financial information. This chapter begins the study of accounting by looking at the activities organizations engage in, and the importance of accounting in organizational decision making. Your overall objective in this chapter is to understand the role that accounting plays in communicating financial information about various forms of enterprise.

## Learning Objectives

**LO 1**  Identify the primary users of accounting information and their needs.

**LO 2**  Explain the purpose of each of the financial statements and the relationships among them, and prepare a set of simple statements.

**LO 3**  Identify and explain the primary assumptions made in preparing financial statements.

**LO 4**  Describe the various roles of accountants in organizations.

## Key Textbook Exhibits

**Exhibit 1-1** identifies various users, common decisions they face, and relevant questions they ask. *Self-Test:* How can financial statements be utilized to help these users answer their questions?

**Exhibits 1-2 and 1-4** give Ben & Jerry's principal financial statements. *Self-Test:* What is the function of each statement and what type of information does each statement present?

**Exhibit 1-3** summarizes the relationship between the accounting equation and the balance sheet. Note that all assets, liabilities, and owner's equity accounts are reported on the balance sheet. *Self-Test:* Study the various balance sheet accounts, testing yourself whether they should be classified as assets, liabilities, or owners' equity.

**Exhibit 1-5** identifies the links between the income statement, balance sheet, and statement of retained earnings. *Self-Test:* What is the purpose of each of the three statements identified and what is the relationship between them?

**Exhibit 1-6** identifies some of the various roles accountants play in society. *Self-Test:* What is the purpose of each position and how are they related?

**Exhibit 1-7** illustrates the Independent Auditors' Report for Ben & Jerry's. *Self-Test:* What is the purpose of an audit report and who is authorized to issue one?

## Review of Key Concepts

**LO 1** Users of financial information are traditionally split into two groups: internal users and external users. **Internal users** are the management of the company and can obtain any information they need in a form that meets their needs. **Management accounting** is the branch of accounting concerned with providing information to internal users for planning and controlling a business.

External users include groups with very diverse motivations and interests. Stockholders need financial information that will help in choosing among competing alternative investments. Before buying a **bond**, a bondholder needs financial information to help determine whether the company will be able to repay the amount owed at maturity plus interest. Before lending money, a banker needs financial information that will help to determine the company's ability to repay the loan plus interest. The Internal Revenue Service needs financial information to determine the tax on income. The Securities and Exchange Commission regulates the financial reporting for public companies. External users do not have day-to-day access to the financial information of the company, and must therefore use information presented to them by the company management. **Financial accounting** is the branch of accounting concerned with providing financial information to external users.

### Sixty Second Quiz!

**Question:** Does financial accounting and reporting provide all the information needed by people and institutions who make economic decisions about business enterprises?

**Answer:** People and institutions who use financial information for business and economic decisions need to combine information provided by financial reporting with pertinent information from other sources; for example, information about general economic conditions or expectations, political events and political climate, or industry outlook.

**LO 2** The fundamental equation underlying the entire accounting system is as follows:

$$\textbf{Assets} \quad = \quad \textbf{Liabilities} \quad + \quad \textbf{Owners' Equity}$$

The left-hand side of the equation identifies the resources controlled by the company, and the right-hand side identifies the parties having claims against these resources (**creditors** and investors). When the financial statements relate to a corporation, the owners' equity is called **stockholders' equity.** Stockholders' equity usually consists of the amount contributed by the **stockholders** when the stock was first purchased (**capital stock**) and **retained earnings,** which are defined as the accumulated earnings of a business minus any **dividends** paid to stockholders.

**LO 2** The three principal financial statements prepared for external users are the income statement, the balance sheet, and the statement of retained earnings. The three statements are inextricably linked, as changes in one will impact either one or both of the other two statements. Note in Exhibit 1-5 that the net income (income statement) is added to retained earnings (balance sheet). Total retained earnings (statement of retained earnings) is equal to the retained earnings on the balance sheet. If the income statement reports a net loss, then the net loss would be subtracted from retained earnings (opposite of net income).

- The **balance sheet** summarizes the assets, liabilities, and owners' equity of the business at a specific point in time. Both sides of the balance sheet must be equal. That is, assets must equal liabilities plus owners' equity.
- The **income statement** summarizes the **revenues** and **expenses** of the business over a period of time and shows whether or not the business made a profit or loss over that period. Note that the income statement is prepared on an **accrual basis**. This means that revenues and expenses appear on the income statement during the period they are earned or incurred, even though the related cash is not received or paid during that period.
- The **statement of retained earnings** summarizes the changes in retained earnings over a time period. These changes derive from profits or losses for the period (summarized in the income statement) minus dividends paid to stockholders. Remember that dividends (declared or paid) are not an expense, and as a result are never included on the income statement.

## Sixty Second Quiz!

**Question**: What are the principal differences between the balance sheet and the income statement?

**Answer**: The balance sheet reports the resources owned by the company and the obligations owed by the company at a point in time. The income statement reports on the operations (profit or loss) of the company for a period of time, for example, a year.

**LO 3** The conceptual framework of accounting is intended to provide a framework of objectives and fundamental principles that will be the basis for developing financial accounting and reporting standards.

- The **economic entity concept** is based on the premise that business entities are separate economic units from their owners and must have separate and distinct accounting records.
- The **cost principle** requires that assets are recorded and carried on the balance sheet at their original (historic) cost.
- The **going concern assumption** states that the business entity will continue to exist indefinitely.
- The **time period assumption** states that measurement of financial condition and results of operations can be made at relatively short intervals, such as one year. Users of the statements demand information about the entity on a regular basis.
- The **monetary unit** that is used to prepare financial statements is assumed to have a constant value.

**Generally accepted accounting principles (GAAP)** refer to the set of methods, rules, practices, and procedures that have evolved over time and regulate the preparation of financial statements.

**LO 3** Several bodies are jointly responsible for determining GAAP:

- The **Securities and Exchange Commission (SEC)** was set up in 1934 by an act of Congress and has the ultimate authority to determine how and when financial statements are to be prepared and reported. The SEC, however, has delegated authority for setting accounting principles to the **Financial Accounting Standards Board (FASB)**.
- FASB is an independent group of seven individuals who have the authority to set accounting standards. Currently, the board has issued more than one hundred thirty standards dealing with a variety of financial reporting issues.

- The **American Institute of Certified Public Accountants (AICPA)** is the professional organization of certified public accountants. It has an advisory role in setting GAAP but is responsible for setting auditing standards.
- The **International Accounting Standards Committee (IASC)** is the body that is attempting to develop worldwide accounting standards. A major constraint on its effectiveness is that compliance with its standards is voluntary, and it therefore does not have the authority that FASB has in the United States.

## Sixty Second Quiz!

**Question:** How are the accounting standards related to the conceptual framework?

**Answer:** The conceptual framework is intended to establish the objectives and concepts that the Financial Accounting Standards Board will use in developing standards of financial accounting and reporting.

**LO 4** In business entities, accountants can work in three related areas. The **controller** has the responsibility for the overall operations of the accounting system. The **treasurer** ensures the safekeeping and efficient use of the company's cash (liquid resources). The **internal audit function** is responsible for the review and appraisal of the company's accounting and administrative controls. In **nonbusiness entities**, accountants have a major role to play in reporting on the assets, liabilities, and operations of the entity even though the profit motive is not paramount.

**LO 4** **Certified Public Accountants (CPA)** provide many services to their clients.
- **Auditing** is the process of examining financial statements and testing the supporting records in order to render an opinion as to whether or not the statements are fairly presented. Remember that the **auditors' report** is an opinion and not a statement of fact.
- Accountants provide a variety of tax services, which include the preparation of tax returns and advice on tax planning strategies.
- Many public accounting firms also provide management consulting services to their clients.

**LO 4** Education is another major area in which accountants are employed. The **American Accounting Association** is a professional organization of accounting educators and has a major influence on both accounting education and academic research.

Remember that the primary goal of accounting is to provide useful information to aid in the decision-making process. Financial statements are prepared for external parties who must rely on them to provide information on which to base important decisions. Accountants must exercise judgement in deciding which accounting method to select or how to report a certain item in the statements. Keep in mind the trust placed on the accountant by various financial statement users.

## Sixty Second Quiz!

**Question:** What are the three basic types of services performed by public accounting firms?

**Answer:** Auditing, tax, and management consulting services are the three basic services performed by public accountants. However, accounting firms continue to expand into other business opportunities (e.g. internal auditing, legal services, etc).

# Review of Key Terms

| | |
|---|---|
| **Accounting** | The process of identifying, measuring, and communicating economic information to various users. |
| **Accrual basis** | Revenues appear on the income statement during the period they are earned, even though the related cash has not been received during that period. Expenses appear on the income statement during the period they are incurred, even though the related cash has not been paid during that period. |
| **American Accounting Association (AAA)** | The professional organization for accounting educators. |
| **American Institute of Certified Public Accountants (AICPA)** | The professional organization for certified public accountants. |
| **Asset** | Resources owned by an entity. A probable future economic benefit obtained or controlled by a particular entity as a result of past transactions or events. See Exhibit 1-2 for examples of asset accounts. |
| **Auditing** | The process of examining the financial statements and the underlying records of an entity in order to render an opinion as to whether or not the statements are fairly presented. |
| **Auditors' report** | The opinion rendered by a pubic accounting firm concerning the fairness of the presentation of the financial statements. |
| **Balance sheet** | A statement that summarizes the assets, liabilities, and owners' equity at a specific point in time. |
| **Bond** | A certificate issued by corporations representing the promise to repay a certain amount of money and interest in the future. |
| **Capital stock** | The amounts contributed to a corporation by the stockholders. |
| **Certified Public Accountant (CPA)** | The professional designation for public accountants. |
| **Controller** | The chief accounting officer of a company. |
| **Cost principle** | Assets recorded at the cost of acquiring them. |
| **Creditor** | Someone to whom the entity owes a debt. |
| **Dividends** | A distribution of the net income (earnings) of a corporation to its owners (stockholders). |
| **Economic entity concept** | The assumption that requires that an enterprise be accounted for separately from its owners. |
| **Expense** | An outflow of assets resulting from the sale of goods or services, or carrying out other activities that constitute the entity's ongoing major or central operations. |
| **External users** | Includes users other than management, such as stockholders, creditors, and some governmental agencies. |

| | |
|---|---|
| **Financial accounting** | The branch of accounting concerned with the preparation of general-purpose financial statements for both internal and external users. |
| **Financial Accounting Standards Board (FASB)** | The group in the private sector with the authority to set accounting standards. |
| **Generally accepted accounting principles (GAAP)** | The methods, rules, and practices that regulate the preparation of financial statements. |
| **Going concern** | The assumption that an entity has an infinite life. |
| **Income statement** | A statement that summarizes revenues and expenses. |
| **Internal audit** | The department in a company responsible for the review and appraisal of the company's accounting and administrative controls. |
| **Internal users** | Managers are described as "internal users." |
| **International Accounting Standards Committee (IASC)** | The organization formed to develop worldwide accounting standards. |
| **Liability** | An obligation of an entity. Probable future economic sacrifices of a particular entity as a result of past transactions or events.  See Exhibit 1-2 for examples of liability accounts. |
| **Management accounting** | The branch of accounting concerned with providing management of entities with information to help in planning and controlling the enterprise. |
| **Monetary unit** | The measurement unit used in financial statements: the dollar in the United States. For financial reporting, the monetary unit is not adjusted for changes in purchasing power over time. |
| **Nonbusiness entity** | An organization operated for some reason other than to earn a profit. |
| **Owners' equity** | The owners' claim on the assets of the entity. |
| **Retained earnings** | The part of the owners' equity that represents the income earned less dividends paid over the life of the entity. |
| **Revenue** | An inflow of assets resulting from the sale of goods or services, or other activities that constitute the entity's ongoing major or central operations. |
| **Securities and Exchange Commission (SEC)** | The federal agency with ultimate authority over the preparation of financial statements by publicly held corporations. |
| **Statement of retained earnings** | A statement that summarizes the changes in retained earnings over the accounting period. |
| **Stockholder** | One of the owners of a corporation. |
| **Stockholders' equity** | The owners' equity in a corporation. |
| **Time period** | The segment of the calendar for which financial statements are prepared. |
| **Treasurer** | The financial officer responsible for safeguarding and efficient use of the company's liquid resources. |

## Practice Test
## Questions and Problems

**Circle the alternative that best answers the question:**

**LO 1** 1. Which certificate provides evidence of a long-term loan to the company?
    a) A bond
    b) A share of stock
    c) An invoice
    d) An account

**LO 3** 2. Which of the following organizations is responsible for the setting of accounting standards?
    a) The Financial Accounting Standards Board
    b) The American Accounting Association
    c) The Securities and Exchange Commission
    d) The American Institute of Certified Public Accountants

**LO 3** 3. Which of the following organizations has the ultimate authority to determine how and when accounts of public companies are to be prepared and reported?
    a) The Financial Accounting Standards Board
    b) The American Accounting Association
    c) The Securities and Exchange Commission
    d) The American Institute of Certified Public Accountants

**LO 2** 4. Which of the following types of information would you expect to see reported on a balance sheet?
    a) Stockholders' equity, bonds, plant and equipment, inventory
    b) Revenues, depreciation expense, tax expense, cost of goods sold
    c) Cash used in investing activities, cash provided by operations, cash provided by financing activities
    d) Earnings for current year, dividends, retained earnings brought forward from previous periods

**LO 2** 5. Which of the following types of information would you expect to see reported on an income statement?
    a) Stockholders' equity, bonds, plant and equipment, inventory
    b) Revenues, depreciation expense, tax expense, cost of goods sold
    c) Cash used in investing activities, cash provided by operations, cash provided by financing activities
    d) Earnings for current year, dividends, retained earnings brought forward from previous periods

LO 2  6.  Which of the following types of information would you expect to see reported on a statement of retained earnings?
   a)  Stockholders' equity, bonds, plant and equipment, inventory
   b)  Revenues, depreciation expense, tax expense, cost of goods sold
   c)  Cash deposits and cash withdrawals
   d)  Earnings for current year, dividends, retained earnings brought forward from previous periods

LO 1  7.  Internal users of financial information include?
   a)  Stockholders
   b)  Management
   c)  Bondholders
   d)  Internal Revenue Service

LO 1  8.  The branch of accounting concerned with providing internal users with information to facilitate planning and control?
   a)  Auditing
   b)  Financial accounting
   c)  Tax accounting
   d)  Managerial accounting

LO 1  9.  Which user would most likely ask the question: "Can the company afford to give me a raise?"
   a)  Supplier
   b)  Stockholder
   c)  Employee
   d)  Management

LO 4  10.  The usual services provided by public accounting firms include?
   a)  Auditing
   b)  Tax
   c)  Management consulting
   d)  All of the above

*Use the following information to answer questions 11 through 15:*

Terra Corporation's financial statements for the year ended July 31, 2001, are as follows:

## Terra Corporation

## Income statement for the year to July 31, 2001

| | |
|---|---|
| Revenues | $15,000 |
| Cost of sales | ? |
| Gross margin | 6,500 |
| Selling and administrative expenses | ? |
| Net income | $4,300 |

## Terra Corporation
## Balance sheet on July 31, 2001

**Assets**

| | |
|---|---:|
| Cash | ? |
| Inventories | 1,800 |
| Total current assets | 5,100 |
| Land and buildings | 1,100 |
| *Total assets* | ? |

**Liabilities**

| | |
|---|---:|
| Accounts payable | $200 |
| Accrued salaries and wages | 1,000 |
| Total current liabilities | 1,200 |
| Long-term liabilities | 600 |
| Total liabilities | 1,800 |

**Stockholders' equity**

| | |
|---|---:|
| Capital stock | ? |
| Retained earnings | 4,300 |
| Total stockholders' equity | 4,400 |
| *Total liabilities and stockholders' equity* | ? |

**LO 2** 11. Gross margin is defined as the difference between revenues and cost of sales. Terra Corporation's cost of sales for the year ended July 31, 2001, was:

 a) $12,000

 b) $8,500

 c) $15,500

 d) $3,500

**LO 2** 12. Net income is found by deducting selling and administrative expenses from gross margin. Terra Corporation's selling and administrative expenses for the year ended July 31, 2001, are:

 a) $3,500

 b) $1,300

 c) $4,800

 d) $2,200

**LO 2** 13. Terra Corporation's cash balance on July 31, 2001, is:

 a) $3,300

 b) $6,300

 c) $4,800

 d) $1,500

**LO 2** 14. Terra Corporation's total assets on July 31, 2001, are:

 a) $6,200

 b) $1,500

 c) $4,800

 d) $3,300

`LO 2`  15. Terra Corporation's capital stock on July 31, 2001, is:
    a) $4,300
    b) $ 100
    c) $4,800
    d) $9,100

## Indicate whether each of the following statements is true or false:

`LO 1`  16. Because stockholders can gain unlimited access to the company's records, they are mostly concerned with management accounting concepts.

`LO 1`  17. Creditors, bondholders, labor unions, and government agencies are all external users of accounting information.

`LO 2`  18. An alternative title for the balance sheet is the statement of financial position.

`LO 2`  19. The statement of retained earnings summarizes the cash effect of the company's operations over the period.

`LO 3`  20. The time period assumption states that one should take into account the fact that the company may discontinue operations in the near future.

`LO 3`  21. The monetary unit in which accounts are prepared is assumed to have a constant value over time.

`LO 4`  22. Public accounting firms provide only audit services for their clients.

`LO 4`  23. Changes in a company's assets over a period can be found by comparing the income statements at the beginning and end of the period.

`LO 3`  24. The International Standards Committee has the same degree of authority in the world as the Financial Accounting Standards Board has in the USA.

`LO 2`  25. If the income statement shows a company has made a loss in a year and the company pays no dividend in that year, the balance on retained earnings will decrease from the beginning to the end of the year.

`LO 3`  26. The cost principle ensures that even if a company's land has increased in value since it was purchased, the amount the land is reported at in the balance sheet is the original cost.

`LO 1`  27. Internal users of accounting information include both management and stockholders.

`LO 4`  28. The primary goal of accounting is to provide useful information to aid in the decision-making process.

`LO 4`  29. Any individual or firm can issue and sign an Audit Report. They do not need to be a Certified Public Accountant.

`LO 3`  30. The American Institute of Certified Public Accountants (AICPA) sets the accounting standards (GAAP) in the United States.

## Complete each of the following statements:

**LO 1** 31. _____ is the branch of accounting concerned with the preparation of financial statements for both external and internal users.

**LO 2** 32. Entities that are organized for reasons other than to make a profit are called _____.

**LO 2** 33. If an entity has net earnings for a year of $10,000, and pays no dividend to stockholders during that year, the effect on its retained earnings balance is $_____.

**LO 2** 34. Revenues and expenses are reported on an entity's _____.

**LO 3** 35. The _____ is a government body that has the ultimate authority over how publicly held corporations present their financial statements.

**LO 2** 36. The amount in the balance sheet of a corporation that represents both the amount contributed by the stockholders and retained earnings is _____.

**LO 3** 37. The assumption that business entities are separate and distinct from their owners is known as the _____ concept.

**LO 4** 38. The financial officer responsible for safeguarding, and the efficient use of, the company's liquid resources is called the _____.

**LO 2** 39. The financial statement that summarizes the resources of the enterprise and the claims against those resources by both creditors and owners is the _____.

**LO 2** 40. The _____ reports on the revenues and expenses of the business during the period.

**LO 3** 41. The methods, rules, and practices that regulate the preparation of financial statements are called _____.

**LO 2** 42. On a company's balance sheet, total assets are reported as $15,000, total liabilities are $8,000, and stockholders' equity is _____.

**LO 3** 43. The _____ sets the accounting standards in the United States.

**LO 4** 44. _____ is the process of examining the financial statements and the underlying records of a company in order to render an opinion as to whether the statements are fairly presented.

**LO 1** 45. _____ is "the process of identifying, measuring, and communicating economic information to various users."

## Answer each of the following problems:

**LO 1** 46. Alpha Corporation is a large manufacturing firm, producing steel rods for the fastener industry. Their primary manufacturing is carried out in California and Illinois, and they are currently considering expanding their manufacturing capacity by building a new factory in Texas. The new factory will require that the company raise more capital, probably by issuing bonds. Which of the following items from the company's most recent financial statements would stockholders be interested in to help them assess the advisability of bond issue? Code each line in the stockholders' column as

    A. Need to know

    B. Helpful to know

    C. Not necessary to know

|     | INFORMATION | STOCKHOLDERS |
| --- | --- | --- |
| 1. | Ten-year record of sales | |
| 2. | Ten-year record of earnings | |
| 3. | Interest expense | |
| 4. | Long-term debt | |
| 5. | Cash on hand | |
| 6. | Wages expense | |
| 7. | Dividends paid | |
| 8. | Property, plant and equipment | |
| 9. | Stockholders' equity | |
| 10. | Accounts payable | |

**LO 2** 47. The following items appear in the financial statements of the Dillon Department Stores Company for the year ended December 31, 2001. In the table below, indicate whether the item is an asset, liability, owners' equity, revenue, or expense, and whether it appears on the balance sheet or income statement. Then use this information to prepare the income statement and balance sheet for that year. (Hint! Remember that receivables and payables appear on the balance sheet, and that expenses and revenues appear on the income statement.)

| ACCOUNT | | ASSET, LIABILITY, OWNERS' EQUITY, REVENUE OR EXPENSE | INCOME STATEMENT OR BALANCE SHEET |
|---|---|---|---|
| Accounts payable | $ 700 | | |
| Accounts receivable | 2,400 | | |
| Land and buildings | 1,500 | | |
| Cash | 900 | | |
| Capital stock | 200 | | |
| Furniture | 1,900 | | |
| Interest expense | 300 | | |
| Long-term notes payable | 3,000 | | |
| Inventories | 1,500 | | |
| Retained earnings | 4,300 | | |
| Revenues | 12,000 | | |
| Selling expenses | 2,200 | | |
| Cost of sales | 8,500 | | |

## Critical Thinking Problem

**LO 2**    48. The income statement of the Walt Disney Company for the years ended September 30, 1999, 1998, and 1997 are presented below.

## Walt Disney Company
## Consolidated Statement of Income

| Business Segments | Year Ended September 30 | | |
|---|---|---|---|
| (In millions, except per share data) | **1999** | 1998 | 1997 |
| *Revenues* | | | |
| Media Networks | $      7,512 | $      7,142 | $      6,522 |
| Studio Entertainment | 6,548 | 6,849 | 6,981 |
| Theme Parks and Resorts | 6,106 | 5,532 | 5,014 |
| Consumer Products | 3,030 | 3,193 | 3,782 |
| Internet and Direct Marketing | 206 | 260 | 174 |
|         Total Revenues | 23,402 | 22,976 | 22,473 |
| | | | |
| *Cost and expenses* | | | |
| Media Networks | 5,901 | 5,396 | 4,823 |
| Studio Entertainment | 6,432 | 6,080 | 5,902 |
| Theme Parks and Resorts | 4,660 | 4,244 | 3,878 |
| Consumer Products | 2,423 | 2,392 | 2,889 |
| Internet and Direct Marketing | 299 | 354 | 230 |
|         Total Costs and Expenses | 19,715 | 18,466 | 17,722 |
| | | | |
| *Operating income* | | | |
| Media Networks | 1,611 | 1,746 | 1,699 |
| Studio Entertainment | 116 | 769 | 1,079 |
| Theme Parks and Resorts | 1,446 | 1,288 | 1,136 |
| Consumer Products | 607 | 801 | 893 |
| Internet and Direct Marketing | (93) | (94) | (56) |
| Amortization of intangibles | (456) | (431) | (439) |
| | 3,231 | 4,079 | 4,312 |
| Restructuring charges | (132) | (64) | ---- |
| Gain on sale of Starwave | 345 | ---- | ---- |
| Gain on sale of KCAL | ---- | ---- | 135 |
|         Total Operating Income | 3,444 | 4,015 | 4,447 |
| | | | |
| Corporate and other activities | (196) | (236) | (367) |
| Equity in Infoseek loss | (322) | ---- | ---- |
| Net interest expense | (612) | (622) | (693) |
| Income before income taxes | 2,314 | 3,157 | 3,387 |
| | | | |
| Income taxes | (1,014) | (1,307) | (1,421) |
| Net income | $      1,300 | $      1,850 | $      1,966 |
| | | | |
|     Earnings per share | | | |
|       Diluted | $      0.62 | $      0.89 | $      0.95 |
|       Basic | $      0.63 | $      0.91 | $      0.97 |

**Required**

1. Over the three years, which of the five main activities in the income statement (media networks, studio entertainment, theme parks and resorts, consumer products, and internet and direct marketing) provided Disney with the largest sales volume? Which activity generated the largest total operating income? Which activity generated the largest operating income relative to its sales? Can you use this analysis to advise Disney on which, if any, of its activities it should expand?

2. Why do you suppose that Disney reported the Corporate and other activities loss, Infoseek loss, and Net interest expense separately from its other activities? If Disney had not made the large loss on Infoseek, what would its income before income taxes have been for the year to September 30, 1999?

3. The Internet and Direct Marketing segment is reporting negative operating income for all three years. Can you think of any reasons why Disney should not discontinue this segment?

## Solutions

### Multiple Choice

| | | | | |
|---|---|---|---|---|
| 1. | a | | 9. | c |
| 2. | a | | 10. | d |
| 3. | c | | 11. | b |
| 4. | a | | 12. | d |
| 5. | b | | 13. | a |
| 6. | d | | 14. | a |
| 7. | b | | 15. | b |
| 8. | d | | | |

### True/False

**COMMENT/EXPLANATION**

| | | |
|---|---|---|
| 16. | False | Only the corporation's management can gain unlimited access to the records, and they are the group mostly concerned with management accounting. |
| 17. | True | |
| 18. | True | |
| 19. | False | The statement of retained earnings summarizes changes in the retained earnings balance on the balance sheet over the accounting period. |
| 20. | False | The time period assumption states that financial statements should be prepared for specific time periods. |
| 21. | True | |
| 22. | False | Public accounting firms provide audit, tax, and business consulting services for their clients. |
| 23. | False | Changes in a company's assets can be found by comparing the balance sheet at the beginning and end of the period. The income statement summarizes operating activities over the period. |
| 24. | False | The IASC is advisory only and has no legal authority over its members. |
| 25. | True | |
| 26. | True | |
| 27. | False | Stockholders are external users of accounting information, since they are remote from the day-to-day operations of the enterprise. |
| 28. | True | |
| 29. | False | Only a Certified Public Accountant can issue and sign an Auditor Report on the fairness of the presentation of financial statements. |
| 30. | False | The FASB sets the accounting standards. The AICPA sets the auditing standards to be followed by public accounting firms. |

## Fill in the Blanks

31. Financial accounting
32. Nonbusiness entities
33. $10,000 increase
34. Income statement
35. Securities and Exchange Commission
36. Stockholders' equity
37. Economic entity
38. Treasurer

39. Balance sheet
40. Income statement
41. Generally accepted accounting principles
42. $7,000
43. Financial Accounting Standards Board
44. Auditing
45. Accounting

## Problem 46

One set of answers to this problem appears below. However, your answers may differ from these and can still be correct since the questions are open to interpretation. The main purpose of this question is to encourage you to realize that different users have different needs.

| | INFORMATION | STOCKHOLDERS |
|---|---|---|
| 1. | Ten-year record of sales | C |
| 2. | Ten-year record of earnings | B |
| 3. | Interest expense | A |
| 4. | Long-term debt | A |
| 5. | Cash on hand | B |
| 6. | Wages expense | C |
| 7. | Dividends paid | A |
| 8. | Property, plant and equipment | C |
| 9. | Stockholders' equity | A |
| 10. | Accounts payable | C |

## Problem 47

| ACCOUNT | | ASSET, LIABILITY, OWNERS' EQUITY, REVENUE OR EXPENSE | INCOME STATEMENT OR BALANCE SHEET |
|---|---|---|---|
| Accounts payable | $ 700 | Liability | Balance sheet |
| Accounts receivable | 2,400 | Asset | Balance sheet |
| Land and buildings | 1,500 | Asset | Balance sheet |
| Cash | 900 | Asset | Balance sheet |
| Capital stock | 200 | Stockholders' equity | Balance sheet |
| Furniture | 1,900 | Asset | Balance sheet |
| Interest expense | 300 | Expense | Income statement |
| Long-term liabilities | 3,000 | Liability | Balance sheet |
| Inventories | 1,500 | Asset | Balance sheet |
| Retained earnings | 4,300 | Stockholders' equity | Balance sheet |
| Revenues | 12,000 | Revenue | Income statement |
| Selling expenses | 2,200 | Expense | Income statement |
| Cost of sales | 8,500 | Expense | Income statement |

## Dillon Department Stores Company
## Income statement for the year to December 31, 2001

| | |
|---|---:|
| Revenues | $12,000 |
| Cost of sales | (8,500) |
| Gross margin | 3,500 |
| Selling expenses | (2,200) |
| Interest expense | (300) |
| Net income | $1,000 |

## Dillon Department Stores Company
## Balance sheet on December 31, 2001

**Assets**

| | |
|---|---:|
| Cash | $900 |
| Accounts receivable | 2,400 |
| Inventories | 1,500 |
| Total current assets | 4,800 |
| Furniture | 1,900 |
| Land and buildings | 1,500 |
| Total long-term assets | 3,400 |
| *Total assets* | $8,200 |

**Liabilities**

| | |
|---|---:|
| Accounts payable | $700 |
| Long-term liabilities | 3,000 |
| Total liabilities | 3,700 |
| **Stockholders' equity** | |
| Capital stock | 200 |
| Retained earnings | 4,300 |
| Total stockholders' equity | 4,500 |
| *Total liabilities and stockholders' equity* | $8,200 |

## Critical Thinking Problem 48

1.  The following table summarizes the performance of the five business segments of the Walt Disney Company for 1999, 1998, and 1997:

| Media Networks | 1999 | 1998 | 1997 |
|---|---|---|---|
| Revenues | 7,512 | 7,142 | 6,522 |
| Percentage increase from prior year | 5.2% | 9.5% | |
| Operating income | 1,611 | 1,746 | 1,699 |
| Percentage increase from prior year | -7.7% | 2.8% | |
| Operating income as a percentage of revenues | 21.4% | 24.4% | 26.1% |

| Studio Entertainment | 1999 | 1998 | 1997 |
|---|---|---|---|
| Revenues | 6,548 | 6,849 | 6,981 |
| Percentage increase from prior year | -4.4% | -1.9% | |
| Operating income | 116 | 769 | 1,079 |
| Percentage increase from prior year | -84.9% | -28.7% | |
| Operating income as a percentage of revenues | 1.8% | 11.2% | 15.5% |

| Theme Parks and Resorts | 1999 | 1998 | 1997 |
|---|---|---|---|
| Revenues | 6,106 | 5,532 | 5,014 |
| Percentage increase from prior year | 10.4% | 10.3% | |
| Operating income | 1,446 | 1,288 | 1,136 |
| Percentage increase from prior year | 12.3% | 13.4% | |
| Operating income as a percentage of revenues | 23.7% | 23.3% | 22.7% |

| Consumer Products | 1999 | 1998 | 1997 |
|---|---|---|---|
| Revenues | 3,030 | 3,193 | 3,782 |
| Percentage increase from prior year | -5.1% | -15.6% | |
| Operating income | 607 | 801 | 893 |
| Percentage increase from prior year | -24.2% | -10.3% | |
| Operating income as a percentage of revenues | 20.0% | 25.1% | 23.6% |

| Internet and Direct Marketing | 1999 | 1998 | 1997 |
|---|---|---|---|
| Revenues | 206 | 260 | 174 |
| Percentage increase from prior year | -20.8% | 49.4% | |
| Operating income | (93) | (94) | (56) |
| Percentage increase from prior year | -1.1% | 67.9% | |
| Operating income as a percentage of revenues | -45.1% | -36.2% | -32.2% |

1.  Media Networks and Studio Entertainment provided the largest revenues in all three years. Media Networks also had the largest operating income in the last three years; however, Studio Entertainment had the smallest operating income in 1999. Relative to sales, Theme Parks and Resorts had the largest operating income as a percentage of revenues (23.7% in 1999), with Media Networks close behind (21.4% for 1999). Theme Parks and Resorts have also experienced the largest revenue growth from 1998 to 1999 of 10.4%.

    Given both the increase in revenues over the three years and the high profitability in Theme Parks and Resorts, it would appear that Disney should continue to expand this segment. Before making that recommendation, however, we would need to know other information, such as how large the potential market is, who Disney's competitors are in this market, and what impact the Theme Parks and Resorts segment has on the other segments of Disney's operations.

2. These three charges (reduction) to income were reported separately so that it would not distort the results of Disney's main operations. Excluding the Infoseek loss would have resulted in an income before taxes of $2,636 million. Reporting these losses separately allowes the users of the financial statements to assess the performance of Disney's main activities apart from its' incidental and other activities.

3. The Internet and Direct Marketing revenues only account for approximately 1% of total revenues. For the year ended September 30, 1999, the segment generated a loss of $93 million. Disney will continue to operate this segment if they feel there is potential for future profitability. With the size of Disney and the growth of the Internet, it is likely the Internet and Direct Marketing segment will be a growth area for the company.

# Chapter 2

# Financial Statements and the Annual Report

The objective of financial reporting is to meet the needs of various types of decision makers and its success is measured by how well it meets that objective. This chapter explores how the annual report and the various financial statements it contains help to achieve this objective. Your overall aim in this chapter is to understand the form, content, and purpose of the annual report and of the various financial statements it contains.

## Learning Objectives

**LO 1** Describe the objectives of financial reporting.

**LO 2** Describe the qualitative characteristics of accounting information.

**LO 3** Explain the concept and purpose of a classified balance sheet and prepare the statement.

**LO 4** Use a classified balance sheet to analyze a company's financial position.

**LO 5** Explain the difference between a single-step and a multiple-step income statement and prepare each type of income statement.

**LO 6** Use a multiple-step income statement to analyze a company's operations.

**LO 7** Identify the components of the statement of retained earnings and prepare the statement.

**LO 8** Identify the components of the statement of cash flows and prepare the statement.

**LO 9** Read and use the financial statements and other elements in the annual report of a publicly held company.

## Key Textbook Exhibits

**Exhibit 2-2** provides a summary of the qualitative characteristics of accounting information. *Self-Test:* How important is each of these characteristics to the quality of the information provided to you as an investor?

**Exhibit 2-9** shows Gateway's Comparative Balance Sheets. *Self-Test:* How are the assets, liabilities, and stockholders' equity of the company classified and presented? Can you calculate the measures of liquidity (working capital and current ratio) for this firm?

**Exhibit 2-10** shows Gateway's Comparative Income Statements. *Self-Test:* Do you understand how the statement is presented and how to use the statement to calculate the various profitability measures (gross profit, profit margin, and earnings per share)?

## Review of Key Concepts

**LO 1** The primary objective of financial reporting is to provide economic information to permit users of that information to make informed decisions. People who use the information contained in financial reports include the management of the company (internal users) and people not involved in the daily management of the company such as investors, banks, and customers (external users). General-purpose financial statements provide both internal and external users with information about the activities of the company. The types of information needed by users include:

**Likely future cash receipts to investors and creditors.**

Investors decide whether to buy or sell the company's shares and bonds on the basis of the likely future cash flow they will receive. These cash flows could include future interest and dividend payments made by the company as well as estimates of the future price at which the company's stocks could be sold.

**Likely future cash flows to the company.**

These are useful since there is a relationship between the cash flow the company receives and the cash flow it can generate for its investors and creditors.

**Resources and claims on resources.**

Users wish to know both the resource base of the company and the claims against it. For example, potential investors may wish to know how much the company has invested in new equipment and whether or not these purchases have been financed by borrowing.

**LO 2** In order to be useful, accounting information must have certain attributes. These characteristics ensure that the information is of the highest possible quality and will therefore be most useful to users. The qualitative characteristics that accounting information should display are:

**Understandability** - The information must be comprehensible to the reasonably informed user.

**Relevance** - The information should be able to make a difference in a decision.

**Reliability** - Users should be able to depend on the information. In order to fulfill this requirement, information should satisfy three criteria that together indicate reliability. First the information should be verifiable, and free from error. Secondly, the information should faithfully represent the underlying economic conditions; and thirdly, it should be neutral in that it is not slanted to portray the company in any particular light, either good or bad.

**Comparability and consistency** - Users should be able to compare the accounts of different companies within the same time period as well as accounts of the same company over time. Note that comparability does not require all companies to use exactly the same accounting principles and methods; rather, companies provide enough information about their accounting methods for users to be able to make meaningful comparisons.

**Materiality** - Information is material if a user's judgment is affected by the omission or misstatement of the information. What constitutes material information will vary according to the type and size of the organization.

**Conservatism** – In a choice between alternative but equally likely ways of presenting information, the method that provides the lowest asset valuation or the least amount of income should be chosen.

**LO 3** Having reviewed both the purpose of financial statements, and the desirable qualities they should display, we turn to a consideration of the financial statements themselves. The first of these statements that we will consider is the **classified balance sheet**. It is constructed by distinguishing long-term from short-term items, and to do so requires understanding a company's **operating cycle**. The operating cycle begins when cash is invested in inventory and ends when cash is collected from customers. For example, assume that a company pays cash for inventory on July 15, 1999, sells the inventory on credit on August 1, 1999, and receives cash from its customer on September 15, 1999. In this case the operating cycle is 62 days consisting of 17 days between the cash purchase and 45 days between the sale and the receipt of cash from the customer.

## Sixty Second Quiz!

**Question**: Operating cycles vary in length between businesses. Which of the following types of business would you expect to have the shortest operating cycle? Which would you expect to have the longest?

Grocery store

Toy retailer

Automobile manufacturer

Engineering contractor building freeways and other large projects

**Answer**: We could expect the grocery store to have the shortest operating cycle and the engineering contractor to have the longest.

Having defined the operating cycle of a business, we can now use this definition to identify the different components of the balance sheet.

**Current assets** are those assets that are expected to be converted to cash, sold, or consumed either within the normal operating cycle of the business or within one year if the operating cycle is shorter than one year. Examples of current assets are cash, inventory, accounts receivable, prepaid expenses, and marketable securities.

**Noncurrent assets** are all assets that do not fall within the category of current assets. Examples are investments in other companies and property, plant, and equipment. Another group of noncurrent assets is **intangible assets** that, unlike other noncurrent assets, lack physical substance. The process of spreading the cost of a long-term, tangible asset over its useful life is called **depreciation**. **Amortization** refers to spreading the cost of an intangible asset over its useful life.

**Current liabilities** are obligations of the business that must be satisfied within one year. If, however, the operating cycle is shorter than one year, current liabilities are those liabilities that mature within the operating cycle. Examples of current liabilities are accounts payable and wages payable.

**Long-term liabilities**, as the name suggests, are liabilities of the company that mature in more than one year. If, however, the operating cycle is greater than one year, long-term liabilities are defined as liabilities that do not mature within the operating cycle. Bonds issued by the company are the most common form of long-term liability, but obligations under certain types of leasing arrangements and notes payable are also classified as long-term liabilities.

**Stockholders' equity** represents owners' claims on the business and is composed of two principal parts: **capital stock** and **retained earnings**. Capital stock is money or other assets that have been paid into the company by the stockholders. Retained earnings are earnings that the company has made since its inception less any dividends it has paid. Note that capital stock can also be split into two parts: **par value** and **paid-in capital in excess of par value**. Together these amount to the total that stockholders have paid for the stock the company has issued.

## Sixty Second Quiz!

**Question:** At what amount should intangible assets be shown on the balance sheet and what principle is being applied?

**Answer:** Intangibles should be shown at the cost of acquiring them. This is an application of the cost principle. If the intangible asset has not been acquired through a formal transaction, it will not have a cost assigned to it and will not appear on the balance sheet. For example, the Coca Cola Company's most valuable asset is its trademark and, because it was not formally acquired through a purchase, it does not appear as an asset on the Coca Cola Company's balance sheet.

**LO 4** The classified balance sheet can be used to analyze a company's financial position.

**Liquidity** measures the company's ability to pay its debts. Two possible measures of liquidity are:

| | | |
|---|---|---|
| Working capital | = | Current Assets - Current Liabilities |
| Current ratio | = | $\dfrac{\text{Current Assets}}{\text{Current Liabilities}}$ |

## Sixty Second Quiz!

**Question:** Which of the two measures of liquidity is better for making comparisons both across time for the same company and across companies?

**Answer:** The current ratio. Because it is a ratio, you can compare companies of different size and changes in a single company over time. Working capital is a dollar amount, which may or may not be useful for comparisons.

**LO 5** The **income statement** is used to summarize the results of the entity's operations over a period by reporting revenues, expenses, and the difference between them. If revenues exceed expenses, the company reports a net income or earnings; if expenses exceed revenues, the company reports a loss. In a **single-step income statement**, all expenses are added together and the total is deducted from the total revenues to arrive at net income. In a **multiple-step income statement**, revenues and expenses are subdivided to provide more information for the user.

**LO 6** Multiple-step income statements can be used to analyze the company's **profitability**.
Both the gross profit ratio and the profit margin give insights into how much margin or profit the company is generating from each dollar of sales. The gross profit ratio indicates how much is left after paying for the goods that have been sold. The profit margin indicates how much is left after *all* expenses have been paid.

| | | |
|---|---|---|
| Gross profit ratio | = | $\dfrac{\text{Gross Profit}}{\text{Sales}}$ |
| Profit margin | = | $\dfrac{\text{Net Income}}{\text{Sales}}$ |

**LO 7**    **A statement of stockholders' equity** explains the changes in stockholders' equity, both in capital stock and retained earnings, over the accounting period. If there are no changes to capital stock, **a statement of retained earnings** can be presented instead. This statement explains the changes in retained earnings between the beginning and end of the period. Both of these statements provide the link between the balance sheet and income statement since they explain the change in retained earnings on the balance sheet in terms of the net income for the period as reported in the income statement.

**LO 8**    The **statement of cash flows** summarizes the cash effects of the company's operating, investing, and financing activities for the period.

- **Operating activities** are those activities necessary to acquire, produce, and sell products and services. Examples include a house builder buying timber, a bank processing loan applications, and an insurance company paying sales commissions to its sales force.

- **Investing activities** are those activities that relate to the acquisition and disposal of long-term assets. Examples include the purchase of plant and equipment, and the sale of stocks or bonds held as investments.

- **Financing activities** are those activities resulting in changes in the debt or equity of the company. Examples include the issue of stocks or bonds, the repayment of bonds, and the repurchase of the company's own stock.

**LO 9**    Annual reports are prepared by the company to provide information for stockholders about the company's activities during the financial period. They contain the following information in addition to the financial statements discussed above.

In the **management discussion and analysis**, the company management discusses and explains certain aspects of the company's performance.

The **report of management,** on the other hand, sets out the responsibilities of the company's management. In particular, the report points out that the responsibility for the information in the annual report rests with the management of the company.

The **report of the independent accountants** or **auditors** expresses the opinion of the independent auditor on the fairness of the financial statements. Note that the independent auditors do not certify the accuracy of the financial statements; rather, they express an opinion as to whether or not there is material misstatement in the financial reports.

The **footnotes** to the financial statements provide essential details about how the accounting numbers were calculated. For example, the footnotes contain information on how the company writes off, or depreciates, its long term assets, how it values its inventory, and its obligations under certain types of long-term contracts such as operating leases. The footnotes are an essential part of the financial reports and you will find as you progress in your study of accounting that they are an invaluable aid to understanding and analyzing financial reports.

# Review of Key Terms

| | |
|---|---|
| **Comparability** | The quality of accounting information that allows a user to analyze two or more companies and look for similarities and differences. |
| **Conservatism** | The practice of using the least optimistic estimate when two or more possible estimates are equally likely. |
| **Consistency** | The quality of accounting information that allows a reader to compare two or more accounting periods for a single company. |
| **Current asset** | An asset that is expected to be realized in cash, sold, or consumed during the operating cycle, or within one year if the cycle is shorter than one year. |
| **Current liability** | An obligation that will be satisfied within the operating cycle, or within one year if the cycle is shorter than one year. |
| **Current ratio** | Current assets divided by current liabilities. |
| **Depreciation** | The allocation of the cost of a tangible, long-term asset over its useful life. |
| **Gross profit** | The difference between revenues and cost of goods sold. |
| **Gross profit ratio** | Gross profit divided by sales |
| **Liquidity** | The ability of a company to pay its debts as they come due. |
| **Materiality** | The magnitude of an omission or misstatement in accounting information that will affect the judgment of someone relying on the information. |
| **Multiple-step income statement** | An income statement that provides the reader with classifications of revenues and expenses as well as with important subtotals. |
| **Operating cycle** | The period of time between the purchase of inventory and the collection of any receivable from the sale of the inventory. |
| **Profit margin** | Net income divided by sales. |
| **Relevance** | The capacity of information to make a difference in a decision. |
| **Reliability** | The quality of accounting information that makes it dependable in reporting what it purports to represent. |
| **Single-step income statement** | An income statement in which all expenses are added together and subtracted from total revenues. |
| **Understandibility** | The quality of accounting information that makes it comprehensible to readers willing to spend the necessary time. |
| **Working capital** | The difference between current assets and current liabilities. |

## Practice Test
## Questions and Problems

### Circle the alternative that best answers the question:

**LO 3**  1.  Which of the following contains only liabilities?
- a)  Accounts payable, taxes payable, notes payable
- b)  Retained earnings, capital stock, paid-in capital in excess of par value
- c)  Sales revenue, cost of goods sold, net income
- d)  Plant and equipment, inventory, cash

**LO 3**  2.  Which of the following contains only assets?
- a)  Accounts payable, taxes payable, notes payable
- b)  Retained earnings, capital stock, paid-in capital in excess of par value
- c)  Sales revenue, cost of goods sold, net income
- d)  Plant and equipment, inventory, cash

**LO 5**  3.  Which of the following contains items that would only be found in the income statement?
- a)  Accounts payable, taxes payable, notes payable
- b)  Retained earnings, capital stock, paid-in capital in excess of par value
- c)  Sales revenue, cost of goods sold, net income
- d)  Plant and equipment, inventory, cash

**LO 3**  4.  Which of the following economic events results in a corporation acquiring an asset?
- a)  The corporation buys merchandise on credit.
- b)  The corporation declares a dividend to be paid in two months.
- c)  The corporation announces a pay increase for the following year for its hourly paid workers.
- d)  The corporation pays an amount it owes a customer.

**LO 2**  5.  Which of the following statements best describes the principle of reliability?
- a)  When uncertainty exists, understating assets, overstating liabilities, accelerating recognition of losses, and delaying recognition of gains is preferred.
- b)  Similar events are measured using identical accounting procedures from period to period.
- c)  Different firms use identical accounting measurement methods for similar events.
- d)  The measurement of an event is verifiable and dependable.

**LO 2** 6. Which of the following accounting principles is being applied when a firm delays recognition of a sale made to a customer who has declared bankruptcy until cash is received from the customer?
a) Matching
b) Objectivity
c) Going concern
d) Conservatism

**LO 3** 7. Which of the following best describes the amount that appears on the balance sheet as stockholders' equity?
a) What the company owes and must pay in the future
b) Cash that stockholders have contributed
c) The shareholders' claim on the assets of the firm
d) The total past earnings minus the amount distributed in dividends

**LO 3** 8. Which of the following best describes the amount that appears on the balance sheet as retained earnings?
a) What the company owes and must pay in the future
b) Cash or other assets that stockholders have contributed to the company in exchange for shares
c) The shareholders' claim on the assets of the firm
d) The total past earnings minus the amount distributed in dividends

**LO 9** 9. A statement that "in our opinion the financial statements present fairly, in all material respects, the financial position of X Corporation " would most likely be found in:
a) the auditor's report.
b) the management's discussion and analysis.
c) the management letter.
d) the president's letter to the stockholders.

**LO 3** 10. Which of the following is a creditor of Beta Corporation?
a) A customer of Beta Corp that buys goods on credit.
b) A bank that lends money to Beta Corp.
c) An investor who sells their stock in Beta Corp.
d) An investor who buys stock in Beta Corp.

**LO 3** 11. Which of the following best describes the amount that appears on the balance sheet as liabilities?
a) What the company owes and must pay in the future
b) Cash that stockholders have contributed
c) The shareholders' claim on the assets of the firm
d) The total past earnings minus the amount distributed in dividends

**LO 4**  12.  Liquidity:
  a)  is the cash flow from operations minus cash flow used in investment activities.
  b)  deals with the ability of the company to pay its debts as they come due.
  c)  is the amount of cash that the company has available.
  d)  equals current assets minus current liabilities.

*Use the following information to answer questions 13 through 15:*
The following items appear in the balance sheet of Company A at the end of Year 1 and Year 2:

|  | Year 2 | Year 1 |
|---|---|---|
| Current assets | $ 5,000 | $ 2,000 |
| Long-term assets | 8,000 | 5,000 |
| Current liabilities | 2,000 | 6,000 |
| Long-term liabilities | 7,000 | 0 |
| Stockholders' equity | ? | ? |

**LO 3**  13.  Company A's stockholders' equity was:
  a)  $22,000 in Year 2 and $13,000 in Year 1.
  b)  $4,000 in Year 2 and $1,000 in Year 1.
  c)  $8,000 in Year 2 and $13,000 in Year 1.
  d)  None of the above.

**LO 3**  14.  Between Year 1 and Year 2:
  a)  Company A's total liabilities and current liabilities both increased.
  b)  Company A's total liabilities and current liabilities both decreased.
  c)  Company A's total liabilities increased and its current liabilities decreased.
  d)  Company A's total liabilities decreased and its current liabilities increased.

**LO 4**  15.  Between Year 1 and Year 2:
  a)  Company A's working capital and current ratio both increased.
  b)  Company A's working capital and current ratio both decreased.
  c)  Company A's working capital increased and its current ratio decreased.
  d)  Company A's working capital decreased and its current ratio increased.

## Indicate whether each of the following statements is true or false:

**LO 4**  16.  A company's current ratio has changed from 2:1 at the beginning of the period to 2.5:1 at the end. Over the same period, its current liabilities have also increased. The company's current assets must also have increased over the same period.

**LO 8**  17.  A company's income may or may not equal its cash flows from operations.

**LO 3**  18.  A fast food restaurant could be expected to have a shorter operation cycle than a furniture store.

**LO 5**  19.  A multiple-step income statement may not be as useful to investors and other users as a single-step income statement.

**LO 3** 20. Accounts payable are current assets resulting from a firm selling inventory but not yet having received the money from the customer.

**LO 3** 21. All tangible fixed assets must be depreciated.

**LO 2** 22. Consistency refers to the feature of accounting that ensures that every company conforms to the same set of accounting standards.

**LO 6** 23. If a company's gross profit ratio increases, its profit margin must also increase.

**LO 4** 24. If a company's working capital decreases, its current ratio increases.

**LO 6** 25. If a firm has retained earnings of $3,000, then it must have cash available to pay dividends of at least $3,000.

**LO 8** 26. If you wish to find the amount of cash that a firm generated from its operations during the accounting period, you should look in the income statement.

**LO 5** 27. Investors and other users of financial statements are primarily concerned with the cash a company can generate, so there is no need to provide any statement other than the statement of cash flows.

**LO 2** 28. Purchase of inventory on credit increases current assets and increases current liabilities.

**LO 3** 29. Retained earnings is a measure of the total earnings of the business since its inception less all dividends the company has paid to its shareholders.

**LO 9** 30. If a company shows a cash flow from operations of $55 million in its cash flow statement, its net income must also be $55 million in its income statement.

## Complete each of the following statements:

**LO 3** 31. _____ is a method of allocating the cost of a long-term asset over its useful life.

**LO 8** 32. The statement of cash flows shows the cash flows resulting from the company's _____, _____, and _____ activities over the period.

**LO 6** 33. Company Z has sales of $100,000, cost of sales of $60,000, and net income of $20,000. Its gross profit ratio is _____, and its profit margin is _____.

**LO 4** 34. A company's current assets are $20,000 and its working capital is $15,000. Its current liabilities are _____ and its current ratio is _____.

**LO 2** 35. A company buys inventory for cash on February 1, 1999, sells it on credit on February 28, 1999, and receives cash from the customer on March 15, 1999. The company's operating cycle is _____ days.

**LO 5** 36. A single-step income statement provides less information to users than a _____ income statement.

**LO 4** 37. Company A's current assets are $20,000, its current liabilities are $10,000. Company B's current assets are $200,000 and its current liabilities are $150,000. As measured by its current ratio, Company A is _____ liquid than Company B.

**LO 4** 38. Of the two measures, working capital and the current ratio, the one that is better for making comparisons across different companies is _____.

**LO 3** 39. Intangible assets are carried on the balance sheet at _____. This is an application of the _____.

**LO 5** 40. _____ is the difference between sales and cost of goods sold; selling expenses and general and administrative expenses are deducted to find _____ .

**LO 9** 41. The _____ provides an independent opinion on the fairness of the financial statements.

**LO 6** 42. If a company's gross margin is 30%, and its cost of goods sold is $14,000, its sales are _____.

**LO 2** 43. _____ is the practice of using the least optimistic estimate when two or more possible estimates are about equally likely.

**LO 3** 44. The element of the balance sheet that consists of the two main components, capital stock and retained earnings, is _____.

**LO 9** 45. The income statement, unlike the statement of cash flows, reports only on the _____ activities of the business.

## Answer each of the following problems:

**LO 4,5** 46. Complete the table below to show the effect of each transaction on current and long-term assets, current and long-term liabilities, or stockholders' equity.

Use + if the item increases, - if the item decreases, 0 if the event has no effect on the item, and ? if the effect of the event cannot be determined.

The first one is done for you.

| | CURRENT ASSETS | LONG-TERM ASSETS | CURRENT LIABILITIES | LONG-TERM LIABILITIES | STOCKHOLDERS' EQUITY |
|---|---|---|---|---|---|
| Cash collections from accounts receivable | + Cash<br>- Accounts receivable | | | | |
| Cash payment of accounts payable | | | | | |
| Cash payment of taxes payable | | | | | |
| Issue of bonds for cash | | | | | |
| Issue of capital stock for cash | | | | | |
| Purchase of inventory for cash | | | | | |
| Purchase of inventory on credit | | | | | |
| Purchase of building for cash | | | | | |
| Repayment of bonds | | | | | |

**LO 5,6** 47. The consolidated statement of earnings for Ben & Jerry's Corporation for three financial years include the following amounts:

## BEN & JERRYS HOMEMADE INC
**Values are in thousands, except where noted.**

| Year Ended | 12/25/99 | 12/26/98 | 12/27/97 |
|---|---|---|---|
| Gross profit | 91,752 | 72,978 | 59,922 |
| Income before income taxes | 5,208 | 9,776 | 6,284 |
| Cost of sales | (145,291) | (136,225) | (114,284) |
| Income taxes | (1,823) | (3,534) | (2,388) |
| Selling, general and administrative expenses | (78,623) | (63,895) | (53,520) |
| Special charge | (8,602) | | |
| Net income | 3,385 | 6,242 | 3,896 |
| Net sales | 237,043 | 209,203 | 174,206 |
| Other income (expense) including interest | 681 | 693 | (118) |

**Required**

1. Prepare in good form a multiple-step income statement for each period.

2. Restate each item in the multiple-step income statements as a percentage of sales.

3. Calculate the gross profit ratio and profit margin for each year.

4. On the basis of your calculations, compare the company's profitability over the three years and explain why it is more meaningful to use ratios to compare these statements than to directly compare the total numbers in each statement.

**LO 5** 48. Alyssa Lopez has been in business as a beautician for a year and believes she has found a lucrative niche in providing on-site beautician services to retirement homes. She now wants to expand the business by employing an additional beautician but the new employee would need a new car. She therefore wants you to invest in the business by either lending her money or becoming a partner. She shows you the following "income statement" for the year, which she has drawn up by summarizing her personal checkbook:

| | |
|---|---|
| Revenues | $45,000 |
| Expenses | 25,000 |
| Net income | $20,000 |

You examine the statement and talk to Alyssa who gives you the following additional information:

a) She owes $10,000 to Beta Beauty Supplies for beauty supplies that have already been used but not paid for.

b) She used her own car for the business at a cost of $3,000 for the year.

c) The revenue figure in her income statement does not include cash of $5,000 received from customers that Alyssa has used for her own living expenses.

**Required**

1. Alyssa has clearly not provided you with an income statement. What has she given you?

2.      Draw up the income statement for the year for Alyssa's business.

3.      Would you be willing to invest money in Alyssa's business? What problems do you see? Would you prefer to lend her money or become a partner? Why?

## Critical Thinking Problem

**LO 4**    49.    We show below extracts from the consolidated balance sheets of Ben & Jerry's Homemade Inc. on 12/25/99 and 12/26/98. The numbers are in thousands of dollars.

**BEN & JERRYS HOMEMADE INC**
**Balance Sheet**

|  | 12/25/99 | 12/26/98 |
|---|---|---|
| **ASSETS** | | |
| Current assets: | | |
| Cash and cash equivalents | $25,260 | $25,111 |
| Short-term investments | 21,331 | 22,118 |
| Trade accounts receivable (less allowance of $966 in 1999 and $979 in 1998 for doubtful accounts) | 18,833 | 11,338 |
| Inventories | 13,937 | 13,090 |
| Deferred income taxes | 5,609 | 7,547 |
| Prepaid expenses and other current assets | 2,377 | 3,105 |
| Total current assets | $87,347 | $82,309 |
| | | |
| **LIABILITIES & STOCKHOLDERS' EQUITY** | | |
| Current liabilities: | | |
| Accounts payable and accrued expenses | $38,915 | $28,662 |
| Current portion of long-term debt and obligations under capital leases | 5,627 | 5,266 |
| Total current liabilities | $44,542 | $33,928 |

**Required**

1.  Calculate Ben & Jerry's working capital and current ratio for the two years.

2.  By considering both your answer to question 1 and changes in the components of Ben & Jerry's current assets and current liabilities over the year, comment on whether or not you think that Ben & Jerry's liquidity has improved over the period.

## Solutions

### Multiple Choice

| | | | | |
|---|---|---|---|---|
| 1. | a | | 9. | a |
| 2. | d | | 10. | b |
| 3. | c | | 11. | a |
| 4. | a | | 12. | b |
| 5. | d | | 13. | b |
| 6. | d | | 14. | c |
| 7. | c | | 15. | a |
| 8. | d | | | |

### True/False

| | | |
|---|---|---|
| 16. | True | |
| 17. | True | |
| 18. | True | |
| 19. | False | The multiple-step income statement provides more information for users. |
| 20. | False | Accounts receivable, an asset, result from selling goods on credit. |
| 21. | False | Land need not be depreciated. |
| 22. | False | Consistency refers to the feature of accounting that ensures that users are able to compare the accounts of different companies within the same time period and accounts of the same company over time. |
| 23. | False | For example, selling and administrative expenses can increase disproportionately and reduce net income for the period although the gross profit ratio has increased. |
| 24. | False | Both working capital and the current ratio move in the same direction. |
| 25. | False | Retained earnings does not represent cash available. |
| 26. | False | Cash flow from operations is found in the statement of cash flows. |
| 27. | False | Investors are also interested in the assets and liabilities shown in the balance sheet and the net income, the measure of operating performance shown in the income statement. |
| 28. | True | |
| 29. | True | |
| 30. | False | Net income represents both cash received and paid, and amounts owed and receivable. |

## Fill in the Blanks

| | | | |
|---|---|---|---|
| 31. | depreciation | 39. | original cost, cost principle |
| 32. | operating, investing, financing | 40. | gross profit, income from operations |
| 33. | 40%, 20% | 41. | auditors' report |
| 34. | $5,000, 4.0 | 42. | $20,000 |
| 35. | 43 | 43. | conservatism |
| 36. | multiple-step | 44. | stockholders' equity |
| 37. | more | 45. | operating |
| 38. | current ratio | | |

## Problem 46

| | CURRENT ASSETS | LONG-TERM ASSETS | CURRENT LIABILITIES | LONG-TERM LIABILITIES | STOCKHOLDERS' EQUITY |
|---|---|---|---|---|---|
| Cash collections from accounts receivable | + Cash<br>- Accounts receivable | | | | |
| Cash payment of accounts payable | - Cash | | - Accounts payable | | |
| Cash payment of taxes payable | - Cash | | - Taxes payable | | |
| Issue of bonds for cash | + Cash | | | + Bonds | |
| Issue of capital stock for cash | + Cash | | | | + Capital Stock |
| Purchase of inventory for cash | - Cash<br>+ Inventory | | | | |
| Purchase of inventory on credit | + Inventory | | + Accounts payable | | |
| Purchase of building for cash | - Cash | + Building | | | |
| Repayment of bonds | - Cash | | | - Bonds | |

## Problem 47

1.

| Year Ended | 12/25/99 | 12/26/98 | 12/27/97 |
|---|---|---|---|
| Net sales | $237,043 | $209,203 | $174,206 |
| Less: Cost of sales | (145,291) | (136,225) | (114,284) |
| Gross profit | 91,752 | 72,978 | 59,922 |
| Less: Selling, general and administrative expenses | (78,623) | (63,895) | (53,520) |
| Less: Special charge | (8,602) | | |
| Other income (expense) including interest | 681 | 693 | (118) |
| Income before income taxes | 5,208 | 9,776 | 6,284 |
| Less: Income taxes | (1,823) | (3,534) | (2,388) |
| Net income | $ 3,385 | $ 6,242 | $ 3,896 |

2.

| Year Ended | 12/25/99 | 12/26/98 | 12/27/97 |
|---|---|---|---|
| Net sales | 100.0% | 100.0% | 100.0% |
| Less: Cost of sales | (61.3%) | (65.1%) | (65.6%) |
| Gross profit | 38.7% | 34.9% | 34.4% |
| Less: Selling, general and administrative expenses | (33.2%) | (30.5%) | (30.7%) |
| Less: Special charge | (3.6%) | | |
| Other income (expense) including interest | 0.3% | 0.3% | (0.1%) |
| Income before income taxes | 2.2% | 4.7% | 3.6% |
| Less: Income taxes | (0.8%) | (1.7%) | (1.4%) |
| Net income | 1.4% | 3.0% | 2.2% |

3. The gross profit ratio and profit margin for each year can be found from the table above.

| Year Ended | 12/25/99 | 12/26/98 | 12/27/97 |
|---|---|---|---|
| Gross profit ratio | 38.7% | 34.9% | 34.4% |
| Profit margin | 1.4% | 3.0% | 2.2% |

4. Ben & Jerry's sales have continued to grow over the three years and their gross profit ratio has also increased, indicating that their manufacturing operations have continued to be profitable. However, an increase in the percentage paid for selling and administration in 1999 and the special charge in 1999 has resulted in the profit margin ratio decreasing significantly in 1999. Note that if the company had not had the special charge, the profit margin would have been 5%, a significant increase over previous years. If you are analyzing Ben & Jerry's income statements to help predict future profitability, then you would probably use this figure since the special charge is a one-time expense that is not expected to repeat.

Using ratios lets you see the relationship between sales and expense over the three accounting periods, which is particularly helpful in this case where the sales and expenses are rising.

## Problem 48

1. Alyssa has provided you with a partial summary of cash payments and receipts, which is more like a statement of cash flows than an income statement. However, the statement she has provided you with is not complete, and therefore it cannot even be called a statement of cash flows.

2.  **Income statement**

| | | |
|---|---|---|
| Sales | | $50,000 |
| Expenses | 25,000 | |
| Supplies expense | 10,000 | |
| Car expenses | 3,000 | |
| Total expenses | | 38,000 |
| **Net income** | | **$12,000** |

Note: Sales equals $45,000, as reported, plus $5,000 taken for Alyssa's use.

3.  The business is clearly not as profitable as Alyssa had claimed, and therefore you would probably be reluctant to invest money in it until you could see some further results. However, of greater concern is the confusion of Alyssa's personal accounts with the business accounts. A system of accounting for the business separate from Alyssa's personal spending should be established. Until such a system is operational, you cannot put much reliance on the information provided by her. If you were to invest, probably a loan would be preferable, especially if it could be secured on an asset such as her car.

## Critical Thinking Problem 49

1.

| | 1999 | 1998 |
|---|---|---|
| Working capital ($ thousands) | 42,805 | 48,381 |
| Current ratio | 1.96 | 2.43 |

2.  The two components of Ben & Jerry's working capital that have increased over the period are accounts receivable (from $18,833 to $11,338) and accounts payable (from $38,915 to $28,662). Overall however, Ben & Jerry's working capital position seems fairly satisfactory since it has almost twice as much in current assets as it does in current liabilities. However, the change in both accounts receivable and accounts payable should be monitored to ensure that the situation does not continue to worsen.

# Chapter 3

# Processing Accounting Information

Accounting information is the result of a process that begins with an economic event and ends with the production of financial reports. This chapter starts the exploration of that process. Your overall aim is to understand the basic accounting tools and procedures that are needed to record accounting information.

## Learning Objectives

**LO 1** Explain the difference between an internal and an external event.

**LO 2** Explain the role of source documents in an accounting system.

**LO 3** Analyze the effects of transactions on the accounting equation.

**LO 4** Define the concept of a general ledger and understand the use of the T account as a method for analyzing transactions.

**LO 5** Explain the rules of debit and credit.

**LO 6** Explain the purposes of a journal and the posting process.

**LO 7** Explain the purpose of a trial balance.

## Key Textbook Exhibits

**Exhibit 3-1** illustrates the impact of various transactions on the accounting equation. Note how each entry maintains the equality of the basic accounting equation. *Self-Test:* In transaction number 5, the $5,000 from "court fees" is recorded as an increase in the Retained Earnings column. Remember that Retained Earnings is classified within owners' equity on the balance sheet. In Exhibit 3-3, the same $5,000 is shown under the Revenues classification. Remember that Revenues is an income statement account. Is this inconsistent?

$$\text{Assets} = \text{Liabilities} + \text{Owners' Equity}$$
$$\text{Revenue} - \text{Expenses} = \text{Net Income}$$

**Exhibit 3-3** illustrates the income statement for Glengarry Health Club that would be prepared from the transactions in Exhibit 3-1. *Self-Test:* How is this income statement prepared from the transactions in Exhibit 3-1 when the accounts in Exhibit 3-1 are all from the balance sheet?

**Exhibit 3-4** illustrates a sample **chart of accounts** for a Theater company. Note that the asset accounts begin with a 1, the liabilities with a 2, the equities with a 3, the revenues with a 4, and the expenses with a 5. *Self-Test:* Do you think the asset account numbers used by most companies begin with a 1, the liability account numbers with a 2, the equity account numbers with a 3, etc.? Why?

**Exhibit 3-5** illustrates how transactions are posted from the journal to the ledger. Make sure you can follow the logic of the **posting** from the journal to each ledger account. *Self-Test:* Why is it necessary to accumulate the debits and credits from the journal entries, in the General Journal, in individual General Ledger accounts, such as Cash and Court Fee Revenue?

**Exhibit 3-6** illustrates the trial balance for Glengarry Health Club. Remember that a trial balance is a list of each account and its balance and is used to prove the equality of debits and credits. *Self-Test:* Where did the accountants of Glengarry get the amounts used in the trial balance?

## Review of Key Concepts

**LO 1**   Any event that is recognized in a set of financial statements is called a **transaction.** Transactions are the basic building blocks of any accounting system. **Internal events**, such as the transfer of material to production or the use of a piece of equipment, occur entirely within the enterprise. **External events**, such as the purchase of inventory or a stock issue for cash, involve interactions with an outside party or group. All events must be measured to be recognized. If the amount or value of the event cannot be determined, the event is not recognized in the financial records.

**LO 2**   **Source documents** are used to identify transactions. For external transactions, source documents may be generated externally, for example, an invoice from a supplier; or internally, as with a receipt for payment received from a customer. For internal transactions, source documents are generated internally. Material requisitions used to transfer goods from inventory to production are examples of source documents generated internally.

**LO 3**   The Cost Principle requires that we record an asset at the cost to acquire it and continue to show the cost amount on the balance sheet until the company disposes of the asset. The cost of an asset can be verified by an independent observer and is much more objective and verifiable than market value.

**LO 3**   One way of analyzing the impact of economic events on the accounts is to use the accounting equation:

$$\textbf{Assets} \ = \ \textbf{Liabilities + Owners' Equity}$$

Every transaction has a *dual effect* on the accounting equation. If assets increase, then there must also be an increase in liabilities or owners' equity and vice versa. If assets decrease, then there must also be a decrease in liabilities or owners' equity and vice versa. Note that the increase and decrease may both be in the same term of the equation. For example, if inventory is bought for cash, one asset (inventory) increases and another asset (cash) decreases by the same amount. The accounting equation must always balance after each transaction has been recorded.

To illustrate, let us analyze the transactions of the Pacioli Corporation. The Pacioli Corporation, a retailer of accounting software, was incorporated on January 1, 2001. Pacioli's transactions for its first year of operations ended December 31, 2001 included the following:

1. Stockholders invested $225,000 cash in exchange for 225,000 common shares with a par value of $1 each.
2. Merchandise inventory was bought over the year totaling $195,000. All purchases were made on credit.
3. Office furniture was bought for $40,000 cash on February 2, 2001. The furniture has a three-year life and no residual value.
4. Pacioli paid its vendors $170,000 in cash.

| | **Assets** | | | **Liabilities** | **Stockholders' Equity** | |
| | Cash | Merchandise Inventory | Furniture | Accounts Payable | Capital Stock | |
|---|---|---|---|---|---|---|
| 1. | +225,000 | | | | +225,000 | Both the assets and stockholders' equity increase. |
| 2. | | +195,000 | | +195,000 | | Both assets and liabilities increase. |
| 3. | -40,000 | | +40,000 | | | One asset (furniture) increases and one asset (cash) decreases. Total assets are unaffected. |
| 4. | -170,000 | | | -170,000 | | Both cash and accounts payable are reduced. |
| | 15,000 | +195,000 | + 40,000 = | 25,000 + | 225,000 | Balance |

**LO 5** It is impractical to use the accounting equation to analyze and record large volumes of transactions. Therefore, in practice two main tools are used: **ledger accounts** and **journal entries**.

• An **account** is a record used to accumulate detailed information about changes in each type of asset, liability, owners' equity (balance sheet), revenue, and expense (income statement). A chart of accounts lists all the accounts that an entity uses. Each entity will have its own unique chart of accounts. See the sample chart of accounts in Exhibit 3-4.

• A **general ledger** is a book, file, hard drive, or other device that contains the accounts of a business.

• A **debit** is the name given to increasing an asset or expense account, and to decreasing a liability, owners' equity, or revenue account. By convention, debits are recorded on the left side of an entry or account.

• A **credit** is the name given to decreasing an asset or expense account, and to increasing a liability, owners' equity, or revenue account. By convention, credits are recorded on the right side of an entry or account.

| | **BALANCE SHEET** | | | **INCOME STATEMENT** | |
| | **Assets** | **Liabilities** | **Equity** | **Revenues** | **Expenses** |
|---|---|---|---|---|---|
| **Debit** | Increase | Decrease | Decrease | Decrease | Increase |
| **Credit** | Decrease | Increase | Increase | Increase | Decrease |

The Balance Sheet includes assets, liabilities, and owners' equity. The Income Statement includes revenues and expenses. Remember assets and expenses are the only two types of accounts that increase on the debit side. All other account types decrease on the debit side. Also note that for each account type in the chart, credits operate opposite of debits, (i.e. when debits increase, credits decrease and vice versa).

- A **T account** is a convenient way of symbolizing a general ledger account. In practice, general ledger accounts come in many different forms, such as computer files. We illustrate the recording of transactions in T accounts using the Pacioli Corporation example.

| CASH | | | CAPITAL STOCK | | |
|---|---|---|---|---|---|
| 1. | 225,000 | | | 1. | 225,000 |
| Bal. | 225,000 | | | Bal. | 225,000 |

Cash is increased; therefore the asset account, cash, is debited. Capital stock also increases and the owners' equity account, capital stock, is credited.

| MERCHANDISE INVENTORY | | | ACCOUNTS PAYABLE | | |
|---|---|---|---|---|---|
| 2. | 195,000 | | | 2. | 195,000 |
| Bal. | 195,000 | | | Bal. | 195,000 |

Merchandise inventory is increased and the asset account, merchandise inventory, is debited. Liabilities increased and therefore the liability account, accounts payable, is credited.

| CASH | | | | OFFICE FURNITURE | | |
|---|---|---|---|---|---|---|
| 1. | 225,000 | 3. | 40,000 | 3. | 40,000 | |
| Bal. | 185,000 | | | Bal. | 40,000 | |

Office furniture increased and the asset account, office furniture, is debited. Cash decreased and the asset account, cash, is credited.

| CASH | | | | ACCOUNTS PAYABLE | | | |
|---|---|---|---|---|---|---|---|
| 1. | 225,000 | 3. | 40,000 | 4. | 170,000 | 2. | 195,000 |
| | | 4. | 170,000 | | | | |
| Bal. | 15,000 | | | | | Bal. | 25,000 |

Cash decreases and therefore the asset account, cash, is credited. Accounts payable decreases and the liability account, accounts payable, is debited.

**LO 6** Even though T accounts are a convenient way of symbolizing how a transaction affects a general ledger account, in practice, the **journal** is the place where transactions are recorded. Transactions are first recorded in the journal, which is therefore called a book of original entry. Once the journal entries are complete, the effects of the transactions are posted to the ledger accounts. Journal entries are recorded in the order they occur and take the following general form (with xxx representing the dollar sum involved):

| | | Debit | Credit |
|---|---|---|---|
| Date | [Account(s) to be debited] | xxx | |
| | [Account(s) to be credited] | | xxx |
| | *Explanation of transaction* | | |

For example, the journal entries for the transactions for Pacioli Corporation are as follows:

| | Date | Account Titles and Explanations | Post Ref. | Debit | Credit |
|---|---|---|---|---|---|
| 1. | 2001 | Cash | 1. | 225,000 | |
| | | Capital stock | | | 225,000 |
| | | Sale of company stock | | | |
| 2. | 2001 | Merchandise inventory | | 195,000 | |
| | | Accounts payable | | | 195,000 |
| | | Purchase of inventory on credit | | | |
| 3. | 2001 | Office furniture | | 40,000 | |
| | | Cash | 1. | | 40,000 |
| | | Purchase of furniture for cash | | | |
| 4. | 2001 | Accounts payable | | 170,000 | |
| | | Cash | | | 170,000 |
| | | Payment of accounts payable | | | |

Once the journal entries are complete, the ledger accounts are posted with the effects of the transactions. As this continues throughout the accounting period, each ledger account builds into a complete record of all transactions relating to that account that have taken place during the period. The ledger accounts can then be used as the basis for preparing the periodic financial statements. To illustrate the posting of transactions to ledger accounts, we show the postings to the cash account of the Pacioli Company's transactions using a **running balance form of account**:

### General Ledger
#### Cash                              **Account No. 1**

| Date | Explanation | Post. Ref. | Debit | Credit | Balance |
|---|---|---|---|---|---|
| 2001 | Stock issued | 1. | 225,000 | | 225,000 |
| 2001 | Purchase of office furniture | 3. | | 40,000 | 185,000 |
| 2001 | Payment of accounts payable | 4. | | 170,000 | 15,000 |

Note that in this form of ledger account, the account balance is clearly seen after each transaction is posted, hence the name "running balance".

**LO 7**  A **trial balance** is a list of account balances at a particular point in time, and is usually drawn up at the end of a period. It is not itself a financial statement, but simply a convenient device to help detect errors. During the **journalizing** and posting of transactions, total debits should always equal total credits. If, when the trial balance is drawn up, the total of the credit balances does not equal the total debit balances, then there must have been a mistake made either in journalizing or posting the transactions. An imbalance in the trial balance can therefore be used to help detect and correct errors. The following is the trial balance for Pacioli Corporation on December 31, 2001:

**Pacioli Corporation**

| Trial balance on 12/31/01 | Debit | Credit |
|---|---|---|
| Cash | 15,000 | |
| Merchandise inventory | 195,000 | |
| Furniture | 40,000 | |
| Accounts payable | | 25,000 |
| Capital stock | | 225,000 |
| | $250,000 | $250,000 |

All of the information needed to prepare the balance sheet comes from the trial balance.

**Pacioli Corporation**
**Balance Sheet**
**December 31, 2001**

| Assets | | | Liabilities and Owners' Equity | | |
|---|---|---|---|---|---|
| Cash | $ | 15,000 | Accounts payable | $ | 25,000 |
| Merchandise inventory | | 195,000 | Capital stock | | 225,000 |
| Office furniture | | 40,000 | | | |
| | | | Total liabilities and | | |
| Total assets | $ | 250,000 | owners' equity | $ | 250,000 |

None of the transactions involved revenue or expense accounts so an income statement is not prepared.

## Review of Key Terms

| | |
|---|---|
| **Account** | The record used to accumulate the monetary amounts for each individual asset, liability, revenue, expense, and component of owners' equity. |
| **Chart of accounts** | A list of all the accounts used by a company. |
| **Credit** | The name given to decreasing an asset or expense account, and to increasing liability, owners' equity, or revenue, account. It is recorded on the right side of an account. |
| **Debit** | The name given to increasing an asset or expense account, and to decreasing a liability, owners' equity, or revenue account. It is recorded on the left side of an account. |
| **Double-entry system** | An accounting system in which every transaction is recorded with equal debits and credits, and the accounting equation is kept in balance. |
| **Event** | A happening of consequence to an entity. |
| **External event** | An event involving the interaction between an entity and its environment. |
| **General journal** | A journal used in lieu of a specialized journal. |
| **General ledger** | A book, file, magnetic tape, or disc containing all of a company's accounts. |
| **Internal event** | An event occurring entirely within the business. |
| **Journal** | A chronological record of transactions (journal entries), also known as the book of original record. |
| **Journalizing** | The process of recording journal entries. |
| **Posting** | The process of transferring the amounts from a journal to the appropriate ledger accounts. |
| **Source document** | A piece of paper used as evidence to record a transaction. |
| **Transaction** | Any event, internal or external, that is recognized in a set of financial statements. |
| **Trial balance** | A worksheet showing the balance in each account. |

## Practice Test
## Questions and Problems

### Circle the alternative that best answers the question:

**LO 5**   1.   Which of the following describes the purchase of $1,000 of supplies on credit?
   a)   Increase assets and increase owner's equity for $1,000
   b)   Decrease owners' equity for $1,000 and decrease assets for $1,000
   c)   Increase assets and increase liabilities for $1,000
   d)   Decrease liabilities and decrease assets for $1,000

**LO 3**    2.    The effect on the balance sheet of paying accounts payable with cash is that:
- a) total assets increase and total liabilities increase.
- b) total assets decrease and total liabilities decrease.
- c) total assets increase and total liabilities decrease.
- d) total assets decrease and total liabilities increase.

**LO 4**    3.    The ledger is:
- a) the book of the original entry in which debit and credit descriptions of events that change assets, liabilities, and owners' equity are recorded.
- b) the place where economic information is accumulated with respect to the accounts affected.
- c) a summary of accounts and their balances, which is used to prepare financial statements.
- d) a record of all events that affect the company.

**LO 3**    4.    The effect on the balance sheet of issuing stock for cash is that:
- a) total assets increase and total liabilities increase.
- b) stockholders' equity increases and total liabilities decrease.
- c) total assets are unaffected.
- d) stockholders' equity increases and total assets increase.

**LO 7**    5.    The trial balance is:
- a) the book of the original entry in which debit and credit descriptions of events that change assets, liabilities, and owners' equity are recorded.
- b) the place where economic information is accumulated with respect to the accounts affected.
- c) a summary of accounts and their balances that is used to prepare financial statements.
- d) a record of all events that affect the company.

**LO 3**    6.    Which of the following changes describes the receipt of $1,000 from the issue of bonds?
- a) Assets and owners' equity increase by $1,000
- b) Assets and owners' equity decrease by $1,000
- c) Assets and liabilities increase by $1,000
- d) Assets and liabilities decrease by $1,000

**LO 5**    7.    An asset account:
- a) has a debit balance.
- b) is decreased with a credit.
- c) is a balance sheet account.
- d) All of the above are correct.

**LO 3**    8.    The effect on the balance sheet of buying furniture on credit is that:
- a) total assets increase and total liabilities increase.
- b) total assets decrease and total liabilities decrease.
- c) total assets increase and total liabilities decrease.
- d) total assets decrease and total liabilities increase.

**LO 5** 9. When you deposit money in the bank, the teller informs you that your account has been credited. You are now totally confused because in your accounting class you have just learned that a debit increases your assets and therefore the bank should have debited your account. Which statement best clarifies your confusion?

a) The definitions of debits and credits given by your instructor are wrong.

b) The bank is increasing its liability to you by accepting your money and is therefore recording an increase in the bank's liability to you with a credit.

c) This situation is one of life's great mysteries that we will never fully understand.

d) The banks are attempting to change the definition of credit to be consistent with everyday usage, as in "she is a credit to her family".

**LO 5,6** 10. Which of the following statements is true?

a) The double entry system means that for every debit, there must be a corresponding credit; therefore, the total debits posted to the general ledger must equal the total credits.

b) Accounts that normally have credit balances include capital stock, long-term liabilities, and expenses.

c) The general ledger is the book of original entry.

d) Journal entries must include the accounts to be debited and credited, and may include the relevant dollar amounts.

**LO 7** 11. Which of the following statements is true?

a) If the total debits equals the total credits in a trial balance, then there is an error in the ledger, the journal, or the trial balance, or in the posting from one to the other.

b) The trial balance is a tool used to prove the equality of debits and credits in the general ledger.

c) A trial balance is a supplement to the balance sheet that provides more timely information for investors.

d) Financial statements should be prepared before the trial balance is balanced.

**LO 3** 12. The effect on the balance sheet of selling inventory for cash at a profit is that:

a) total assets decrease and total liabilities increase.

b) total liabilities decrease.

c) total assets are unaffected.

d) stockholders' equity increases.

**LO 6** 13. The journal is:

a) the book of original entry in which debit and credit descriptions of events that change assets, liabilities and owners' equity are recorded.

b) the place where economic information is accumulated with respect to the accounts affected.

c) a summary of accounts and their balances that is used to prepare financial statements.

d) a record of all events that affect the company.

**LO 7** 14. Alpha Corporation buys $35,000 worth of computer equipment for cash. All of the following journal entries incorrectly record this transaction. Which of them will lead to the debit balance on the trial balance being greater than the credit balance?

| | | Debit | Credit |
|---|---|---|---|
| a) | Computer equipment | $38,000 | |
| | Cash | | $35,000 |
| b) | Cash | $35,000 | |
| | Computer equipment | | $35,000 |
| c) | Computer equipment | $33,000 | |
| | Cash | | $33,000 |
| d) | Computer equipment | $35,000 | |
| | Cash | | $38,000 |

**LO 3** 15. The effect on the balance sheet of receiving cash for accounts receivable is that:
   a) total assets decrease and total liabilities increase.
   b) total liabilities decrease.
   c) total assets are unaffected.
   d) stockholders' equity increases.

## Indicate whether each of the following statements is true or false:

**LO 4** 16. The difference between a manual system and a computerized accounting system is the form in which the accounts are stored.

**LO 5** 17. Dividends and expense accounts normally have debit balances.

**LO 1** 18. The only events that require source documents are external events.

**LO 1** 19. Internal events need not be recorded in journal entries but can be posted straight to ledger accounts.

**LO 1** 20. Only events that can be measured reliably should be recorded in the accounts.

**LO 5** 21. In accounting, as in common usage, credits imply something positive has happened to the organization.

**LO 6** 22. A journal entry is the first formal record of a transaction made in the accounting system.

**LO 4** 23. A T account is a form of account used to analyze transactions and is so called because it contains the total transactions for each account.

**LO 2** 24. Time sheets are used as source documents to identify wages payable to employees.

**LO 6** 25. Specialized journals are used to record repetitive transactions in which the debit or the credit is always to the same account.

**LO 3** 26. When cash is received to satisfy an account receivable, total assets increase.

**LO 3** 27. When bonds are issued for cash, stockholders' equity decreases.

**LO 3** 28. When inventory is bought for cash, the current ratio increases.

**LO 3** 29. When common stock is issued for cash, stockholders' equity decreases.

**LO 3** 30. When accounts payable are paid in cash, working capital decreases.

## Complete each of the following statements:

**LO 3** 31. The record used to accumulate monetary amounts for each asset, liability, and component of owners' equity is called an _____.

**LO 3** 32. The numerical list of all of the accounts used by an entity is the _____.

**LO 4** 33. A general ledger is often supplemented by a _____, which contain detailed accounts for a particular class of accounts such as accounts receivable.

**LO 1** 34. The transfer of raw materials into production, the use of plant and equipment in manufacturing and the movement of finished goods into a company's own retail stores are examples of _____ events.

**LO 6** 35. The _____ is where transactions are first recorded in preparation for posting to ledger accounts.

**LO 7** 36. The _____ is a preliminary list of all accounts and their balances, and is a way of proving the equality of debit and credit account balances.

**LO 2** 37. Time cards, invoices received from suppliers, and cash register tapes are examples of _____ that provide evidence needed to record a transaction.

**LO 1** 38. The sale of bonds, the payment of wages to employees, and the transfer of finished goods to customers are examples of _____ events.

**LO 5** 39. Increasing an asset or expense and decreasing a liability, owners' equity, or revenue account all require the account to be _____.

**LO 6** 40. In _____ journal entries, more than one account is either debited or credited.

**LO 4** 41. If the cash account is _____, cash has been received.

**LO 3** 42. Every transaction has a _____ on the accounting equation.

**LO 4** 43. When cash is paid to satisfy an account payable, the cash account is _____ and the accounts payable account is _____.

**LO 5** 44. By convention, _____ are recorded on the left side of an entry or account, and _____ are recorded on the right side of an entry or account.

## Answer each of the following problems:

**LO 5** 46. The following economic events took place in the year ended June 30, 1999, for Computit Corporation, a retailer of computer equipment. Match each event with the correct type of accounting entry:

*Accounting Entry*

A. increase assets and increase liabilities
B. increase assets and increase capital stock
C. increase assets and increase retained earnings
D. decrease liabilities and decrease assets
E. decrease capital stock and decrease assets
F. decrease retained earnings and decrease assets
G. increase one asset and decrease another asset
H. is not communicated by the formal accounting system

| ECONOMIC EVENT | ACCOUNTING ENTRY |
|---|---|
| 1. Sold computer equipment for cash | |
| 2. Market share increased 25% from last year | |
| 3. Paid interest to the bondholders on due date | |
| 4. Declared and paid dividends to the owners of the company | |
| 5. Paid vendors for goods purchased on account | |
| 6. Postage stamps were bought and used to send invoices | |
| 7. The chairman of the company resigned | |
| 8. Received cash from the sale of stock | |
| 9. Received cash from the issuance of bonds | |
| 10. Purchased computer equipment on credit | |

LO 1,2   47.      Refer to the transactions in Problem 46.

**Required**

For the transactions that **are** recorded in the accounts:

1.  Identify at least one source document that is generated from the event.
2.  Identify which information on the source document is most useful in recording the events in the accounts.

| ECONOMIC EVENT | SOURCE DOCUMENTS | INFORMATION |
|:---:|:---:|:---:|
| 1. | | |
| 2. | | |
| 3. | | |
| 4. | | |
| 5. | | |
| 6. | | |
| 7. | | |
| 8. | | |
| 9. | | |
| 10. | | |

**LO 3,4** 48. Larry, Curly, and Moe started Stooge Inc., a bookkeeping and accounting service business on January 1, 2001. During January the following transactions took place:

a) Larry, Curly, and Moe each provided $7,000 cash in return for 7,000 shares of $1 par value capital stock of Stooge Inc.

b) An office and furniture were rented. Rent of $2,500 cash was paid for the month of January.

c) Services of $20,000 were performed for customers; 80% was paid in cash and the remainder was still outstanding at the end of January.

d) Office stationery supplies of $400 were bought. The supplies were bought on credit, and at the end of the month no payment had been made to the supplier. The supplies had all been used by month end.

e) A computer was bought at the end of the month for $2,000 cash.

f) Larry, Curly, and Moe had agreed that each would receive a monthly salary of $5,500. Salaries were paid at the end of the month.

**Required**

1. Complete the table below showing the impact of each transaction on the accounting equation.

| | **Assets** | | | = | **Liabilities +** | **Owners' Equity** | |
| | *Cash* | *Computer* | *Accounts Receivable* | | *Accounts Payable* | *Capital Stock* | *Retained Earnings* |
|---|---|---|---|---|---|---|---|
| a) | | | | | | | |
| b) | | | | | | | |
| c) | | | | | | | |
| d) | | | | | | | |
| e) | | | | | | | |
| f) | | | | | | | |
| Bal. | | | | = | | | |

2. Prepare a trial balance on January 31, 2001, an income statement for the month of January and a balance sheet as of January 31, 2001. On the basis of the statements you have prepared, do you think that the business is viable with the present arrangements?

## Critical Thinking Problem

LO 4   49.   Pacioli Company's summary transactions for its first year of operations to December 31, 2001, are summarized below.

1. Stockholders invested $300,000 cash in exchange for 300,000 shares of Pacioli's common stock with a par value of $1 each.
2. Inventory was bought over the year totaling $210,000. All purchases were made on credit.
3. Office furniture was bought for $31,000 cash on February 2, 2001. The furniture has a three-year life and zero residual value.
4. Pacioli paid its vendors $150,000 in cash.
5. The first year's rental of $72,000 on a retail store was paid on January 2, 2001. The payment was not made on January 1st because that's a holiday and everyone should be home watching football. Shouldn't they?
6. During the year total sales were $440,000, of which $90,000 were in cash and the remainder were on credit.
7. Pacioli received $75,000 from customers who had previously purchased inventory from Pacioli on account (number 6. above).
8. Salaries and wages of $62,000 for the year were paid in cash.
9. Utilities for the year of $11,000 were paid in cash.

Pacioli's bookkeeper prepared journal entries for these transactions and posted them to ledger accounts. He asks you for help to find his $10,000 mistake when his trial balance did not balance.

|    |                                              | Debit $ | Credit $ |
|----|----------------------------------------------|---------|----------|
| 1. | Cash                                         | 300,000 |          |
|    |     Capital stock        |         | 300,000  |
|    | Receipt of cash in exchange for stock issued |         |          |
| 2. | Inventory                                    | 210,000 |          |
|    |     Accounts payable     |         | 210,000  |
|    | Purchase of inventory on credit              |         |          |
| 3. | Office furniture                             | 31,000  |          |
|    |     Cash                 |         | 31,000   |
|    | Purchase of furniture for cash               |         |          |
| 4. | Accounts payable                             | 150,000 |          |
|    |     Cash                 |         | 150,000  |
|    | Cash payment to vendors                      |         |          |
| 5. | Cash                                         | 72,000  |          |
|    |     Rent expense         |         | 72,000   |
|    | Cash payment for rent                        |         |          |
| 6. | Cash                                         | 90,000  |          |
|    | Accounts receivable                          | 250,000 |          |
|    |     Sales                |         | 440,000  |
|    | Cash and receivables from sales              |         |          |
| 7. | Accounts receivable                          | 75,000  |          |
|    |     Cash                 |         | 75,000   |
|    | Cash received from customers on account      |         |          |

| 8. | Salaries and Wages expense | 62,000 | |
| | Cash | | 62,000 |
| | Cash paid for wages and salaries | | |

| 9. | Utilities expense | 11,000 | |
| | Cash | | 11,000 |
| | Cash paid for utilities | | |

| | **CASH** | | | | | **CAPITAL STOCK** | |
|---|---|---|---|---|---|---|---|
| 1. | 310,000 | 3. | 31,000 | | | 1. | 300,000 |
| 5. | 72,000 | 4. | 150,000 | | | | |
| 6. | 90,000 | 8. | 62,000 | | | | |
| 7. | 75,000 | 9. | 11,000 | | | | |
| Bal | 293,000 | | | | | | |

| | **ACCOUNTS PAYABLE** | | | | | **RENT EXPENSE** | |
|---|---|---|---|---|---|---|---|
| 4. | 250,000 | 2. | 210,000 | | | 5. | 72,000 |
| 6. | 350,000 | | | | | | |
| Bal | 390,000 | | | | | | |

| | **OFFICE FURNITURE** | | | **ACCOUNTS RECEIVABLE** | |
|---|---|---|---|---|---|
| 3. | 31,000 | | 7. | 75,000 | |

| | **UTILITIES EXPENSE** | | | **SALARIES AND WAGES EXPENSE** | |
|---|---|---|---|---|---|
| 9. | 11,000 | | 8. | | 52,000 |

| | **INVENTORY** | | | **SALES** | |
|---|---|---|---|---|---|
| 2. | 210,000 | | | 6. | 440,000 |

| **Trial balance on 12/31/2001** | **Debit** | **Credit** |
|---|---|---|
| Cash | $ 293,000 | |
| Rent expense | | $ 72,000 |
| Sales | | 440,000 |
| Salaries and wages expense | 52,000 | |
| Utilities expense | 11,000 | |
| Accounts receivable | | 75,000 |
| Office furniture | 31,000 | |
| Inventory | 210,000 | |
| Capital stock | | 300,000 |
| Accounts payable | 390,000 | |
| | $987,000 | $887,000 |

**Required**

The bookkeeper has made errors in the journal entries, the posting and balancing of the ledger accounts. Help the bookkeeper by completing the following tasks:

a.  Prepare corrected journal entries.

| No. | Account Titles and Explanations | Debit | Credit |
|-----|--------------------------------|-------|--------|
| 1.  |                                |       |        |
|     |                                |       |        |
|     |                                |       |        |
|     |                                |       |        |
|     |                                |       |        |
| 2.  |                                |       |        |
|     |                                |       |        |
|     |                                |       |        |
|     |                                |       |        |
|     |                                |       |        |
| 3.  |                                |       |        |
|     |                                |       |        |
|     |                                |       |        |
|     |                                |       |        |
|     |                                |       |        |
| 4.  |                                |       |        |
|     |                                |       |        |
|     |                                |       |        |
|     |                                |       |        |
|     |                                |       |        |
| 5.  |                                |       |        |
|     |                                |       |        |
|     |                                |       |        |
|     |                                |       |        |
|     |                                |       |        |
| 6.  |                                |       |        |
|     |                                |       |        |
|     |                                |       |        |
|     |                                |       |        |
|     |                                |       |        |
| 7.  |                                |       |        |
|     |                                |       |        |
|     |                                |       |        |
|     |                                |       |        |
|     |                                |       |        |
| 8.  |                                |       |        |
|     |                                |       |        |
|     |                                |       |        |
|     |                                |       |        |
|     |                                |       |        |

| 9. | | | |
|----|---|---|---|
| | | | |
| | | | |
| | | | |

b. Prepare correct postings to the T accounts.

c.  Prepare a corrected trial  balance.

| Trial balance on 12/31/2001 | Debit | Credit |
|---|---|---|
|  |  |  |
|  |  |  |
|  |  |  |
|  |  |  |
|  |  |  |
|  |  |  |
|  |  |  |
|  |  |  |
|  |  |  |
|  |  |  |
|  |  |  |
|  |  |  |
|  |  |  |

# Solutions

## Multiple Choice

| | | | | |
|---|---|---|---|---|
| 1. | c | | 9. | b |
| 2. | b | | 10. | a |
| 3. | b | | 11. | b |
| 4. | d | | 12. | d |
| 5. | c | | 13. | a |
| 6. | c | | 14. | a |
| 7. | d | | 15. | c |
| 8. | a | | | |

## True/False

### COMMENT/EXPLANATION

| 16. | True | |
|---|---|---|
| 17. | True | |
| 18. | False | Although not all recognizable events generate a standard source document, some form of documentation must be generated for all transactions. |
| 19. | False | All transactions must be recorded in journal entries. |
| 20. | True | |
| 21. | False | A credit is simply a shorthand way of saying that there is an increase in a liability or owners' equity account or a decrease in an asset account. |
| 22. | True | |
| 23. | False | A T account is so called because it is in the shape of a T. |
| 24. | True | |
| 25. | True | |
| 26. | False | The increase in cash equals the reduction in accounts receivable, so the net effect on total assets is zero. |
| 27. | False | Stockholders' equity is unaffected by a bond issue, but assets and liabilities would both increase. |
| 28. | False | The net effect on total assets is zero so the current ratio does not change. |
| 29. | False | When stock is issued for cash, common stock increases. |
| 30. | False | Current assets and current liabilities change in the same amount. Therefore there is no change in working capital. |

## Fill in the Blanks

31. account
32. chart of accounts
33. subsidiary ledger
34. Internal
35. Journal
36. trial balance
37. source documents
38. External

39. debited
40. compound
41. debited
42. dual effect
43. credited, debited
44. debits, credits
45. $197,000

## Problems 46 and 47

| ECONOMIC EVENT | ACCOUNTING ENTRY | SOURCE DOCUMENTS | INFORMATION |
|---|---|---|---|
| 1. | G | Receipt from vendor | Cost of computer |
| 2. | H | | |
| 3. | F | Lists of bondholders and interest paid to each | Total interest paid |
| 4. | F | Lists of stockholders and dividends paid to each | Total dividends paid |
| 5. | D | Invoice or statement from vendor | Amount of invoice or statement |
| 6. | F | Receipt from post office | Total cost of stamps used |
| 7. | H | | |
| 8. | B | Checks received from stockholders | Total dollar amount of checks received |
| 9. | A | Checks received from bondholders | Total dollar amount of checks received |
| 10. | A | Invoice from supplier | Amount of purchase |

## Problem 48

1.

| | Assets | | | = | Liabilities + | Owners' Equity | |
|---|---|---|---|---|---|---|---|
| | *Cash* | *Computer* | *Accounts Receivable* | | *Accounts Payable* | *Capital Stock* | *Retained Earnings* |
| a) | $+21,000 | $ | $ | | $ | $ +21,000 | $ |
| b) | -2,500 | | | | | | -2,500 |
| c) | +16,000 | | +4,000 | | | | +20,000 |
| d) | | | | | +400 | | -400 |
| e) | -2,000 | +2,000 | | | | | |
| f) | -16,500 | | | | | | -16,500 |
| Bal. | 16,000 | 2,000 | 4,000 | = | 400 | 21,000 | 600 |

**Note to Student:**  Notice that for some transactions, all accounts either increase (see a) and c)) or decrease (see b) and f)). For other transactions, some accounts increase and some decrease (see d) and e)).  Each transaction will affect the accounts in one of these three patterns.

| Trial balance on January 31, 2001 | Debit | Credit |
|---|---|---|
| Cash | $16,000 | |
| Computer | 2,000 | |
| Accounts receivable | 4,000 | |
| Accounts payable | | $    400 |
| Capital stock | | 21,000 |
| Retained earnings | | 600 |
| **Totals** | **$22,000** | **$22,000** |

## 2. Income statement for the month of January 31, 2001

### Stooge Inc.
### Income Statement
### For the Month Ended January 31, 2001

| | | |
|---|---:|---:|
| **Service revenues** | | $20,000 |
| **Costs and expenses:** | | |
| Salary expense | $16,500 | |
| Rent expense | 2,500 | |
| Stationery expense | 400 | |
| **Total expenses** | | 19,400 |
| **Net income** | | $600 |

## Balance sheet on January 31, 2001

### Stooge Inc.
### Balance Sheet
### January 31, 2001

| | | | | |
|---|---:|---|---:|---:|
| Cash | $16,000 | Accounts payable | | $  400 |
| Accounts receivable | 4,000 | *Stockholders' equity* | | |
| *Current assets* | 20,000 | Capital stock | $21,000 | |
| Computer | 2,000 | Retained earnings | 600 | |
| | | | | 21,600 |
| | | **Total liabilities and** | | |
| **Total assets** | $22,000 | **stockholders' equity** | | $22,000 |

The income statement shows a small positive net income after the owners' salaries have been paid. The future viability of the enterprise depends on whether or not revenues will grow so that this level of salary payments can be maintained. If these salaries cannot be paid from future revenues, then the owners will have to decide if the salary payments they are receiving from the new company are comparable with what they could earn elsewhere. If they are, then they should probably accept an alternative job offer; if they are not, then they should consider reducing the salaries they are receiving from the company to a level comparable to their alternative employment.

## Critical Thinking Problem 49

a.  The following are the corrected entries for Pacioli for the year ended 12/31/2001:

|  |  | Debit | Credit |
|---|---|---|---|
| 1. | Cash | 300,000 | |
| | Capital stock | | 300,000 |
| | Receipt of cash in exchange for stock issued | | |
| 2. | Inventory | 210,000 | |
| | Accounts payable | | 210,000 |
| | Purchase of inventory on credit | | |
| 3. | Office furniture | 31,000 | |
| | Cash | | 31,000 |
| | Purchase of furniture for cash | | |
| 4. | Accounts payable | 150,000 | |
| | Cash | | 150,000 |
| | Cash payment to vendors | | |
| 5. | Rent expense | 72,000 | |
| | Cash | | 72,000 |
| | Cash payment for rent | | |
| 6. | Cash | 90,000 | |
| | Accounts receivable | 350,000 | |
| | Sales | | 440,000 |
| | Cash and receivables from sales | | |
| 7. | Cash | 75,000 | |
| | Accounts receivable | | 75,000 |
| | Cash received from customers on account | | |
| 8. | Wages and salaries expense | 62,000 | |
| | Cash | | 62,000 |
| | Cash paid for salaries and wages | | |
| 9. | Utilities expense | 11,000 | |
| | Cash | | 11,000 |
| | Cash paid for utilities | | |

b.  The following are the corrected T-accounts for Pacioli for the year ended 12/31/2001:

| | CASH | | | | CAPITAL STOCK | |
|---|---|---|---|---|---|---|
| 1. | 300,000 | 3. | 31,000 | | 1. | 300,000 |
| 6. | 90,000 | 4. | 150,000 | | | |
| 7. | 75,000 | 5. | 72,000 | | | |
| | | 8. | 62,000 | | | |
| | | 9. | 11,000 | | | |
| Bal | 139,000 | | | | | |

|  | ACCOUNTS PAYABLE | | |
|---|---|---|---|
| 4. | 150,000 | 2. | 210,000 |
| | | Bal | 60,000 |

|  | RENT EXPENSE | |
|---|---|---|
| 5. | 72,000 | |

|  | OFFICE FURNITURE | |
|---|---|---|
| 3. | 31,000 | |

|  | ACCOUNTS RECEIVABLE | | |
|---|---|---|---|
| 6. | 350,000 | 7. | 75,000 |
| Bal | 275,000 | | |

|  | UTILITIES EXPENSE | |
|---|---|---|
| 9. | 11,000 | |

|  | WAGES EXPENSE | |
|---|---|---|
| 8. | 62,000 | |

|  | INVENTORY | |
|---|---|---|
| 2. | 210,000 | |

|  | SALES | |
|---|---|---|
| | | 6. 440,000 |

c. The following is the corrected trial balance for Pacioli for the year ended 12/31/2001:

| Trial Balance on 12/31/2001 | Debit | Credit |
|---|---|---|
| Cash | 139,000 | |
| Accounts receivable | 275,000 | |
| Inventory | 210,000 | |
| Office furniture | 31,000 | |
| Accounts payable | | 60,000 |
| Capital stock | | 300,000 |
| Sales | | 440,000 |
| Rent expense | 72,000 | |
| Wages expense | 62,000 | |
| Utilities expense | 11,000 | |
| | $800,000 | $800,000 |

# Chapter 4

# Income Measurement and Accrual Accounting

This chapter continues the exploration of the accounting process started in Chapter 3 by considering how income is measured and accounted for. You have two overall goals in this chapter. First, understand the conceptual framework for measuring income and how, within that framework, accounting for income is carried out. Second, review the entire accounting process, called the accounting cycle, from the initial step of recording an event through the final step of preparing financial statements.

## Learning Objectives

**LO 1** Explain the significance of recognition and measurement in the preparation and use of financial statements.

**LO 2** Explain the differences between the cash and accrual bases of accounting.

**LO 3** Describe the revenue recognition principle and explain its application in various situations.

**LO 4** Describe the matching principle and the various methods for recognizing expenses.

**LO 5** Identify the four major types of adjusting entries, and prepare them for a variety of situations.

**LO 6** Explain the steps in the accounting cycle and the significance of each step.

**LO 7** Explain why and how closing entries are made at the end of an accounting period.

**LO 8** Understand how to use a work sheet as a basis for preparing financial statements.

## Key Textbook Exhibits

**Exhibit 4-2** illustrates the essential differences between the cash and accrual bases of accounting. *Self-Test:* Does the accrual basis reflect the economic or the cash impact of transactions?

**Exhibit 4-3** shows the income statement and partial cash flow statement for the Glengarry Health Club. *Self-Test:* How does the cash measure of performance differ from the accrual-based measure? Why are they different?

**Exhibit 4-4** gives an illustration of the relationship between costs, assets, and expenses. When costs are incurred, assets are created and the use of those assets generates expenses. For example, a piece of equipment will be used over several periods, and spreading the cost of that asset over the asset's useful life (through charging depreciation) results in depreciation expense for each period.

**Exhibit 4-5** summarizes the types of adjustments that are necessary to implement the accrual basis of accounting.

**Exhibit 4-8** summarizes the steps in the complete accounting cycle. *Self-Test:* When are these steps carried out?

## Review of Key Concepts

**LO 1**  During a financial period, many events occur that affect the company. In preparing financial statements for the period, two related issues must be considered. First, determine which events to record. **Recognition** refers to the process by which accountants depict the effects of economic events on the entity.

Once an event is recognized, it is then necessary to **measure** it, to quantify its impact on the entity. In measuring assets, two conceptual issues must be addressed:

- *The basis of measurement must be decided.* Two possible measures of value are **historical cost** (the original cost of the item) and **current value** (the amount that could be received now if the asset were sold). The choice between them involves a trade-off between reliability and relevance. Although historical cost is more reliable, current value is likely to be more relevant to many decisions.

- *The monetary unit may not have a stable value.* Inflation, or a rise in the general level of prices in the economy, may result in distortions in the accounting numbers reported.

### Sixty Second Quiz!

**Question:**   A company owns two pieces of land that both appear in its balance sheet at historical cost. One piece of land was bought twenty years ago, the other last year, and for each, the company paid $100,000. Both pieces of land are therefore shown in the balance sheet at $100,000. Does this mean that they are equally valuable today?

**Answer:**   Probably not. Land that was bought twenty years ago is unlikely to be worth $100,000 today. Inflation (an increase in the general price level) could have increased the number of dollars needed to buy the land over twenty years. In addition, there could have been increases or decreases in value that were related to the particular piece of land (development potential, discovery of oil, deterioration in the area, etc.). Consequently, the historical costs that appear in the balance sheet cannot be used as reliable measures of current value.

**LO 2**  The **measurement of income** provides a way to communicate information about how the business has performed over the period. Two possible ways of measuring income are the **accrual basis** and the **cash basis**. The two methods differ in when revenue and expenses are recognized. For an income statement prepared on the cash basis, revenues and expenses are recognized when the associated cash is received or paid. For an income statement prepared on an accrual basis, revenue is recognized when it is earned, and expense is recognized when it is incurred.

**LO 3**  Under the accrual basis of income measurement, revenues are recognized according to the **principle of revenue recognition**, which requires that two conditions must be met. First, the revenues must have been earned (i.e. the costs associated with generating the revenues must have been incurred or be capable of being reliably estimated). Second, the revenues must have been realized or be realizable (i.e., cash or claims to cash must have been received in exchange for the goods or service).

The revenue recognition principle means that revenue is often recognized before cash is received. Consequently, the net income reported in the income statement often differs from the cash flows from operations reported in the statement of cash flows.

The following table summarizes some special applications of the principle of revenue recognition.

| Event | Revenue recognition |
|---|---|
| Long-term contracts | For long-term contracts, such as large civil engineering projects, the percentage-of-completion method is used. Revenue is recognized in proportion to the amount of the contract completed. |
| Franchises | The franchiser recognizes revenue when "substantial performance" of its obligation has been completed. |
| Commodities | For commodities, the production method is used. This allows revenues to be recognized as soon as the commodity is produced. This is one of the few examples where revenue can be recognized before the point of sale. |
| Installment sales | Where payment is received from customers by installments, for example for the sale of automobiles, there is a higher probability that customers will default and not pay all the money owed. In these cases, the installment sales method of revenue recognition may be used. Under this method, revenue is only recognized when cash is received. |
| Rent and interest | Rent and interest are earned continuously, and the recognition of revenue for these items is also continuous. |

**LO 4**    Under the **matching principle**, costs for a period are matched against the revenues they have helped to generate during that period. The determining factor, therefore, in charging an expense in any period is whether it can be matched against revenue. Expenses can come from two sources: from using an asset or from incurring a liability.

## Sixty Second Quiz!

**Question**:    A retail store has the following information about sales of Product A for January 1999:

|  |  |
|---|---|
| Sales to customers on credit (no cash was received in January) | $20,000 |
| Cash sales to customers | $10,000 |
| Inventory of Product A - January 1, 1999 | $0 |
| Cash purchases during January | $40,000 |
| Inventory of Product A - January 31, 1999 | $10,000 |

How much revenue would be recognized under the cash basis of income recognition? How much under the accrual basis? What expenses would be recognized under each basis of income recognition?

**Answer**:

|  | Cash basis | Accrual basis |
|---|---|---|
| Revenues | $10,000 | $30,000 |
| Expenses | $40,000 | $30,000 |

Under the cash basis of accounting, only the cash received for sales would be recognized. Under the accrual basis, all sales would be recognized provided that the costs associated with generating the revenues have been incurred or can be reliably estimated, and that claims to cash have been received. The expenses recognized under each method would also vary. Under the cash basis, all cash paid for purchases ($40,000) is charged as an expense for the month. Under the accrual basis, the matching principle results in only those goods that were sold during the period being expensed. Goods on hand at the end of the period ($10,000) are not, so the expense (called cost of goods sold) is the difference between the goods purchased and the closing inventory ($40,000 - $10,000).

**LO 5** **Adjustments** are journal entries made at the end of the accounting period that ensure the proper matching of costs and revenues for companies using the accrual basis of accounting. They are not necessary for companies using a cash basis. There are four distinct types of adjustments corresponding to when the cash for an expense or revenue is paid or received during the accounting period. Note that these adjustments never involve the cash account.

**Deferred expense**

When cash is paid for an expense before the expense is incurred, an asset account is created at the time of payment. At the end of the period, this asset must be reduced (credited) and an expense account increased (debited) by the amount of the cost that has expired over the period. The adjusting entry involves:

| | | |
|---|---|---|
| Debit expense | xxx | |
| Credit asset | | xxx |

To illustrate, Pacioli Company made a cash payment of $500 on July 1, 2000, to pay the premium on a one-year fire insurance policy. On that date, the following journal entry was made to record the payment. The entry resulted in the creation of an asset account, prepaid insurance.

| | | | |
|---|---|---|---|
| 7/1/00 | Prepaid insurance | 500 | |
| | Cash | | 500 |

On December 31, 2000, at the end of the accounting period, an adjusting entry must be made to reduce the asset account by the amount of the insurance policy used up during the accounting period. In this case, the company has used six months of a twelve-month policy. Therefore exactly half, or $250, of the policy benefit has been used. The adjusting entry both reduces the asset and increases (or creates) an insurance expense account.

| | | | |
|---|---|---|---|
| 12/31/00 | Insurance expense | 250 | |
| | Prepaid insurance | | 250 |

**Deferred revenue**

Similarly, when cash is received before revenue is earned, a liability account is created. At the end of the period, the liability must be reduced (debited) and a revenue account increased (credited) by the amount of the revenue that has been earned during the period. The adjusting entry involves:

| | | |
|---|---|---|
| Debit liability | xxx | |
| Credit revenue | | xxx |

Pacioli Company received $25,000 from a customer on December 1, 2000, for work that was to be done over the next two months. The following journal entry was made to record the receipt of cash. Note that the journal entry creates a liability account called "revenues received in advance."

| | | | |
|---|---|---|---|
| 12/1/00 | Cash | 25,000 | |
| | Revenue received in advance | | 25,000 |

On December 31, 2000, exactly half of the work has been completed and therefore an adjusting entry is needed to record the amount of revenue that has been earned. The adjusting entry both reduces the liability account and increases (or creates) the revenue account.

| | | | |
|---|---|---|---|
| 12/31/00 | Revenue received in advance | 12,500 | |
| | Revenue | | 12,500 |

### Accrued liability

When expense is incurred before cash is paid, an entry to record the amount owed must be made. A liability account must therefore be increased (credited), and an expense account must be increased (debited). The adjusting entry involves:

| | | |
|---|---|---|
| Debit expense | xxx | |
| Credit liability | | xxx |

Pacioli Company owes its employees $2,000 in unpaid wages on December 31, 2000. The adjusting entry creates a liability account called wages payable and increases (or creates) wages expense.

| | | | |
|---|---|---|---|
| 12/31/00 | Wages expense | 2,000 | |
| | Wages payable | | 2,000 |

### Accrued asset

When revenue is earned before cash is received, an entry to record the amount to be received must be made. An asset account is therefore increased (debited), and a revenue account is increased (credited). The adjusting entry involves:

| | | |
|---|---|---|
| Debit asset | xxx | |
| Credit revenue | | xxx |

On December 1, 2000, Pacioli Company accepted a $10,000 note receivable from a customer. Interest on the note is 6% per annum, and it will be paid on the maturity of the note on February 1, 2001. Interest on the note for the month of December has not been paid. The adjusting entry to record the interest due on the note increases (or creates) an interest receivable account and an interest revenue account.

| | | | |
|---|---|---|---|
| 12/31/00 | Interest receivable | 50 | |
| | Interest revenue | | 50 |
| | (6% x 10,000 x 1/12) | | |

Adjusting entries are extremely important in testing your understanding of the logic of the accounting process. Make sure that you understand them.

## Sixty Second Quiz!

**Question:** Can you identify two features that are common to the four types of adjustments?

**Answer:** All four types of adjustments involve a balance sheet account (asset or liability) and an income statement account (revenue or expense). In addition, none of the four entries involves cash.

**LO 6** The accounting cycle is the name given to the entire accounting process, which starts with the recording of an economic event in a source document and ends with the preparation of a set of financial statements. The steps in the accounting cycle can be represented as follows:

| Step | Performed |
|---|---|
| 1. Collect and analyze information from source documents | Continuously |
| 2. Journalize transactions | Continuously |
| 3. Post transactions to accounts in the ledger (daily, weekly or immediately in a computerized system) | Periodically |
| 4. Prepare work sheet | End of period |
| 5. Record and post adjustments | End of period |
| 6. Close the accounts | End of period |
| 7. Prepare financial statements | End of period |

Step 6 involves closing the accounts so that financial statements can be prepared. A key element in this last step is deciding which accounts should be reported in the income statement and which in the balance sheet. Balance sheet accounts are called **real accounts** because they are permanent in nature. Revenue and expense accounts, which are reported in the income statement, are called **nominal or temporary accounts** because they are closed at the end of the period. The closing process results in both the net income or loss for the period being calculated, and the balances in all temporary accounts returning to zero ready for the start of the new cycle.

**LO 7** At the end of the accounting cycle, **closing entries** achieve two goals. First, all revenue and expense accounts (**nominal** or **temporary** accounts) are closed to an income summary account so that the temporary accounts start the new period with zero balances. Secondly, the net income or loss from the income summary is transferred to the retained earnings account. The steps in the closing process are as follows:

**Step 1: Close revenue and expense accounts to income summary**

| | | |
|---|---|---|
| Debit revenue accounts | xxx | |
| Credit income summary | | xxx |
| Debit income summary | xxx | |
| Credit expense accounts | | xxx |

Note that if revenues exceed expenses, the company has net income and the balance in income summary at this point is a credit. If expenses exceed revenues, the company has a net loss and the balance in income summary at this point is a debit.

**Step 2: Close income summary to retained earnings**

If the company has made a profit:

| | | |
|---|---|---|
| Debit income summary | xxx | |
| Credit retained earnings | | xxx |

Or, if the company has made a loss:

| | | |
|---|---|---|
| Debit retained earnings | xxx | |
| Credit income summary | | xxx |

**Step 3: Close the dividend account to retained earnings:**

| | | |
|---|---|---|
| Debit retained earnings | xxx | |
| Credit dividends | | xxx |

To illustrate the use of closing entries, assume that the following is an extract from the adjusted trial balance of Platox Company on December 31, 2000.

|  | $ Debit | $ Credit |
|---|---|---|
| Retained Earnings |  | 50,000 |
| Sales |  | 200,000 |
| Cost of Goods Sold | 150,000 |  |
| Wages Expense | 20,000 |  |
| Utilities Expense | 5,000 |  |
| Rent Expense | 3,000 |  |

**Step 1: Close revenue and expense accounts to income summary**

|  |  | Debit | Credit |
|---|---|---|---|
| 12/31/00 | Sales | 200,000 |  |
|  | Cost of goods sold |  | 150,000 |
|  | Wages expense |  | 20,000 |
|  | Utilities expense |  | 5,000 |
|  | Rent expense |  | 3,000 |
|  | Income summary |  | 22,000 |

**Step 2: Close income summary to retained earnings**

|  |  | Debit | Credit |
|---|---|---|---|
| 12/31/00 | Income summary | 22,000 |  |
|  | Retained earnings |  | 22,000 |

**Step 3: Close the dividend account to retained earnings**

|  |  | Debit | Credit |
|---|---|---|---|
| 12/31/00 | Retained earnings | 10,000 |  |
|  | Dividend |  | 10,000 |

The T account for retained earnings is as follows:

| RETAINED EARNINGS | | | |
|---|---|---|---|
|  |  | beg. bal. | 50,000 |
| 12/31/00 | 10,000 | 12/31/00 | 22,000 |
|  |  | end. bal. | 62,000 |

**LO 8** Worksheets can be used to prepare financial statements by recording adjusting and closing entries. Typically, but not necessarily, work sheets have ten columns: two for the unadjusted trial balance, two for recording adjusting entries, two for the adjusted trial balance, two for recording the closing entries, and two for the balance sheet.

# Review of Key Terms

| | |
|---|---|
| **Accounting cycle** | A series of steps performed each period culminating in the preparation of a set of financial statements. |
| **Accrual** | Cash that has not yet been paid or received for an expense that has been incurred or a revenue earned. |
| **Accrual basis** | A system of accounting in which revenues are recognized when they are earned, and expenses are recognized when they are incurred. |
| **Accrued asset** | An asset resulting from the recognition of revenue before the receipt of cash. |
| **Accrued liability** | A liability resulting from the recognition of an expense before the payment of cash. |
| **Adjusting entries** | Journal entries made at the end of a period by companies using the accrual basis of accounting. |
| **Cash basis** | A system of accounting that recognizes revenue when cash is received, and expenses when cash is paid. |
| **Closing entries** | Journal entries made at the end of a period to return the balance in all nominal accounts to zero, and to transfer the net income or loss and the dividends of the period to retained earnings. |
| **Contra account** | An account with a balance that is opposite to that of a related account. |
| **Current value** | The amount of cash or its equivalent that could be received currently by selling an asset. |
| **Deferral** | Cash has either been paid or received, but expense or revenue has not yet been recognized. |
| **Deferred expense (Prepaid expense, prepaid asset)** | An asset resulting from the payment of cash before the expense is incurred. |
| **Deferred revenue (Unearned revenue)** | A liability resulting from the receipt of cash before the recognition of revenue. |
| **Expenses** | Outflows or other uses of assets or incurrences of liabilities resulting from delivering goods, rendering services, or carrying out other activities. |
| **Historical cost (Original cost)** | The original cost of an asset. |
| **Installment method** | The method by which revenues are recognized at the time cash is collected. |
| **Interim statements** | Financial statements prepared monthly, quarterly, or at other intervals less than a year in duration. |
| **Matching principle** | The association of revenue for a period with all of the costs expended in generating that revenue. |
| **Nominal accounts (Temporary accounts)** | The name given to revenue, expense, and dividend accounts because they are temporary and are closed at the end of the period. |
| **Percentage-of-completion method** | The method used by contractors to recognize revenues before the completion of a long-term contract. |
| **Production method** | The method whereby revenue is recognized when a commodity is produced rather than when it is sold. |

| | |
|---|---|
| **Real accounts**<br>**(Permanent accounts)** | The name given to balance sheet accounts because they are permanent and are not closed at the end of the period. |
| **Recognition** | The process of recording an item in the financial statements as an asset, liability, revenue, expense, or the like. |
| **Revenue recognition**<br>**principle** | Revenues are recognized on the income statement when they are realized, or realizable, and earned. |
| **Revenues** | Increases in assets or reductions in liabilities from delivering or producing goods or services. |
| **Straight-line method** | The assignment of an equal amount of depreciation to each period. |
| **Work sheet** | A device used at the end of the period to gather the information needed to prepare financial statements without actually recording and posting adjusting entries. |

## Practice Test
## Questions and Problems

## Circle the alternative that best answers the question:

**LO 2**  1.  The following information is available for Company A during March 2000:

| | |
|---|---|
| Cash sales to customers | $150,000 |
| Inventory of Product A - March 1, 2000 | $0 |
| Cash purchases during March | $120,000 |
| Inventory of Product A - March 31, 2000 | $20,000 |

The net income reported under the accrual basis of accounting for Company A for the month of March, 2000 was:

a) $150,000

b) $120,000

c) $30,000

d) $50,000

**LO 2**  2.  On the morning of June 27, 2000, you purchased a sweater (that was originally priced at $120) on sale for $50 cash. In the afternoon, you accepted an offer of $80 for it, which you will receive on July 1, 2000. You are certain that you will receive the money. For the day of June 27, 2000, under the accrual method, your net income and cash flow, respectively, were:

a) $30 and $30

b) $70 and $30

c) $0 and -$50

d) $30 and -$50

**LO 7**  3.  After closing is complete:

a) all temporary accounts have a zero balance.

b) the net income or net loss and the dividends for the period have been transferred to the retained earnings account.

c) all accounts with a non-zero balance will be communicated in the balance sheet.

d) All of the above are correct.

**LO 7** 4. The net income for the period is $400, and dividends paid amount to $600. Which of the following statements is true?
a) The company paid out more in dividends than the cash it generated from its operations.
b) The company paid out more in dividends than it earned in income.
c) The company paid out less in dividends than it earned in income.
d) The company paid out less in dividends than the cash it generated from its operations.

**LO 7** 5. A revenue or sales account is:
a) a temporary account that is closed at the end of the accounting period.
b) communicated on the income statement.
c) an increase in retained earnings.
d) All of the above are correct.

**LO 7** 6. Which of the following accounts is closed at the end of the accounting period but is not found in the income statement?
a) Sales revenue
b) Accounts receivable
c) Dividends paid
d) Rent expense

**LO 5** 7. Which of the following could not be an adjusting entry?
a) Increase insurance expense, decrease prepaid insurance
b) Increase rent expense, decrease prepaid rent
c) Decrease accounts payable, decrease cash
d) Increase depreciation expense, increase accumulated depreciation

**LO 5** 8. During the adjusting process, failing to enter an adjustment for supplies inventory used during the period would:
a) overstate the liabilities and understate net income.
b) understate liabilities and overstate net income.
c) overstate assets and net income.
d) understate assets and net income.

**LO 2** 9. During 2000, Smite Company paid $12,000 to its landlord for rent. On January 1, 2000, prepaid rent was $3,000 and on December 31, 2000, prepaid rent was $4,000. Rent expense for 2000 was:
a) $10,000
b) $11,000
c) $12,000
d) $13,000

**LO 4** 10. Which of the following statements is true?

a) For commodities, revenue may be recognized before the point of sale.

b) For installment sales, revenue is recognized before cash has been received.

c) For long-term contracts, revenue should be recognized when cash payments are received from the customer.

d) For franchising operations, revenue from initial franchise fees may be recognized before the franchiser has made substantial performance of its obligations.

**LO 5** 11. Ceres Company fails to make an adjusting entry for depreciation at the end of the accounting period. The effect of this is that:

a) the current ratio at the end of the period is overstated.

b) net income is understated.

c) the profit margin is overstated.

d) both b) and c) are correct.

**LO 5** 12. During January 2000, Smilla Company's interim income statement reported salary expense of $28,000. On January 1, 2000, the balance on the salaries payable account was $8,000, and on January 31, 2000, the balance was $4,000. The cash paid in salaries during January, 2000 was:

a) $24,000

b) $32,000

c) $36,000

d) $32,000

**LO 5** 13. The net book value of Jura Corporation's plant and machinery was $20,000 on January 1, 2000, and was $30,000 on December 31, 2000. During the year the company bought plant and machinery for $14,000, and did not sell any of its existing plant or machinery. The depreciation expense for 2000 was:

a) $4,000

b) $24,000

c) $16,000

d) $6,000

**LO 5** 14. Isaly Company's balance on its inventory account on January 1, 2000 was $3,000, and on December 31, 2000 it was $1,000. All purchases were for cash, and it paid $54,000 cash to its suppliers during the year. The cost of goods sold on its income statement was:

a) $52,000

b) $56,000

c) $55,000

d) $57,000

**LO 5** 15. Adjusting entries are an application of:

a) the revenue recognition principle.

b) conservatism.

c) the matching principle.

d) relevance.

## Indicate whether each of the following statements is true or false:

`LO 5`    16. Adjustments are concerned with ensuring that the cash account is up to date at the end of the period.

`LO 5`    17. An adjusting entry does not include an entry to the cash account.

`LO 1`    18. Current value is both more relevant and more reliable than historical cost.

`LO 5`    19. Deferred expense is an asset that results from the payment of cash before the expense is incurred.

`LO 4`    20. Expenses may come both from using an asset and by incurring a liability.

`LO 5`    21. Failing to adjust for depreciation in a period will overstate net income in that period and understate total assets at the end of the period.

`LO 2`    22. If a company has positive net income during a period, its retained earnings balance on the balance sheet will increase from the previous year.

`LO 4`    23. If a company only ever makes cash sales, then revenues and reported income are identical under both the cash and accrual bases of accounting.

`LO 1`    24. Inflation may have a significant impact on the validity of reported income.

`LO 7`    25. Revenue and expense accounts are also known as nominal or permanent accounts.

`LO 7`    26. Internal statements are financial statements prepared monthly, quarterly, or at other intervals of less than a year.

`LO 3`    27. Revenues or sales in the financial statements measures the cash received from customers during the accounting period.

`LO 6`    28. The only steps in the accounting cycle that are carried out continuously throughout the accounting period are collecting and analyzing information from source documents and journalizing transactions.

`LO 3`    29. The percentage-of-completion method is the method by which revenues are recognized at the time cash is collected.

`LO 3`    30. The installment method is the revenue recognition method by which revenues are recognized at the time a commodity is produced rather than when it is sold.

## Complete each of the following statements:

**LO 3**  31. The principle of revenue recognition requires that revenues must have been both _____ and _____.

**LO 4**  32. Under the _____, costs for a period are matched against the revenues they helped to generate during the period.

**LO 5**  33. The four types of adjustments are _____, _____, _____, and _____.

**LO 6**  34. The entire accounting process from the recording of an economic event to the preparation of financial statements is called the _____.

**LO 3**  35. _____ is the method used by contractors to recognize revenues before the completion of a long-term contract.

**LO 1**  36. _____ is the original cost of an asset; _____ is the amount of cash or cash equivalent that could be received now by selling the asset.

**LO 7**  37. Financial statements prepared for any period less than a year are called _____.

**LO 1**  38. _____ is the process of recording an item in the financial statements as an asset, liability, equity, revenue, or expense.

**LO 5**  39. Adjusting entries are _____ transactions and therefore never involve _____.

**LO 5**  40. _____ is used to refer to a situation where cash has either been paid or received, but where recognition of the expense or revenue is delayed to a later time.

**LO 4**  41. _____ involve the use of assets or incurring of liabilities in delivering goods and services.

**LO 5**  42. _____ is used to refer to a situation in which no cash has yet been paid or received, but it is necessary to recognize an expense and the associated liability, or a revenue and the associated asset.

**LO 4**  43. _____ is the name given to allocating the cost of a long-term asset over its life.

**LO 7**  44. _____ is the name given to revenue, expense, and dividend accounts because they are temporary and are closed at the end of the period.

**LO 1**  45. The _____ is the original cost of an asset.

## Answer each of the following problems:

**LO 5,6** 46. On January 1, 2000, IntelliGent was incorporated as a network-consulting firm. During its first year of operations, the following summary events occurred:

1. Stockholders invested $170,000 cash, in exchange for capital stock.
2. Two years' rent of $19,200 was paid in advance on January 1, 2000.
3. Supplies of $3,500 were purchased on credit and used immediately.
4. Office furniture, fixtures, and equipment were purchased for $30,000 cash.
5. Fees earned during the year were $115,000, of which $70,000 was on credit and the remainder was for cash.
6. Utilities expense for the year amounted to $1,700 and was paid in cash.
7. Salaries of $33,000 were paid in cash during the year.
8. On July 1, the firm purchased a comprehensive three-year insurance policy for $6,000 cash.
9. The firm provided services of $15,000 for a client. These fees are in addition to the fees identified in item 5. For these services, IntelliGent accepted a $15,000 note receivable on August 1, 2000. The note has an interest rate of 10%, and both the interest and the capital are due to be paid in one year.
10. IntelliGent Company paid in full for the supplies purchased in item 3.
11. Legal expenses of $1,500 were paid in cash.
12. Cash collections on accounts receivable were $35,000.
13. Cash dividends of $10,000 were paid.

Additional information:

a) Interest on the note receivable must be accrued.
b) The necessary amount of prepaid insurance must be written off.
c) Prepaid rent must be written off.
d) The office furniture, fixtures, and equipment have a five-year life and zero salvage value. The company uses the straight-line method to depreciate its fixed assets.
e) Salaries of $2,300 were earned by staff, but remained unpaid at year-end.
f) Fees of $2,000 were earned at year-end, for which the receivable and the revenue have not yet been recorded.

**Required**

1. Prepare the journal entries for the year, and post them to T accounts.
2. Prepare an unadjusted trial balance.
3. Prepare the adjusting entries, and post them to the ledger accounts.
4. Prepare an adjusted trial balance.
5. Prepare closing entries, and post them to the ledger accounts.
6. Prepare a post-closing trial balance.
7. Prepare an income statement, a statement of retained earnings, and a classified balance sheet as of December 31, 2000.

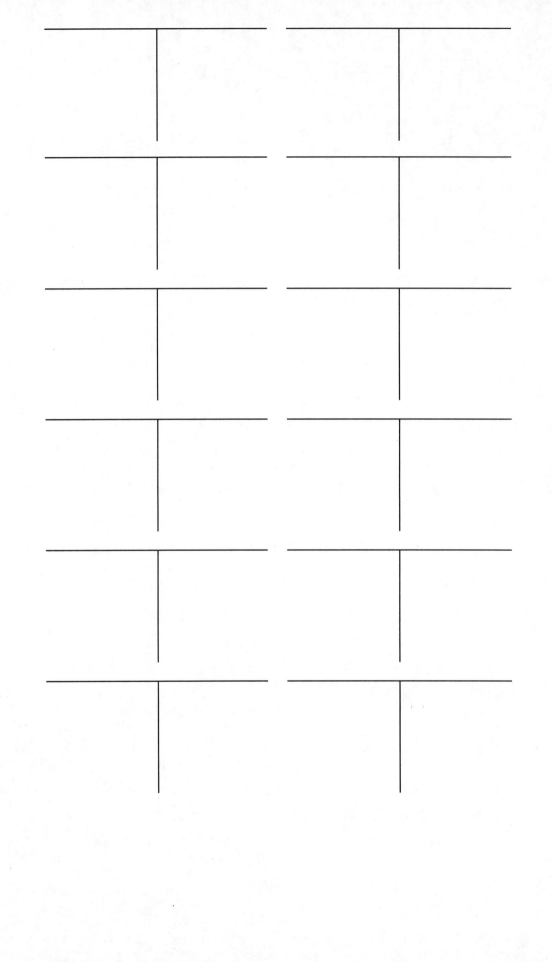

**LO 5** 47. A company is drawing up its annual accounts for the year ended December 31, 2000. The following information must be taken into account:

a) The company owns equipment that originally cost $50,000 three years ago. The company depreciates equipment over a five-year period, assuming straight line depreciation, and zero salvage value.

b) On October 1, 2000, the company contracted to carry out maintenance on an empty building for one year. Payment in advance of $5,000 for the first six months of the contract was received on October 1, 2000. It was expected that revenue would be earned evenly over the six months.

c) Annual property taxes of $4,800 are due to be paid on January 31, 2001. The taxes relate to the year February 1, 2000, to January 31, 2001.

d) The company owns $100,000 of corporate bonds, and a full year's interest at 6% will be received on March 31, 2001. No entry has yet been made for this interest receipt.

**Required**

1. Identify what type of adjustment is needed for each item.

2. Show the effect of each adjustment on the accounting equation.

3. Give the adjusting journal entries.

## Critical Thinking Problem

**LO 5**  48.  What would be the effect on the reported income and balance sheet if the adjustments for the Pacioli Company in **LO 5** in the Review of Key Concepts were not made before the closing process? Analyze the impact using the following table. Note that if net income is overstated or understated, then owners' equity will also be overstated or understated by the same amount, since owners' equity is contributed capital plus retained earnings.

|    | **Effect on Income Statement** | **Effect on Balance Sheet** |
|----|--------------------------------|-----------------------------|
| A. | Revenue:<br><br>Expense:<br><br>Net income: | Assets:<br><br>Liabilities:<br><br>Owners' equity: |
| B. | Revenue:<br><br>Expense:<br><br>Net income: | Assets:<br><br>Liabilities:<br><br>Owners' equity: |
| C. | Revenue:<br><br>Expense:<br><br>Net income: | Assets:<br><br>Liabilities:<br><br>Owners' equity: |
| D. | Revenue:<br><br>Expense:<br><br>Net income: | Assets:<br><br>Liabilities:<br><br>Owners' equity: |

## Solutions

### Multiple Choice

| | | | | |
|---|---|---|---|---|
| 1. | d | | 9. | b |
| 2. | d | | 10. | a |
| 3. | d | | 11. | c |
| 4. | b | | 12. | b |
| 5. | d | | 13. | a |
| 6. | c | | 14. | b |
| 7. | c | | 15. | c |
| 8. | c | | | |

### True/False

**COMMENT/EXPLANATION**

| | | |
|---|---|---|
| 16. | False | Adjustments ensure the correct application of the accrual basis of accounting. |
| 17. | True | |
| 18. | False | Since it can be derived from the original transaction, historical cost is more reliable than current value. However, for many decisions, current value is more relevant than historical cost since it reflects current economic conditions. |
| 19. | True | |
| 20. | True | |
| 21. | False | Failing to adjust for depreciation will overstate both net income and net assets. |
| 22. | False | If dividends in the year are greater than net income, the retained earnings balance will decline. |
| 23. | False | A company with only cash sales will report identical revenues under both the cash and accrual bases of accounting. However, the expenses under both methods may differ, and so reported income under the two methods may be different. |
| 24. | True | |
| 25. | False | Revenue and expense accounts are nominal or temporary accounts. |
| 26. | False | Statements covering a period of less than a year are called interim statements. |
| 27. | False | Revenues are the total sales made during the period, either for cash or on credit. |
| 28. | True | |
| 29. | False | The percentage-of-completion method recognizes revenues in proportion to the relationship between incurred costs and total project costs. |
| 30. | False | The production method is the revenue recognition method used when revenues from commodities are recognized at the point of production rather than sale. |

## Fill in the Blanks

31. earned, realized (or realizable)
32. matching principle
33. accrued liability, accrued asset, deferred expenses, deferred revenues
34. accounting cycle
35. percentage-of-completion
36. historical cost, current value
37. interim statements
38. recognition
39. internal, cash
40. deferral
41. expenses
42. accrual
43. depreciation
44. nominal or temporary
45. historical cost

## Problem 46

Part 1 - Journal Entries

| | | | |
|---|---|---:|---:|
| (1) | Cash | 170,000 | |
| | Capital stock | | 170,000 |
| | | | |
| (2) | Prepaid rent | 19,200 | |
| | Cash | | 19,200 |
| | | | |
| (3) | Supplies expense | 3,500 | |
| | Accounts payable | | 3,500 |
| | | | |
| (4) | Furniture, fixtures & equipment | 30,000 | |
| | Cash | | 30,000 |
| | | | |
| (5) | Cash | 70,000 | |
| | Accounts receivable | 45,000 | |
| | Sales | | 115,000 |
| | | | |
| (6) | Utilities expense | 1,700 | |
| | Cash | | 1,700 |
| | | | |
| (7) | Salaries expense | 33,000 | |
| | Cash | | 33,000 |
| | | | |
| (8) | Prepaid insurance | 6,000 | |
| | Cash | | 6,000 |
| | | | |
| (9) | Note receivable | 15,000 | |
| | Sales | | 15,000 |
| | | | |
| (10) | Accounts payable | 3,500 | |
| | Cash | | 3,500 |
| | | | |
| (11) | Legal expenses | 1,500 | |
| | Cash | | 1,500 |

| | | | | |
|---|---|---|---|---|
| (12) | Cash | 35,000 | | |
| | Accounts receivable | | 35,000 | |
| | | | | |
| (13) | Dividends | 10,000 | | |
| | Cash | | 10,000 | |

**Part 3 - Adjusting Entries:**

| | | | | |
|---|---|---|---|---|
| (a) | Interest receivable | 625 | | |
| | Interest revenue | | 625 | |
| | (5/12 x 10% x 15,000 = $625) | | | |
| | | | | |
| (b) | Insurance expense | 1,000 | | |
| | Prepaid insurance | | 1,000 | |
| | (1/2 x 1/3 x 6,000) | | | |
| | | | | |
| (c) | Rent expense | 9,600 | | |
| | Prepaid rent | | 9,600 | |
| | (19,200 x 1/2) | | | |
| | | | | |
| (d) | Depreciation expense | 6,000 | | |
| | Accumulated depreciation | | 6,000 | |
| | (1/5 x 30,000) | | | |
| | | | | |
| (e) | Salaries expense | 2,300 | | |
| | Salaries payable | | 2,300 | |
| | | | | |
| (f) | Accounts receivable | 2,000 | | |
| | Sales | | 2,000 | |

**Part 5 - Closing Entries:**

| | | | | |
|---|---|---|---|---|
| (i) | Sales | 132,000 | | |
| | Interest revenue | 625 | | |
| | Rent expense | | | 9,600 |
| | Utilities expense | | | 1,700 |
| | Salary expense | | | 35,300 |
| | Insurance expense | | | 1,000 |
| | Supplies expense | | | 3,500 |
| | Legal expense | | | 1,500 |
| | Depreciation | | | 6,000 |
| | Income summary | | | 74,025 |
| | | | | |
| (ii) | Income summary | 74,025 | | |
| | Retained earnings | | 74,025 | |
| | | | | |
| (iii) | Retained earnings | 10,000 | | |
| | Dividends | | 10,000 | |

| CASH | | | |
|---|---|---|---|
| 1. | 170,000 | 2. | 19,200 |
| 5. | 45,000 | 4. | 30,000 |
| 12. | 35,000 | 6. | 1,700 |
| | | 7. | 33,000 |
| | | 8. | 6,000 |
| | | 10. | 3,500 |
| | | 11. | 1,500 |
| | | 13. | 10,000 |
| e.b. | 145,100 | | |

| CAPITAL STOCK | | | |
|---|---|---|---|
| | | 1. | 170,000 |

| SALES | | | |
|---|---|---|---|
| | | 5. | 115,000 |
| | | 9. | 15,000 |
| | | f) | 2,000 |
| (i) | 132,000 | e.b | 132,000 |

| ACCOUNTS PAYABLE | | | |
|---|---|---|---|
| 10. | 3,500 | 3. | 3,500 |

| RENT EXPENSE | | | |
|---|---|---|---|
| c) | 9,600 | (i) | 9,600 |

| FURNITURE | | | |
|---|---|---|---|
| 4. | 30,000 | | |

| ACCOUNTS RECEIVABLE | | | |
|---|---|---|---|
| 5. | 70,000 | 12. | 35,000 |
| f) | 2,000 | | |
| e.b. | 37,000 | | |

| UTILITIES EXPENSE | | | |
|---|---|---|---|
| 6. | 1,700 | (i) | 1,700 |

| SALARIES EXPENSE | | | |
|---|---|---|---|
| 7. | 33,000 | | |
| e) | 2,300 | | |
| e.b. | 35,300 | (i) | 35,300 |

| INTEREST REVENUE | | | |
|---|---|---|---|
| (i) | 625 | a) | 625 |

| INSURANCE EXPENSE | | | |
|---|---|---|---|
| b) | 1,000 | (i) | 1,000 |

| LEGAL EXPENSE | | | |
|---|---|---|---|
| 11. | 1,500 | (i) | 1,500 |

| SUPPLIES EXPENSE | | | |
|---|---|---|---|
| 3. | 3,500 | (i) | 3,500 |

| DEPRECIATION EXPENSE | | | |
|---|---|---|---|
| d) | 6,000 | (i) | 6,000 |

| ACCUMULATED DEPRECIATION | | | |
|---|---|---|---|
| | | d) | 6,000 |

| NOTE RECEIVABLE | | | |
|---|---|---|---|
| 9. | 15,000 | | |

| INTEREST RECEIVABLE | | | |
|---|---|---|---|
| a) | 625 | | |

| PREPAID RENT | | | |
|---|---|---|---|
| 2. | 19,200 | c) | 9,600 |
| e.b. | 9,600 | | |

| PREPAID INSURANCE | | | |
|---|---|---|---|
| 8. | 6,000 | b) | 1,000 |
| e.b. | 5,000 | | |

| SALARIES PAYABLE | | |
|---|---|---|
| | e) | 2,300 |

| DIVIDENDS | | | |
|---|---|---|---|
| 13. | 10,000 | (iii) | 10,000 |

| RETAINED EARNINGS | | | |
|---|---|---|---|
| (iii) | 10,000 | (ii) | 74,025 |
| | | e.b. | 64,025 |

| INCOME SUMMARY | | | |
|---|---|---|---|
| (ii) | 74,025 | (i) | 74,025 |

Calculations

(a)  5/12 x 10% x 15,000 = $625

(b)  1/2 x 1/3 x 6,000 = $1,000

(c)  19,200 x 1/2 = $9,600

(d)  1/5 x 30,000 = $6,000

Part 7 - Financial Statements

## Income Statement for year ended December 31, 2000

| | | |
|---|---|---|
| Sales | | $132,000 |
| Interest revenue | | 625 |
| | | 132,625 |
| Expenses | | |
| Supplies | $3,500 | |
| Salaries | 35,300 | |
| Rent | 9,600 | |
| Utilities | 1,700 | |
| Insurance | 1,000 | |
| Depreciation | 6,000 | |
| Legal | 1,500 | |
| | | 58,600 |
| Net Income | | $74,025 |

## Statement of retained earnings for year ended December 31, 2000

| | |
|---|---|
| Opening retained earnings balance | -0- |
| Net income for current year | 74,025 |
| | 74,025 |
| Less dividends | 10,000 |
| Closing retained earnings balance | $64,025 |

## Balance sheet as of December 31, 2000

### Current assets

| | | |
|---|---|---|
| Cash | $ 145,100 | |
| Accounts receivable | 37,000 | |
| Interest receivable | 625 | |
| Note receivable | 15,000 | |
| Prepaid rent | 9,600 | |
| Prepaid insurance | 5,000 | |
| Total current assets | | $ 212,325 |

### Non-current assets

| | | |
|---|---|---|
| Furniture, fixture & equipment - cost | $ 30,000 | |
| Less accumulated depreciation | (6,000) | 24,000 |
| | | $236,325 |

### Liabilities & stockholders' equity
### Current liabilities

| | | |
|---|---|---|
| Salaries payable | | $ 2,300 |

### Stockholders' equity

| | | |
|---|---|---|
| Capital stock | $ 170,000 | |
| Retained earnings | 64,025 | |
| | | 234,025 |
| | | $236,325 |

Parts 2,4,6 - Trial balances

| | Unadjusted | | Adjusting entries | | Adjusted | | Closing entries | | Post closing | |
|---|---|---|---|---|---|---|---|---|---|---|
| | Dr | Cr. | Dr | Cr. | Dr | Cr. | Dr | Cr. | Dr | Cr. |
| Furniture, fixtures & equipment | 30,000 | | | | 30,000 | | | | 30,000 | |
| Accumulated depreciation | | | | 6,000 | | 6,000 | | | | 6,000 |
| Prepaid rent | 19,200 | | | 9,600 | 9,600 | | | | 9,600 | |
| Prepaid insurance | 6,000 | | | 1,000 | 5,000 | | | | 5,000 | |
| Accounts receivable | 35,000 | | 2,000 | | 37,000 | | | | 37,000 | |
| Note receivable | 15,000 | | | | 15,000 | | | | 15,000 | |
| Interest receivable | | | 625 | | 625 | | | | 625 | |
| Cash | 145,100 | | | | 145,100 | | | | 145,100 | |
| Capital stock | | 170,000 | | | | 170,000 | | | | 170,000 |
| Retained earnings | | | | | | | 10,000 | 74,025 | | 64,025 |
| Dividends | 10,000 | | | | 10,000 | | | 10,000 | | |
| Accounts payable | | | | | | | | | | |
| Salaries payable | | | | 2,300 | | 2,300 | | | | 2,300 |
| | | | | | | | | | | |
| Sales | | 130,000 | | 2,000 | | 132,000 | 132,000 | | | |
| Interest revenue | | | | 625 | | 625 | 625 | | | |
| Rent expense | | | 9,600 | | 9,600 | | | 9,600 | | |
| Utilities expense | 1,700 | | | | 1,700 | | | 1,700 | | |
| Salary expense | 33,000 | | 2,300 | | 35,300 | | | 35,300 | | |
| Insurance expense | | | 1,000 | | 1,000 | | | 1,000 | | |
| Supplies expense | 3,500 | | | | 3,500 | | | 3,500 | | |
| Legal expense | 1,500 | | | | 1,500 | | | 1,500 | | |
| Depreciation expense | | | 6,000 | | 6,000 | | | 6,000 | | |
| | | | | | | | | | | |
| Income summary | | | | | | | 74,025 | 74,025 | | |
| | | | | | | | | | | |
| Total | 300,000 | 300,000 | 21,525 | 21,525 | 310,925 | 310,925 | 216,650 | 216,650 | 242,325 | 242,325 |

## Problem 47

1 and 2

| | Adjustment | Effect on accounting equation | | |
|---|---|---|---|---|
| | | Assets | = Liabilities | + Owners' equity |
| a) | Deferred expense | - 10,000 | | - 10,000 |
| b) | Deferred revenue | | - 2,500 | + 2,500 |
| c) | Accrued liability | | + 4,400 | - 4,400 |
| d) | Accrued asset | + 4,500 | | + 4,500 |

3

a)  Depreciation expense                          10,000
        Accumulated depreciation                        10,000
    To record depreciation for year to December 31, 2000


b)  Unearned revenues                            2,500
        Maintenance revenues                          2,500
    To record recognition of revenues received in advance


c)  Property tax expense                          4,400
        Property tax payable                          4,400
    To record property taxes due for eleven months to December 31, 2000


d)  Interest receivable                          4,500
        Interest revenue                              4,500
    To record interest revenue for nine months to December 31, 2000

## Critical Thinking Problem 48

The table below summarizes the impact on the income statement and balance sheet of failing to make the adjusting entries for Pacioli Company.

|    | **Effect on Income Statement** | | **Effect on Balance Sheet** | |
|----|---------------|-------------|--------------|-------------|
| A. | Revenue: | no effect | Assets: | overstated by $250 |
|    | Expense: | understated by $250 | Liabilities: | no effect |
|    | Net income: | overstated by 250 | Owners' equity: | overstated by $250 |
| B. | Revenue: | understated by $12,500 | Assets: | no effect |
|    | Expense: | no effect | Liabilities: | overstated by $12,500 |
|    | Net income: | understated by $12,500 | Owners' equity: | understated by $12,500 |
| C. | Revenue: | no effect | Assets: | no effect |
|    | Expense: | understated by $2,000 | Liabilities: | understated by $2,000 |
|    | Net income: | overstated by $2,000 | Owners' equity: | overstated by $2,000 |
| D. | Revenue: | understated by $50 | Assets: | understated by $50 |
|    | Expense: | no effect | Liabilities: | no effect |
|    | Net income: | understated by $50 | Owners' equity: | understated by $50 |

# Chapter 5
# Merchandise Accounting and Internal Control

This chapter discusses the accounting issues associated with inventory, particularly in relation to merchandising companies. The need for an efficient system of internal control to safeguard the assets of the company and ensure the validity of its financial reports is also discussed. Your main objectives in this chapter are to understand the measurement and accounting issues associated with purchasing and sales, and to gain an understanding of the role and key elements of an internal control system.

## Learning Objectives

**LO 1** Understand how wholesalers and retailers account for sales of merchandise.

**LO 2** Explain the differences between periodic and perpetual inventory systems.

**LO 3** Understand how wholesalers and retailers account for cost of goods sold.

**LO 4** Explain the importance of internal control to a business.

**LO 5** Describe the basic internal control procedures.

**LO 6** Describe the various documents used in recording purchases of merchandise and their role in controlling cash disbursements.

## Key Textbook Exhibits

**Exhibits 5-4** illustrates the cost of goods sold model for a merchandiser. *Self-Test:* What increases beginning inventory? What decreases it?

**Exhibit 5-6** summarizes the issues related to transportation costs and transfer of title. *Self-Test:* If the merchandise was shipped FOB shipping point, would the goods be included in Horton's inventory on December 31, 2001?

**Exhibit 5-9** illustrates the document flow for the purchasing function. *Self-Test:* How does the supplier of the merchandise use the Purchase Order?

## Review of Key Concepts

**LO 1**  It is necessary, when recording sales for retailers and wholesalers, to recognize the impact of sales returns and allowances, trade and quantity discounts, and credit terms on the total sales recorded.

### Sales returns and allowances

Sales returns refer to goods returned by customers under policies that allow goods to be returned within a specified time. Sales allowances refer to allowances customers may receive for spoiled or damaged goods. Sales returns and allowances are recorded in a separate contra-revenue account. This account has a debit balance and allows the company to monitor the level of returns and allowances.

### Trade discounts and quantity discounts

Trade discounts are special discounts offered to certain classes of customers. For example, some hardware stores offer discounts to contractors. Quantity discounts are offered to customers who buy large quantities of goods. Unlike sales returns and allowances, trade discounts and quantity discounts are not recorded in the accounts, and the net amount is recorded as revenue.

### Sales discounts

Sales discounts are offered by many companies to encourage early payment by customers. They can be accounted for in one of two ways. The gross method assumes that the customer will not take advantage of the discount, and initially records sales at the gross amount. If a customer subsequently takes advantage of the discount, the amount of the discount is credited to a contra-revenue account called Sales discounts. The Sales discounts account reduces owners' equity.

For example, on July 1, 2000, a sale of $5,000 is made with terms that allow for a discount of 3% (or $150) if payment is made within 10 days of the sale, and, if the discount is not taken, the full amount must be paid within 30 days. (Note that this is often written as 3/10, net 30.) If the company uses the gross method, the journal entries are as follows:

|  |  | Debit | Credit |
|---|---|---|---|
| 7/1/00 | Accounts receivable | 5,000 | |
|  | Sales | | 5,000 |
|  | Sale of goods on account | | |

If the discount is taken and the customer pays on July 8, 2000:

|  |  | Debit | Credit |
|---|---|---|---|
| 7/8/00 | Cash | 4,850 | |
|  | Sales discounts | 150 | |
|  | Accounts receivable | | 5,000 |
|  | Receipt of cash for goods sold on account | | |

If the discount is not taken and the customer pays on July 31, 2000:

|  |  | Debit | Credit |
|---|---|---|---|
| 7/31/00 | Cash | 5,000 | |
|  | Accounts receivable | | 5,000 |
|  | Receipt of cash for goods sold on account | | |

**LO 1**  The calculation for **cost of goods sold** for a retailer or wholesaler is as follows:

| | | |
|---|---|---|
| | **Beginning inventory** | Goods on hand at the beginning of the period |
| + | **Purchases** | Goods bought during the period |
| = | **Cost of goods available for sale** | |
| - | **Ending inventory** | Goods not sold during the period |
| = | **Cost of goods sold** | |

**LO 2**  Inventory is accounted for under either the perpetual or the periodic inventory system.

•  Under the **perpetual inventory system**, the inventory account is continually updated whenever a sale or purchase occurs. At the same time as the revenue associated with a sale is recorded, an entry is made which reduces the asset Inventory and increases the cost of goods sold. At any point during the accounting period, the inventory account balance represents the goods that are available for sale. For example, assume in the illustration above that the cost of the goods sold was $3,500. The following additional entry would be made when the sale of $5,000 was recorded:

| | | Debit | Credit |
|---|---|---|---|
| 7/1/00 | Cost of goods sold | 3,500 | |
| | Inventory | | 3,500 |
| | $5,000 sale of goods costing $3,500 | | |

•  Under the **periodic inventory system**, the inventory account is updated only once, at the end of the accounting period. It is necessary to open a separate purchases account in which all purchases made by the company are recorded. A physical count of goods is taken at the end of the period. The inventory account is then updated with the total purchases of the period and the ending inventory for the period. The difference between the cost of goods available for sale (equal to purchases plus beginning inventory) and the cost of goods from the physical count is the figure used for cost of goods sold. During the period therefore, the inventory account balance cannot be relied upon to provide the goods available for sale.

**LO 3**  When recording purchases for retailers and wholesalers, it is necessary to recognize the impact of purchase returns and allowances, purchase discounts, and transportation costs on the total purchases recorded.

**Purchase returns and allowances**

Purchase returns refer to goods returned by the company to its supplier. Purchase allowances refer to allowances customers received for spoiled or damaged goods. Purchase returns and allowances are recorded in a separate account, which is a contra-account to the purchases account.

**Purchase discounts**

Purchase discounts are discounts offered by suppliers to encourage early payment. They are accounted for under either the gross method or the net method, which parallel the methods used for sales discounts. To illustrate the gross method, assume that on December 1, 2000, Company Z buys $3,000 of consumable supplies on terms of 4/5, net 30. The discount available is, therefore, 4% of $3,000, or $120. When the goods are purchased, the impact on the accounting equation is as follows:

| | | Debit | Credit |
|---|---|---|---|
| 12/1/00 | Consumable expenses | 3,000 | |
| | Accounts payable | | 3,000 |
| | Purchase of consumables on account | | |

If the discount is taken and the account is paid within five days:

|  |  | Debit | Credit |
|---|---|---|---|
| 12/5/00 | Accounts payable | 3,000 | |
| | Purchase discounts | | 120 |
| | Cash | | 2,880 |
| | Receipt of cash for goods sold on account | | |

### Transportation costs

Transportation costs can be either the responsibility of the seller (the goods are FOB, or free on board, destination point) or the responsibility of the buyer (FOB shipping point). Where the transportation costs are the responsibility of the buyer, they must be added to the costs of the goods purchased. If they are FOB shipping point, they become the property of the buyer as soon as they leave the shipping point and are therefore included in the buyer's inventory at year-end. Similarly, where goods are in transit at year-end and are FOB destination point, they are not included in the buyer's inventory at year-end.

## Sixty Second Quiz!

**Question**: Omega Inc. orders goods from Delta Corp. FOB shipping point on March 28, 2000 just before both companies' financial year end on March 31, 2000. The goods are in transit at the end of the financial year. Which company includes the goods in transit in its inventory balance on March 31, 2000?

**Answer**: The buyer, Omega Inc., includes the goods in its inventory balance.

**LO 4** An **internal control system** consists of the policies and procedures necessary to ensure that the entity's overall objective is being met by the safeguarding of its assets and the reliability of its accounting records. Management has the primary responsibility for the reliability of the financial statements. The **report of management** to stockholders, which is included in the company's annual report, spells out management's responsibility for the financial information in the annual report. Many companies employ a full-time internal audit staff to monitor and evaluate the internal control system. The independent public accountant's responsibility, on the other hand, is primarily to determine whether or not the accounts are presented fairly. The audit committee of the board of directors provides the contact between the stockholders and the external auditors.

**LO 5,6** The **internal control system** of an organization consists of three elements: the control environment, the accounting system, and internal control procedures. In addition, business documents are a key determinant in the success of both the accounting system and the internal control system.

• The **control environment** refers to the pervasive attitude towards internal control within the organization. Determining factors include management's operating style, personnel policies and practices, and the activities of the audit committee.

• The **accounting system**, whether it is automated or manual, must be capable of supporting the internal control procedures established. In particular, it must be capable of handling both the volume and the complexity of the business's transactions.

• **Internal control procedures** include both **administrative controls,** which are concerned with efficient operation and adherence to management policies, and **accounting controls,** which are concerned with safeguarding assets and ensuring the reliability of the financial statements. The key internal control procedures are as follows:

### Proper Authorizations

Management authorizes certain individuals to carry out certain tasks and can then hold these individuals responsible for the outcome of their actions. For example, only one individual in a retail store may authorize refunds.

### Segregation of Duties

The physical custody of assets should be separated from the accounting for them. For example, the same individual should not be responsible for both delivering goods to a customer and receiving the cash for the goods.

### Independent Verification

The work of one department or individual should act as a check on the work of another. For example, the physical count of inventory in a perpetual inventory system acts as a check on the records of both the storeroom and the individual in the accounting department who maintains the inventory account.

### Safeguarding Assets and Records

Adequate safeguards must be in place to protect assets and accounting records from losses of various kinds. For example, changes in computer code should only be made by properly authorized individuals who can provide the appropriate password.

### Independent Review and Appraisal

Both the independent auditors and the internal audit staff should regularly review, appraise, and report on the effectiveness of the internal control system.

## Review of Key Terms

| | |
|---|---|
| **Accounting control** | A procedure concerned with safeguarding the assets or the reliability of the financial statements. |
| **Accounting system** | The methods and records used to accurately report an entity's transactions and to maintain accountability for its assets and liabilities. |
| **Administrative control** | A procedure concerned with efficient operation of the business and adherence to managerial policies. |
| **Audit committee** | A subset of the board of directors that acts as a direct contact between the stockholders and the independent accounting firm. |
| **Blind receiving report** | A form used by the receiving department to account for the quantity and condition of merchandise received from a supplier. |
| **Board of directors** | The group composed of key officers of a corporation and outside members responsible for the general oversight of the affairs of the entity. |
| **Cost of goods available for sale** | Beginning inventory plus cost of goods purchased. |
| **Cost of goods sold** | Cost of goods available for sale minus ending inventory. |
| **FOB destination point** | Terms that require the seller to pay for the cost of shipping the merchandise to the buyer. |
| **FOB shipping point** | Terms that require the buyer to pay the shipping costs. |
| **Foreign Corrupt Practices Act** | Legislation intended to increase the accountability of management for accurate records and reliable financial statements. |
| **Internal audit staff** | The department responsible for monitoring and evaluating the internal control system. |
| **Internal control system** | Policies and procedures necessary to ensure the safeguarding of an entity's assets, the reliability of its accounting records, and the accomplishment of overall company objectives. |

| | |
|---|---|
| **Invoice** | The form sent by the seller to the buyer as evidence of a sale. |
| **Invoice approval form** | A form the accounting department uses before making payment, to document the accuracy of all the information about a purchase. |
| **Net sales** | Sales revenue less sales returns and allowances and sales discounts. |
| **Periodic inventory system** | The system in which the inventory account is updated only at the end of the period. |
| **Perpetual inventory system** | The system in which the inventory account is increased at the time of each purchase of merchandise and decreased at the time of each sale. |
| **Purchase discounts** | The contra-purchases account used to record reductions in purchase price for early payment to the supplier. |
| **Purchase order** | The form sent by the purchasing department to the supplier. |
| **Purchase requisition form** | The form a department uses to initiate a request to order merchandise. |
| **Purchase returns and allowances** | The contra-purchases account used in a periodic inventory system when a refund is received from a supplier or a reduction is given in the balance owed to the supplier. |
| **Purchases** | The account used in a periodic inventory system to record acquisitions of merchandise. |
| **Quantity discount** | A reduction in selling price for buying a large number of units of a product. |
| **Receiving report** | A form used by the receiving department to account for the quantity and condition of merchandise received from a supplier. |
| **Report of management** | A written statement in the annual report indicating the responsibility of management for the financial statements. |
| **Sales discounts** | The contra-revenue account used to record discounts given to customers for early payment of their accounts. |
| **Sales returns and allowances** | The contra-revenue account used to record both refunds to customers and reductions of their accounts. |
| **Trade discount** | A reduction in selling price offered to a special class of customers. |
| **Transportation-in** | The adjunct account used to record freight costs paid by the buyer. |

## Practice Test
## Questions and Problems

### Circle the alternative that best answers the question.

**LO 2** 1. Jenny Department Store uses a periodic inventory system. What is the impact on the financial statements of an overstatement of ending inventory?
a) Current year's net income will be overstated.
b) Next year's net income will be overstated.
c) Next year's ending inventory will be overstated.
d) Next year's ending inventory will be understated.

**LO 3** 2. Which of the following statements correctly defines the calculation of net purchases?
a) Gross purchases less purchase returns and allowances less purchase discounts plus transportation-in
b) Gross purchases less purchase returns and allowances less purchase discounts less transportation-in
c) Gross purchases plus purchase returns and allowances less purchase discounts plus transportation-in
d) Gross purchases plus purchase returns and allowances plus purchase discounts less transportation-in

**LO 1** 3. In 2000, Alpha Corporation's closing inventory of $20 million was higher than its opening inventory by $5 million. Its net purchases for 2000 were $200 million. What was Alpha's cost of goods sold for the year?
a) $195 million
b) $220 million
c) $215 million
d) $185 million

**LO 3** 4. If goods are purchased FOB shipping point, which of the following costs should not be included in ending inventory?
a) Transportation-in
b) Transportation-out
c) Import duties on imported goods
d) Wages paid to warehouse staff in receiving department

**LO 2** 5. Which of the following is not a feature of periodic inventory systems?
a) Provide up to date information on inventory for management control
b) Cheaper to maintain than perpetual inventory system
c) Require a physical count of inventory at the end of the period
d) Require opening of separate purchases account to record acquisitions of goods during the accounting period

**LO 5** 6. Which of the following is not a type of internal control procedure?
   a) Segregation of duties
   b) Independent verification
   c) Proper authorizations
   d) Review by external auditor

**LO 5** 7. Which of the following pairs of duties could be carried out by one person and still maintain the integrity of the internal control system?
   a) Preparing and signing checks
   b) Making cash sales and recording them in the journal
   c) Preparing and mailing purchase orders
   d) Ordering and receiving inventory

**LO 5** 8. Which of the following does not act as a control mechanism for cash received by a merchandising company?
   a) Cash register displays visible to customers
   b) Cash register tapes locked into the till
   c) Prenumbered cash register receipts
   d) All of the above

**LO 6** 9. Which of the following documents is sent to the supplier when a purchase is made?
   a) Invoice approval form
   b) Receiving report
   c) Purchase order
   d) Purchase requisition

**LO 4** 10. Which of the following groups provides direct contact between the stockholders and the independent audit firm?
   a) The board of directors
   b) The company management
   c) The internal auditors
   d) The audit committee

**LO 1** 11. A build up of inventory can indicate that:
   a) the company's products are less desirable.
   b) the prices of the products are undesirable.
   c) either a) or b).
   d) neither a) nor b).

LO 2    12.    Alpha Company uses a perpetual inventory system, and at the end of the year, its cost of goods sold account has a balance of $230,000, and its inventory account has a balance of $40,000. A physical count of its inventory indicates that its closing inventory balance is in fact $30,000. Which of the following errors could have led to this overstatement of inventory?

a)    Failure to record the cost of a sale in the cost of goods sold and inventory accounts

b)    Failure to record a sale in the sales account

c)    Recording a sale twice in the sales account

d)    Recording the cost of a sale twice in the cost of goods sold and inventory accounts

LO 3    13.    The normal account balances for sales returns and sales discounts are, respectively:

a)    a credit balance and a debit balance.

b)    a debit balance and a credit balance.

c)    both debit balances.

d)    both credit balances

LO 1,3    14.    The normal account balances for purchase returns and purchase discounts are, respectively:

a)    both debit balances.

b)    both credit balances

c)    a credit balance and a debit balance.

d)    a debit balance and a credit balance.

LO 2    15.    Which of the following statements is true?

a)    The periodic inventory method provides an up-to-date figure for cost of goods sold throughout the accounting period.

b)    Point-of-sales terminals in retail stores have led to an increased use of periodic inventory systems.

c)    Under the periodic system, the inventory account is updated each time a sale is made.

d)    The ending inventory under the periodic inventory system is found by physically counting the units on hand at the end of the period.

## Indicate whether each of the following statements is true or false:

**LO 1**    16.   The gross method of accounting for sales discounts is more realistic if customers routinely take advantage of the discounts.

**LO 4**    17.   No system of internal control, however well designed, can be completely foolproof.

**LO 1**    18.   If we add purchases and cost of goods sold and deduct opening inventory, we find the closing inventory.

**LO 2**    19.   Point-of-sales terminals have resulted in more retailers adopting periodic inventory systems.

**LO 3**    20.   When goods are shipped FOB shipping point, freight costs are added to the net purchases for the period.

**LO 5**    21.   The external auditor need not be concerned with assessing the effectiveness of the internal control system, since that is the responsibility of the internal audit staff.

**LO 6**    22.   A purchase order can be used as a source document for recording a purchase and a liability.

**LO 5**    23.   If the cash receipts are greater than the amount recorded on the cash register tape, the excess cash should be kept until the next day to cover any shortage on the next day's receipts.

**LO 5**    24.   An adequate system of internal control would require one person to prepare and sign checks and a different person to mail them.

**LO 5**    25.   Serial numbering of business documents such as checks provides an important internal control device.

**LO 2**    26.   A physical count of inventory is carried out only under the periodic inventory system.

**LO 2**    27.   When the perpetual inventory system is used, cost of goods sold is updated every time a sale is made.

**LO 2**    28.   Under both the periodic and the perpetual systems, ending inventory is entered in the accounts after a physical count.

**LO 5**    29.   If a company employs an external auditor, it need not employ an internal audit staff.

**LO 2**    30.   When a customer returns merchandise, the sales account is debited or reduced by that amount.

## Complete each of the following statements:

**LO 1** 31. The major difference between a retailer's and a service organization's income statement is the inclusion of _____, which on the retailer's income statement is deducted from net sales to get gross margin.

**LO 1** 32. A _____ is offered to customers who buy large quantities;
a _____ is offered to particular types of customer;
a _____ is offered to customers who pay early.

**LO 1** 33. _____ can be thought of as a pool of costs distributed between goods that were sold and goods in ending inventory.

**LO 2** 34. The _____ inventory system allows greater control over inventory at a greater cost.

**LO 3** 35. When goods are shipped FOB _____, it is the responsibility of the seller to pay for transportation costs.

**LO 5** 36. _____ controls focus on the efficiency with which an organization is run, _____ controls focus on safeguarding assets and the reliability of the financial statements.

**LO 4** 37. The internal control structure consists of three basic elements, _____, _____, and _____.

**LO 5** 38. _____ refers to the type of internal control procedure that results in the work of one department acting as a check on the work of another.

**LO 1** 39. The shorthand way of identifying invoice terms that provide for a 2% discount if the invoice is paid within 10 days, or the full amount to be paid within 30 days is _____.

**LO 6** 40. The _____ is used by the accounting department to document the accuracy of the purchase requisition, the purchase order, and the receiving report.

**LO 1** 41. A company buys goods for $3,000, 2/8, net 30, and pays on the fifteenth day after the sale. The amount the company pays is _____.

**LO 1** 42. The _____ of recording sales discounts assumes that customers will not normally take advantage of the discount offered.

**LO 4** 43. The _____ is a subset of the board of directors that acts as a direct contact between the stockholders and the independent accounting firm.

**LO 4** 44. The _____ is a written statement in the annual report indicating the responsibility of management for the financial statements.

**LO 4** 45. _____ are responsible for monitoring and evaluating the internal control system.

## Answer each of the following problems:

**LO 5** 46. The following information is available for DJIMI Discount Warehouse. Fill in the blanks in the table.

|  | 12/31/1998 | 12/31/1999 | 12/31/2000 |
|---|---|---|---|
| Opening inventory | 35,000 | ? | ? |
| Purchases | 100,000 | 120,000 | ? |
| Purchase discounts | 3,000 | ? | 6,000 |
| Cost of goods available for sale | ? | 158,000 | 170,000 |
| Cost of goods sold | ? | 100,000 | ? |
| Ending inventory | 40,000 | ? | 65,000 |

**LO 3** 47. Perry's Parlous Plants operates a periodic inventory system and is preparing its accounts for the year ended December 31, 2000. Complete the following table for items that were in transit at the year-end, showing how the company should deal with each item:

| TRANSACTION | PAY FREIGHT COSTS? | RECORD PURCHASE OR SALE IN 2000 INCOME STATEMENT? | INCLUDE IN INVENTORY IN BALANCE SHEET ON 12/31/2000? |
|---|---|---|---|
| Purchase from Petula Phlox; FOB shipping point | | | |
| Purchase from Georgia Geraniums; FOB destination point | | | |
| Sale to Freddes Firs; FOB destination point | | | |
| Sale to Randy Roses Geraniums; FOB shipping point | | | |

**LO 4,5** 48.     For the following situations, indicate whether or not you believe that the system of internal control is adequate and, if not, what you would do to improve it.

1. Mr. W. is a computer programmer for a small grocery chain. Since he is the only computer-literate member of staff, he is responsible both for designing changes to the computerized accounting system and for programming them into the system.

2. Ms. K. is the accountant for a large discount warehouse. She is known to be a workaholic and has not taken a day off work (even for vacations) for three years. She personally oversees all cash transactions, calculating the total cash takings each day, preparing the bank pay-in slips, and personally lodging cash payments in the bank.

3. Mr. S. is the Receiving Department manager for the same discount warehouse. He is known to be frequently absent from his job and to allow his workers to work without supervision. He is proud of the fact that several of them can imitate his signature so that he does not personally have to sign for all the deliveries that are made.

4. Ms. L. supervises the booking office of a railroad station and has agreed that cash, which appears to be more than recorded takings, should be put in a drawer and used for future shortages. At the end of each month, if there is any cash left in the drawer, it is reported in the monthly returns to the head office, and the drawer is emptied for the beginning of the next month.

## Critical Thinking Problem

**LO 1**    49.    Consider the information in Problem 46. What has happened to the firm's inventory level over the three years? What additional information would you need before you could comment on the advisability of this trend?

# Solutions

## Multiple Choice

| | | | | |
|---|---|---|---|---|
| 1. | a | | 9. | c |
| 2. | a | | 10. | d |
| 3. | a | | 11. | c |
| 4. | b | | 12. | a |
| 5. | a | | 13. | c |
| 6. | d | | 14. | b |
| 7. | c | | 15. | d |
| 8. | d | | | |

## True/False

**COMMENT/EXPLANATION**

| | | |
|---|---|---|
| 16. | False | The net method is more appropriate. |
| 17. | True | |
| 18. | False | Closing inventory equals opening inventory plus purchases minus cost of goods sold. |
| 19. | False | Point-of-sales terminals make using a perpetual inventory systems easier. |
| 20. | True | |
| 21. | False | The external auditor must be satisfied as to the effectiveness of the internal control system because the validity of the accounting system depends on it. |
| 22. | False | Receipt of the goods or an invoice from the supplier is the basis of the purchaser's recognition of a liability. |
| 23. | False | All shortages should be reported on a daily basis so that any pattern indicating fraud can be identified. |
| 24. | False | The preparation and signature of checks should be separated. |
| 25. | True | |
| 26. | False | A physical count is also carried out under the perpetual system to act as a check on the closing balance on the inventory account. |
| 27. | True | |
| 28. | False | Under the perpetual system, the inventory account is continually updated after each sale and therefore ending inventory can be found as the closing balance on the inventory account. As was pointed out above, this balance is confirmed by a physical count carried out at the end of the period. |
| 29. | False | Both are normally needed. The external auditor carries out an examination of the internal control procedures of the entity. Therefore, the more effective the internal audit staff, the more reliance the external auditor can place on the information derived from the accounting system. |
| 30. | False | The sales returns account, which is a contra-sales account, is debited. |

## Fill in the Blanks

| | |
|---|---|
| 31. cost of goods sold | 38. independent verification |
| 32. quantity discount, trade discount, | 39. 2/10, net 30 |
| 33. sales discount | 40. invoice approval form |
| 34. cost of goods available for sale | 41. $3,000 |
| 35. perpetual | 42. gross method |
| 36. destination point | 43. audit committee |
| 37. administrative, accounting | 44. report of management |
| 38. control environment, accounting system, control procedures | 45. internal audit staff |

## Problem 46

| | 12/31/1998 | 12/31/1999 | 12/31/2000 |
|---|---|---|---|
| Opening inventory | 35,000 | 40,000 | 58,000 |
| Purchases | 100,000 | 120,000 | 118,000 |
| Purchase discounts | 3,000 | 2,000 | 6,000 |
| Cost of goods available for sale | 132,000 | 158,000 | 170,000 |
| Cost of goods sold | 92,000 | 100,000 | 105,000 |
| Ending inventory | 40,000 | 58,000 | 65,000 |

## Problem 47

| Transaction | Pay freight costs? | Record purchase or sale in 2000 income statement? | Include in inventory in balance sheet on 12/31/2000? |
|---|---|---|---|
| Purchase from Petula Phlox; FOB shipping point | Yes | Yes | Yes |
| Purchase from Georgia Geraniums; FOB destination point | No | No | No |
| Sale to Freddes Firs; FOB destination point | Yes | No | Yes |
| Sale to Randy Roses Geraniums; FOB shipping point | No | Yes | No |

## Problem 48

1.  The principal of segregation of duties would suggest that Mr. W. should not run the entire computer system, since he would have the opportunity to manipulate it to his own benefit. As an illustration of what someone in that position can do, a programmer for a bank wrote into a program, which calculated interest to be charged on loans, a small routine that credited all the roundings in the calculation to his own account. It was not until several hundred thousand dollars found their way into his account that his fraud was discovered.

2.  No one person, no matter how senior, should be allowed to have full control of cash receipts and paying the cash into the bank. Ms. K. could easily steal some cash and there would be no record, other than those prepared by her, to identify how much money should be paid into the bank. A further suspicious situation is her reluctance to take time off. Many frauds have been discovered when illness kept the individual concerned out of the office for a few days, and other staff members could get access to records that were normally kept under close control.

3.  Mr. S.'s department sounds like a disaster waiting to happen. It is hard to see whether any internal control procedures are either in place or being followed. No one should sign someone else's signature, since it completely defeats the purpose of having someone in a senior position sign for deliveries. Perhaps the best solution is to suggest that Mr. S. find other employment.

4.  Any cash shortages and excesses should be reported on a daily basis, preferably analyzed by employee. In this way, it will be apparent if there is any pattern in the shortages of the office as a whole, or by any individual.

## Critical Thinking Problem 49

The inventory levels have increased steadily over the three years. In general, firms wish to control the amount of inventory they are carrying, since it represents a significant investment. In addition, inventories can become obsolete, and the firm may be unable to realize what it paid for them. For these reasons, the firm should examine whether or not it can reduce its inventory levels.

There are, however, circumstances where increasing inventories are necessary. In particular, if the company's sales are increasing, additional inventories may be needed to provide enough safety stock for the new sales level. This might be the case here since the cost of goods sold has increased, suggesting a higher level of sales activity. To confirm this, the sales figures for the three years would be needed.

# Chapter 6

# Inventories and Cost of Goods Sold

This chapter continues the exploration of accounting for inventory started in Chapter 5 by discussing the various methods that are used to find the cost of inventory. You have two overall aims in this chapter. First, understand the assumptions underlying the different methods used for inventory costing, and how each method is applied in practice. Second, understand the impact of the different methods on reported income and the balance sheet.

## Learning Objectives

**LO 1** Identify the forms of inventory held by different types of businesses and the types of cost incurred.

**LO 2** Explain the relationship between the valuation of inventory and the measurement of income.

**LO 3** Apply the inventory costing methods of specific identification, weighted average, FIFO, and LIFO using a periodic system.

**LO 4** Analyze the effects of the different costing methods on inventory, net income, income taxes, and cash flow.

**LO 5** Analyze the effects of an inventory error on various financial statement items.

**LO 6** Apply the lower-of-cost-or-market rule to the valuation of inventory.

**LO 7** Explain why and how the cost of inventory is estimated in certain situations.

**LO 8** Analyze the management of inventory turnover.

**LO 9** Explain the effects that inventory transactions have on the statement of cash flows.

**LO 10** Explain the differences between a periodic and a perpetual inventory system.

**LO 11** Apply the inventory costing methods using a perpetual system.

## Key Textbook Exhibits

**Exhibit 6-1** contains an illustration of the types of costs and inventories held by merchandising and manufacturing enterprises. *Self-Test:* What are the three types of inventory held by a manufacturing business?

**Exhibit 6-4** summarizes the impact over two years of an overstatement or understatement of first year closing inventory. *Self-Test:* Does the total uncorrected reported income equal the total corrected reported income over the two years? Why?

**Exhibits 6-13 through 6-15** illustrate the use of the perpetual inventory system *Self-Test:* Why does the choice of inventory system, and the inventory costing method, lead to different figures for ending inventory and cost of goods sold?

## Review of Key Concepts

**LO 1** Inventory held by merchandising enterprises differs from inventory held by manufacturing enterprises in terms of both the costs incurred in acquiring the inventory, and the types of inventory held.

- For a merchandiser, goods purchased for resale are normally the only type of inventory held. The costs associated with merchandise inventory are simply those required to buy the inventory (including transportation-in, if appropriate).

- Inventory for a manufacturer consists of three distinct categories: raw materials, work in process and finished goods. A manufacturer incurs three types of cost: direct material, direct labor, and manufacturing overhead.

The costs included in each type of inventory for each type of enterprise are summarized below:

**Retailer/Wholesaler**          **Manufacturer**

| Merchandise Inventory | Raw Materials | Work in Process | Finished Goods |
|---|---|---|---|
| Cost to purchase | Cost to purchase | Cost of the materials, direct labor, and overhead used in the manufacture of unfinished items | Total cost of materials, direct labor, and overhead used to manufacture goods completed but not yet sold |

**LO 2** One of the most fundamental concepts in accounting is the relationship between asset valuation and income measurement. Since assets are unexpired costs, and expenses are expired costs, reducing the value of an asset results in an increase in expenses, with a consequent reduction in income. This general point can be illustrated by exploring the relationship between inventory valuation and income measurement.

Cost of goods sold is found from:

**Beginning Inventory + Purchases - Ending Inventory = Cost of Goods Sold**

The valuation of ending inventory therefore determines the cost of goods sold. In addition, we find net income from

**Sales - Cost of Goods Sold - Other Expenses = Net Income**

Given revenue for the period, net income is determined by cost of goods sold. The higher is cost of goods sold, the lower is net income, and vice versa. As we have seen above, cost of goods sold is a function of the valuation of ending inventory. Reported income is therefore directly related to the valuation of ending inventory.

## Sixty Second Quiz!

**Question**:      Suppose a company can use one of two different inventory valuation methods. Method One gives a higher ending inventory than Method Two. Will reported income be higher or lower under Method One than under Method Two? Can you find a general rule about how reported income is related to cost of goods sold and to ending inventory?

**Answer**:      Under Method One, ending inventory is higher, so cost of goods sold will be lower. Therefore, reported income will be higher under Method One than under Method Two. The general rule is that reported income is inversely related to cost of goods sold, and directly related to ending inventory.

**LO 3**   In some types of business, for example car dealerships, it is possible to **specifically identify** items in ending inventory. In this case, the cost of goods sold and the purchase price of ending inventory are clearly identifiable. In most businesses, however, this inventory costing method is not feasible. An inventory costing method must be chosen on the basis of an assumption about how inventory costs flow through the organization. There are three commonly used inventory costing methods:

- **Weighted Average Cost Method:** The weighted average cost for each period is calculated by dividing cost of goods available for sale during the period (purchases plus beginning inventory) by the units available for sale. This weighted average cost is assigned to all units available for sale during the period, including ending inventory.

- **First-in, First-out Method (FIFO):** This method assumes that the first units sold during the period are the units that were purchased first. Ending inventory cost therefore consists of the items that were most recently purchased.

- **Last-in, First-out Method (LIFO):** In contrast to FIFO, LIFO assumes that the first units sold are those that have been purchased most recently. Ending inventory cost therefore consists of items that may have been purchased several periods before.

To illustrate the use of each method, assume that beginning inventory and purchases during January, 2000 for the Alpat Company are given in the following table. Alpat uses a periodic inventory system, and during the year sold 9,000 units at a selling price of $20 per unit.

|  |  | UNITS | COST PER UNIT |
|---|---|---|---|
| Beginning inventory |  | 2,500 | $10 |
| Purchases: | January 1 | 3,000 | $11 |
|  | January 11 | 2,500 | $12 |
|  | January 25 | 2,000 | $15 |

The total cost of goods available for sale, and the total number of units available for sale during the period is found first.

|                           | NUMBER OF UNITS | COST PER UNIT | TOTAL COST |
|---------------------------|-----------------|---------------|------------|
| Beginning inventory       | 2,500           | $10           | $25,000    |
| Purchases:    January 1   | 3,000           | $11           | $33,000    |
|               January 11  | 2,500           | $12           | $30,000    |
|               January 25  | 2,000           | $15           | $30,000    |
| Goods available for sale  | 10,000          |               | $118,000   |
| Sales                     | 9,000           |               |            |
| Ending inventory          | 1,000           |               |            |

**Weighted Average Cost Method**

**Average cost per unit** is $11.80 and is found by dividing the total cost of goods available for sale ($118,000) by the total units of goods available for sale (10,000 units). This cost per unit is used for both cost of goods sold and ending inventory.

|                    | UNIT COST | UNITS | TOTAL COST |
|--------------------|-----------|-------|------------|
| Ending inventory   | $11.80    | 1,000 | $11,800    |
| Cost of goods sold | $11.80    | 9,000 | $106,200   |

**First-In, First-Out (FIFO)**

Under FIFO, it is assumed that the oldest units are sold first. Ending inventory is therefore assumed to come from the last purchase on January 25. Cost of goods sold is found by subtracting the ending inventory value from the total cost of goods available for sale.

|                    | UNIT COST | UNITS | TOTAL COST |
|--------------------|-----------|-------|------------|
| Ending inventory   | $15       | 1,000 | $15,000    |
| Cost of goods sold |           | 9,000 | $103,000   |
| ($118,000 - $15,000) |         |       |            |

**Last-In, First-Out (LIFO)**

Under LIFO, the latest units purchased are assumed to be sold first. Ending inventory is therefore assumed to come from beginning inventory. Cost of goods sold is found by subtracting the ending inventory value from the total cost of goods available for sale.

|                    | UNIT COST | UNITS | TOTAL COST |
|--------------------|-----------|-------|------------|
| Ending inventory   | $10       | 1,000 | $10,000    |
| Cost of goods sold |           | 9,000 | $108,000   |
| ($118,000 - $10,000) |         |       |            |

The impact of the different inventory valuation methods on income can be seen from the following table. In this example, where prices are rising, FIFO leads to lower cost of goods sold, higher gross margin, and higher ending inventory than LIFO.

|  | AVERAGE COST | FIFO | LIFO |
|---|---|---|---|
| Sales (9,000 units @ $20) | $180,000 | $180,000 | $180,000 |
| COGS | 106,200 | 103,000 | 108,000 |
| Gross margin | 73,800 | 77,000 | 72,000 |
| Ending inventory | $11,800 | $15,000 | $10,000 |

## Sixty Second Quiz!

**Question:**   If a firm uses LIFO, must it first sell the goods it bought most recently?

**Answer:**   No. The cost flow assumptions of each of these inventory costing methods do not necessarily match physical flows of inventory. To reduce spoilage and obsolescence, most organizations sell the oldest inventory first. However, irrespective of the physical flows, they may choose to assume a last-in first-out cost flow.

**LO 4**  The overriding consideration in the choice of an inventory costing method should be the ability of the method to accurately reflect the net income of the period. The following factors, however, also enter into an individual firm's choice:

- **Cash Flow and Taxes:** In a period of rising prices, LIFO can result in higher cost of goods sold and lower reported earnings than under FIFO. Relative to FIFO, taxes can therefore be deferred under LIFO.

- **LIFO Conformity Rule:** If LIFO is used for tax reporting, the IRS requires that the company also use LIFO for reporting to stockholders.

- **LIFO Liquidation:** If in any period, the number of units sold exceeds the number of units purchased, the number of units in ending inventory is lower than in beginning inventory. The difference in units is part of the goods sold during the period. Where LIFO is used as the inventory costing method, these units may have been carried in inventory at their original cost, which could be very much lower than units being bought now. In this case, cost of goods sold will be lower because it contains these units. This is known as LIFO Liquidation and it can result in a relatively low cost of goods sold and a high reported (and taxable) income.

- **Replacement Cost of Inventory:** The use of replacement cost for both cost of goods sold and inventory results in better economic measures of both income and inventory valuation. At a time of rising prices and increasing or stable inventory levels, LIFO results in the best approximation of replacement cost of goods sold, and therefore of economic income in the income statement. FIFO results in the closest approximation to valuing inventory at replacement cost in the balance sheet.

**LO 5**  We can use the above analysis to explore the impact that errors in inventory valuation will have on reported income. Suppose Company A makes a mistake in valuing its inventory in Year 1, the first year of its operations. The error results in the ending inventory in Year 1 being recorded as $10,000 rather than $5,000, the correct amount. Also assume that at the end of Year 2, the inventory is correctly recorded at $15,000. Assume that sales, beginning inventory, purchases, and operating expenses for Company A are as presented in the following table. The effect of the error can be analyzed as follows:

**Effects of Inventory Error in Year 1 on Reported Income and Retained Earnings**

| Year 1 | | Reported | | Corrected |
|---|---|---|---|---|
| Sales | | $100,000 | | $100,000 |
| Cost of Goods Sold | | | | |
| Beginning Inventory | $ 10,000 | | $ 10,000 | |
| Add: Purchases | 50,000 | | 50,000 | |
| Cost of Goods Available for Resale | 60,000 | | 60,000 | |
| Less: Ending Inventory | 10,000 | | 5,000 | |
| Cost of Goods Sold | | 50,000 | | 55,000 |
| Gross Margin | | 50,000 | | 45,000 |
| Less: Operating Expenses | | 10,000 | | 10,000 |
| Net Income | | $ 40,000 | | $ 35,000 |
| | | | | |
| **Retained Earnings** | | | | |
| Balance - Beginning of Year | | $    0 | | $    0 |
| Add: Net Income for Year | | 40,000 | | 35,000 |
| Balance - End of Year | | $ 40,000 | | $ 35,000 |

| Year 2 | | Reported | | Corrected |
|---|---|---|---|---|
| Sales | | $120,000 | | $120,000 |
| Cost of Goods Sold | | | | |
| Beginning Inventory | $ 10,000 | | $ 5,000 | |
| Add: Purchases | 60,000 | | 60,000 | |
| Cost of Goods Available for Resale | 70,000 | | 65,000 | |
| Less: Ending Inventory | 15,000 | | 15,000 | |
| Cost of Goods Sold | | 55,000 | | 50,000 |
| Gross Margin | | 65,000 | | 70,000 |
| Less: Operating Expenses | | 10,000 | | 10,000 |
| Net Income | | $ 55,000 | | $ 60,000 |
| | | | | |
| **Retained Earnings** | | | | |
| Balance - Beginning of Year | | $ 40,000 | | $ 35,000 |
| Add: Net Income for Year | | 55,000 | | 60,000 |
| Balance - End of Year | | $ 95,000 | | $ 95,000 |

As we can see, an overstatement of the valuation of ending inventory in Year 1 results in an overstatement of income for that year. In the following year, the beginning inventory will be overstated. Since the ending inventory for the second year is correct, second year income is understated by the amount of the original error. Note also that although the retained earnings balance at the end of the first year will be overstated by $5,000, the balance on retained earnings at the end of the second year will be correct. The impact of the error therefore dissipates in the second year.

### Sixty Second Quiz!

**Question**:     Can you work through the above argument for the case where Company A erroneously **understates** its ending inventory in Year 1? What will be the impact on the income and retained earnings for both periods, assuming that the ending inventory for Year 2 is correct?

**Answer**:     An understatement of the valuation of ending inventory in Year 1 will result in an understatement of income for that period. Retained earnings will be understated at the end of Year 1. In the following year, the beginning inventory will be understated. If the ending inventory for the second period is correct, the second period income will be overstated by the amount of the original error, and the balance on retained earnings at the end of the second year will be correct. Again, the impact of the error dissipates in the second year.

---

**LO 6**   Where the cost of inventory exceeds its market value, inventory should be marked to market by writing the value of inventory down to replacement cost. This **lower-of-cost-or-market rule** can be applied to the total inventory, to individual items, or to groups of inventory. At the end of each period, using one of the costing methods above, the cost of inventory is compared with the market price (replacement cost) of inventory. If the market price is less than cost, then the inventory is written down to the lower amount.

For example, assume that Company A is preparing its accounts for the year ending December 31, 2001. The cost of inventory under LIFO is $25,000, but the company estimates that the replacement cost of the inventory is $20,000. The following adjusting entry is made. Note that the effect of this entry is to reduce the asset inventory and the owners' equity.

|  | Debit | Credit |
|---|---|---|
| Dec. 31 Loss on decline in value of inventory | 5,000 | |
| Inventory | | 5,000 |
| Decline in value of inventory. | | |

**LO 7**   In some circumstances, it is necessary to estimate the value of inventory. Two principal methods are used:

**Gross Profit Method**

The gross profit method is used in a periodic inventory system to value inventory that has been destroyed or lost and cannot be counted. The validity of the method critically depends on reliable estimation of the gross profit ratio. To illustrate this method, assume that on March 31, 2000, Islay Corporation's warehouse was destroyed by fire, and an estimate of the lost inventory is needed for an insurance claim. The following information is available:

| | |
|---|---|
| Inventory, March 1, 2000 | $150,000 |
| Purchases during March | $350,000 |
| Sales, March | $500,000 |
| Gross margin is 40% of revenue. | |

Cost of goods sold is found by multiplying the cost of sales margin by net sales. Since gross margin is 40% of revenue, cost of sales is (100% - 40%) = 60% of revenue.

| | |
|---|---|
| Sales | $500,000 |
| Cost of sales % | 60% |
| Cost of goods sold | $300,000 |

The ending inventory value is found by deducting cost of goods sold from cost of goods available for sale (beginning inventory plus purchases).

| | |
|---|---|
| Beginning inventory, March 1 | $150,000 |
| *Plus* Purchases | 350,000 |
| Goods available for sale | 500,000 |
| *Less* Cost of goods sold | 300,000 |
| Ending inventory, March 31 | $200,000 |

### Retail Inventory Method

The retail inventory method is used to estimate the cost of inventory in retail organizations where a count of inventory using the retail prices rather than costs is substantially easier. To illustrate, the following information is available for Mull Inc. for the month of June, 2000:

| | COST | RETAIL |
|---|---|---|
| Inventory, June 1 | $10,000 | $13,500 |
| *Plus* Purchases in June | $40,000 | $61,500 |
| Total | $50,000 | $75,000 |

The ratio of cost to retail price is determined from beginning inventory and purchases for the period.

| Ratio of cost to retail | = | $50,000/ $75,000 |
|---|---|---|
| | = | 67% |

The retail price of the ending inventory is determined by a physical count. The ratio of cost to retail is applied to the retail price of ending inventory to estimate the cost of ending inventory.

| Inventory, June 30 at retail | = | $15,000 |
|---|---|---|
| Inventory, June 30 at cost | = | $15,000 x 67% |
| | = | $10,000 |

**LO 8** Inventory is one of the largest assets on the balance sheet of many enterprises. Adequate inventory is essential to efficient manufacturing, since a lack of inventory can result in expensive shutdowns. Further, the availability of inventory to fill orders can be a major factor in ensuring good relations with customers. On the other hand, too much inventory can cause unnecessary storage costs, tie up capital unnecessarily, and increase the risk that inventory becomes obsolete. Management of inventory is therefore a critical part of management's task. When analyzing the financial statements, two ratios, inventory turnover and number of days' sales in inventory, can help in understanding the effectiveness of the company's inventory management. Inventory turnover gives the number of times on average inventory is bought and sold during the year. The number of days' sales in inventory gives how many days on average inventory stays in the enterprise before it is sold. Inventory turnover and number of days' sales in inventory are defined as follows:

| Inventory Turnover Ratio | = | Cost of Goods Sold |
|---|---|---|
| | | Average Inventory |
| Number of Days' Sales in Inventory | = | Number of Days in the Period |
| | | Inventory Turnover Ratio |

To illustrate the calculation of these ratios, assume that Company D's cost of goods sold for Year 3 was $240,000, its inventory at the beginning of Year 3 was $50,000, and its inventory at the end of Year 3 was $70,000.

$$\text{Inventory Turnover Ratio} = \frac{\text{Cost of Goods Sold}}{\text{Average Inventory}}$$

$$= \frac{\$240,000}{(\$50,000 + \$70,000)/2}$$

$$= 4 \text{ times}$$

$$\text{Number of Days' Sales in Inventory} = \frac{\text{Number of Days in the Period}}{\text{Inventory Turnover Ratio}}$$

$$= \frac{360}{4}$$

$$= 90 \text{ days}$$

In deciding whether these ratios represented good inventory management by Company D, we would need to compare them with Company D's previous years' ratios, as well as with inventory turnover and number of days' sales in inventory ratios of other companies in the same industry as Company D.

**LO 9** If a company uses the direct method for its cash flow statement, the cash paid to suppliers of inventory will be shown as a use of cash. Where the company uses the indirect method, cash flow from operations is found by adjusting net income for increases or decreases in both the Inventory and Accounts Payable accounts. The adjustments to be made to net income to find cash flow from operations are as follows:

| ITEM | ADJUSTMENT TO NET INCOME |
|---|---|
| Increase in inventory | Deduct from net income |
| Decrease in inventory | Add to net income |
| Increase in accounts payable | Add to net income |
| Decrease in accounts payable | Deduct from net income |

## Sixty Second Quiz!

**Question:** Assume that Company C's balance sheets for Year 9 and Year 10 contain the following account balances. What adjustments would be made to Company C's Year 10 net income of $50,000 to find cash flow from operations for Year 10?

| Company C - Balance Sheet | Year 9 | Year 10 |
|---|---|---|
| Inventory | $10,000 | $15,000 |
| Accounts Payable | $40,000 | $60,000 |

**Answer:** The following adjustments would be made:

| | |
|---|---|
| Net Income | $50,000 |
| Less: Increase in inventory | (5,000) |
| Plus: Increase in accounts payable | 20,000 |

**LO 10,11** Two systems of inventory management are found in practice: perpetual inventory systems and periodic inventory systems. The following table summarizes the differences between the two methods. Note that all inventory costing methods (LIFO, FIFO, etc.) can be used with each system. If either LIFO or average cost is used, the cost of goods sold and net income may be different under the periodic and perpetual systems.

| Feature | Periodic Inventory System | Perpetual Inventory System |
|---|---|---|
| Count of inventory | Carried out at the end of each period and critical to the allocation of cost between ending inventory and cost of goods sold. | Carried out at the end of each period to confirm valuation of ending inventory. |
| Purchases | Recorded in Purchases Account that is closed at the end of the period. | Recorded direct to Inventory Account. |
| Sales | Under both systems, the Sales account is credited, and Cash or Accounts Receivable debited, with the sale price. | |
| Cost of goods sold | No entry is made for the cost of goods sold at the time the sale is made. | The inventory account is updated each time a sale is made. Cost of goods sold is credited to Inventory account and debited to Cost of Goods Sold account each time. |
| FIFO | The valuation of ending inventory is the same under both systems. | |
| LIFO | Cost of goods sold and ending inventory are based on the cost of the last units sold for the entire period. | Cost of goods sold is based on the last units purchased at the time of each sale. Cost of goods sold and ending inventory will therefore differ from the corresponding figures calculated under the periodic system. |
| Average cost | Cost of goods sold and ending inventory are based on the average cost of goods available for sale for the period as a whole. | The average cost of goods sold is calculated at the time of each purchase. Therefore, for this inventory costing method, the ending inventory and cost of goods sold will differ under the periodic and perpetual inventory systems. |

## Review of Key Terms

| | |
|---|---|
| **FIFO method** | An inventory costing method that assigns the most recent costs to ending inventory. |
| **Finished goods** | The inventory of a manufacturer that is complete and ready for sale. |
| **Gross profit method** | A technique used to establish an estimate of the cost of inventory stolen, destroyed, or otherwise damaged, or the amount of inventory on hand at an interim date. |
| **Inventory profit** | That portion of the gross profit resulting from holding inventory during a period of rising prices. |
| **Inventory turnover ratio** | A measure of the number of times inventory is sold during the period. |
| **LIFO conformity rule** | An IRS requirement that if LIFO is used on the tax return, it must also be used in reporting income to stockholders. |
| **LIFO liquidation** | The result of selling more units than are purchased during the period, which can have negative tax consequences if a company is using LIFO. |
| **LIFO method** | An inventory costing method that assigns the most recent costs to cost of goods sold. |
| **LIFO reserve** | The excess of the value of a company's inventory stated at FIFO, compared with the inventory value stated at LIFO. |
| **Lower-of-cost-or-market (LCM) rule** | A conservative approach to valuing inventory, which is an attempt to anticipate declines in the value of inventory before its actual sale. |
| **Merchandise inventory** | The account wholesalers and retailers use to report inventory held for sale. |
| **Moving average method** | The name given to an average cost method when it is used with a perpetual inventory system. |
| **Number of days' sales in inventory** | A measure of how long it takes to sell inventory. |
| **Raw materials** | The inventory of a manufacturer before the addition of any direct labor or manufacturing overhead. |
| **Replacement cost** | The current cost of a unit of inventory. |
| **Retail inventory method** | A technique used by retailers to convert the retail value of inventory to a cost basis. |
| **Specific identification method** | An inventory costing method that relies on matching unit costs with the actual units sold. |
| **Weighted average cost method** | An inventory costing method that assigns the same unit cost to all units available for sale during the period. |
| **Work in process** | The cost of unfinished products in a manufacturing company. |

# Practice Test
# Questions and Problems

## Circle the alternative that best answers the question:

**LO 5** 1. Jenny Department Store uses a periodic inventory system. What is the impact on the financial statements of an overstatement of ending inventory?
a) Current year's net income will be overstated.
b) Next year's net income will be overstated.
c) Next year's ending inventory will be overstated.
d) Next year's ending inventory will be understated.

**LO 4** 2. If a company uses the LIFO cost flow assumption for its federal income tax return:
a) it must use FIFO on its financial statements.
b) it must use LIFO on its financial statements.
c) it may use any inventory cost flow assumption for its financial statements.
d) LIFO cannot be used for federal tax return computations.

**LO 4** 3. Mr. Albert works for a supermarket chain, and his bonus is calculated as a percentage of gross profit (sales minus cost of goods sold). To maximize his bonus, which of the following cost flow assumptions would Mr. Albert prefer if inventory prices and levels are rising?
a) LIFO.
b) FIFO.
c) Average cost.
d) Inventory cost flow assumption does not affect gross profit.

**LO 4** 4. During a period of steeply rising prices, a company adopts a new method of production, resulting in a dramatic reduction in inventories. The effect of this in the year the change takes place is to:
a) increase current ratio and decrease inventory turnover.
b) decrease current ratio and increase inventory turnover.
c) decrease current ratio and decrease inventory turnover.
d) increase current ratio and increase inventory turnover.

**LO 4** 5. If the market value of inventory is lower than its cost, then application of the lower-of-cost-or-market rule would:
a) increase earnings and decrease current ratio.
b) increase earnings and increase current ratio.
c) decrease earnings and decrease current ratio.
d) decrease earnings and increase current ratio.

**LO 7** 6. In which of the following situations would the retail inventory method be an appropriate way to estimate inventories for companies using the periodic inventory system?

a) A supermarket that has kept records of purchases at both retail and cost prices carries out a physical count of the retail price of the goods on its shelves.

b) A department store has a fire and loses part of its inventory.

c) A company wishes to estimate the value of inventory for interim financial statements.

d) All of the above.

**LO 5** 7. Which of the following should not be included in inventory costs for a car dealership?

a) The costs of transporting the cars from the factory to the dealership

b) Excise and sales taxes

c) The salary cost of the salesman who sells the vehicle

d) The cost of modifications to the vehicles made by the dealer before the vehicle is offered for sale

**LO 4** 8. Which of the following statements about LIFO liquidation is false?

a) LIFO liquidation occurs when a company using LIFO sells more units during the period than it buys.

b) LIFO liquidation results in a high tax bill for the company if prices are rising.

c) A company can avoid LIFO liquidation by buying inventory at the end of the year.

d) LIFO liquidation results in inventory from previous periods, with relatively low prices being included in cost of goods sold when prices are falling.

**LO 4** 9. Assume that a bond covenant states that a company's current ratio may not drop below 1:1. Currently the company's current ratio is 1.1:1. To ensure compliance with its bond covenant, which of the following cost flow assumptions would the company prefer if inventory prices are falling?

a) LIFO.

b) FIFO.

c) Average cost.

d) The company would not be able to influence its current ratio by its inventory cost flow assumption.

**LO 7** 10. A high inventory turnover ratio could result from:

a) collection policies that ensure prompt payment of customers' accounts.

b) a high gross margin.

c) inventory levels being carefully monitored to ensure that they are not too high relative to the volume of sales.

d) the physical flow of inventory ensuring that the oldest units are sold first.

*Use the following information to answer questions 11 through 13:*

Sidlaw Corporation has the following information for its inventory purchases for the month of August, 2001.

| Date | Number of Units Purchased | Unit Cost |
|------|---------------------------|-----------|
| August 8 | 150 | $21 |
| August 20 | ? | ? |
| August 30 | 100 | $24 |

The beginning inventory on August 1 was 100 units at a price per unit of $20, and the company had 100 units in inventory on August 31. Sales for the month were 400 units. Although a purchase took place on August 20, information is not available about how many units were purchased or the cost per unit.

**LO 3**   11.   The number of units purchased on August 20 was:
- a) 50
- b) 250
- c) 150
- d) 100

**LO 3**   12.   If the FIFO cost of goods sold for August is $8,600, the cost per unit of the goods purchased on August 20 is:
- a) $21
- b) $22
- c) $23
- d) $24

**LO 3**   13.   The ending inventory under LIFO is:
- a) $2,000
- b) $2,400
- c) $2,100
- d) $2,300

**LO 8**   14.   A company's cost of goods sold is $300,000, its inventory turnover for the year is 20, and its beginning inventory at the beginning of Year 10 was $10,000. Its ending inventory at the end of Year 10 is:
- a) $ 10,000
- b) $ 20,000
- c) $100,000
- d) $ 17,500

LO 9    15. A company has the following balances on its balance sheets at the beginning and end of Year 5:

Inventory

| December 31, Year 4 | $25,000 |
| December 31, Year 5 | $30,000 |

Accounts payable

| December 31, Year 4 | $10,000 |
| December 31, Year 5 | $ 8,000 |

The company uses the indirect method for its cash flow statement and to find the cash flow from operations, the following adjustments must be made to net income:

a)    Deduct $5,000 from net income and add $2,000 to net income.

b)    Deduct $5,000 from net income and deduct $2,000 from net income.

c)    Add $5,000 to net income and add $2,000 to net income.

d)    Add $5,000 to net income and deduct $2,000 from net income.

## Indicate whether each of the following statements is true or false:

LO 2    16. The cost of goods sold is inversely related to the value of ending inventory.

LO 4    17. Where a company pays tax, short-term cash flow under LIFO will be higher than under other inventory costing methods at a time of rising prices.

LO 7    18. A department store will normally have a higher inventory turnover ratio than a supermarket.

LO 5    19. If a counterbalancing inventory error is made over two accounting periods, the net effect of the error on retained earnings should be zero by the end of the second period.

LO 6    20. Inventory must always be reported at historic cost.

LO 9    21. To find cash flow from operations using the indirect method, increases in inventory should be added to net earnings.

LO 7    22. No interim figures for cost of goods sold and ending inventory are readily available from the accounting records under the periodic system of inventory.

LO 11    23. LIFO will lead to identical cost of goods sold, but different inventory values, under the periodic system and the perpetual system.

LO 1    24. Of the three types of cost incurred by manufacturers, only direct labor and manufacturing overhead form part of work in process.

LO 5    25. Specific identification would be an appropriate method for use by an art gallery.

LO 10    26. Under the perpetual inventory method, no physical count of inventory need be carried out at the end of the accounting period, since this system provides up-to-date information about cost of goods sold and inventory values.

LO 9

27. When the direct method for the cash flow statement is used, a decrease in inventory is deducted from net income to find cash flow from operations.

LO 9

28. When the indirect method for the cash flow statement is used, a decrease in accounts payable is added to net income, and an increase in accounts payable is deducted from net income to find cash flow from operations.

LO 10

29. Under the average cost method, the valuation of ending inventory is the same under both the perpetual and the periodic systems.

LO 3

30. A disadvantage of LIFO is that it could result in physical deterioration of inventory, since the latest purchases are sold first.

## Complete each of the following statements:

LO 1

31. A manufacturer's inventory is composed of three elements: _____, _____, and _____.

LO 2

32. Cost of goods available for sale is found by adding _____ to _____; cost of goods sold is found by deducting _____ from cost of goods available for sale.

LO 5

33. The _____ is the IRS requirement that if LIFO is used on a tax return, it must also be used in external reporting.

LO 6

34. Where the market price of inventory is lower than its historic cost, the _____ rule is applied.

LO 7

35. Inventory value can be estimated in the case of a fire or loss by using the _____ method.

LO 7

36. The _____ method is often used by retailers to value inventory for interim statements by converting the retail value of inventory to cost.

LO 7

37. The _____ ratio is calculated by dividing cost of goods sold by average inventory for the period and is used to measure how often the company replaces its inventory each year.

LO 3

38. The _____ method assigns the same unit cost to all units available for sale during the period.

LO 4

39. The excess of the value of a company's inventory stated at FIFO, compared with LIFO, is called the _____.

LO 4

40. At a time of rising prices, when a company using LIFO sells more units in a period than it purchases, some of the units sold will come from older inventory with a relatively low unit price; this situation results in a low cost of goods sold figure and high gross margin and is referred to as _____.

*Use the following information to answer questions 41 through 45:*

Terra Corporation makes the following purchases in the month of July, 2001:

| Date | Number of Units Purchased | Unit Cost |
|------|---------------------------|-----------|
| July 3 | 100 | $15 |
| July 15 | 100 | $10 |
| July 23 | 100 | $5 |

The beginning inventory on July 1 was 200 units at a price per unit of $20, and the company had 200 units on hand on July 31.

LO 4  41. The company sold _____ units during the month of July.

LO 4  42. Under the weighted average cost method, the average cost assigned to all units available for sale during the period is $_____ per unit.

LO 4  43. The inventory costing method that produces the highest cost of goods sold in these circumstances is _____ .

LO 4  44. The inventory costing method that produces the highest ending inventory in these circumstances is _____ .

LO 4  45. At a time of falling prices, net income under FIFO will be _____ than under LIFO.

## Answer each of the following problems:

LO 7  46. On January 31, 2000, Surfers Store in Santa Teresa was destroyed by an earthquake. Inventory worth $10,000 was subsequently salvaged from the ruins. An estimate of the lost inventory is needed for an insurance claim. The following information is available:

| | |
|---|---|
| Inventory, January 1, 2000 (at cost) | $ 75,000 |
| Purchases during January | $250,000 |
| January sales | $300,000 |

Cost of sales is 75% of revenue.

**Required**

1. Using the gross profit method, estimate the amount of inventory lost in the earthquake, and the loss on inventory after the insurance recovery, if the insurance company finally pays $80,000.

2.  Give the journal entry for recording the inventory loss and the receipt of cash from the insurance company.

 47.  The following is an extract from the Statement of Cash Flows for Toys "R" Us, Inc.:

**TOYS"R"US, INC. AND SUBSIDIARIES**

| **Consolidated Statements of Cash Flows** (In $ millions) | *January 28* *2000* | *January 29* *1999* | *January 30* *1998* |
|---|---|---|---|
| **CASH FLO WS FROM OPERATING ACTIVITIES** | | | |
| Net Earnings/(Loss) | $279 | ($132) | $490 |
| Adjustments to reconcile net earnings/(loss) to net cash provided by operating activities: | | | |
| Depreciation, amortization and asset write-offs | 278 | 255 | 253 |
| Deferred income taxes | 156 | (90) | 18 |
| Restructuring and other charges | -- | 546 | -- |
| Changes in operating assets and liabilities: | | | |
| Accounts and other receivables | 35 | (43) | (40) |
| Merchandise inventories | (192) | 233 | (265) |
| Prepaid expenses and other operating assets | (69) | (27) | (9) |
| Accounts payable, accrued expenses and other liabilities | 497 | 229 | 22 |
| Income taxes payable | (119) | (7) | 40 |
| Net Cash Provided by Operating Activities | 865 | 964 | 509 |

**Required**

1.  Does TOYS "R" US use the direct or indirect method to prepare the operating section of the statement of cash flows?

2. Did inventories increase or decrease during 2000, 1999, 1998? If the opening balance in the inventory account was $1,000 on January 30, 1997, what were the balances on the inventory account on the balance sheets on January 30, 1998, January 29, 1999, and January 28, 2000?

**LO 3**   48.   Clare Corporation's inventory records show the following for the year ended December 31, 2000:

|  | Units | Unit Cost($) |
|---|---|---|
| Beginning inventory | 1,000 | $40 |
| Purchases: |  |  |
| March 31 | 600 | 43 |
| May 27 | 800 | 49 |
| August 26 | 700 | 50 |
| October 19 | 1,000 | 56 |
| December 15 | 900 | 60 |

Clare uses a periodic inventory system and during the year sold 4,500 units at a selling price of $60 per unit. Expenses other than cost of goods sold amounted to $40,000 for the year, and the tax rate is 40%.

**Required**

1. Compute cost of goods sold and ending inventory under each of the following three methods:

   Weighted average

   FIFO

   LIFO

2. Prepare income statements for Clare Corporation under each of the three methods.

3.  If Clare wishes to pay the least amount of taxes for 2000, which method would you recommend?

4.  Suppose you were considering investing in Clare and learned that Clare had switched from LIFO to FIFO. What would be the effect on reported net income of the switch? Would that affect your decision whether or not to invest in the company? Why?

## Critical Thinking Problem

**LO 4**   49.   The footnotes to the financial statements of  Company X for the year ended December 31, 2002, contain the following statements:

"Inventories are stated generally at the lower-of-cost-or-market. The cost of all inventories is determined by the last-in, first-out method. As a result of decreases in inventories over the year, certain LIFO inventory quantities were liquidated. These inventory adjustments favorably affected income before taxes."

**Required**

1.   Explain how liquidating LIFO inventories can favorably affect income before taxes, and explain the effect the LIFO liquidation would have on Company X's 2002 tax liability.

2.   How could Company X have avoided a LIFO liquidation?

# Solutions

## Multiple Choice

| | | | |
|---|---|---|---|
| 1. | a | 9. | a |
| 2. | b | 10. | c |
| 3. | b | 11. | c |
| 4. | b | 12. | c |
| 5. | c | 13. | a |
| 6. | a | 14. | b |
| 7. | c | 15. | b |
| 8. | d | | |

## True/False

**COMMENT/EXPLANATION**

| | | |
|---|---|---|
| 16. | True | |
| 17. | True | |
| 18. | False | Supermarkets sell many perishable items and must therefore turn over much of their inventory within days. Department stores' sales tend to be seasonal, and their inventory may turn over only every few weeks or even months. |
| 19. | True | |
| 20. | False | If the replacement cost of inventory is lower than its historic cost, the inventory is written down to its replacement cost. |
| 21. | False | Increases in inventory should be deducted from net earnings to find cash flow from operations, because an increase in inventory implies that cash is being expended in the buildup of inventory. |
| 22. | True | |
| 23. | False | Cost of goods sold and ending inventory are inextricably linked. A change in one results in a change in the other. Ending inventory values under LIFO will differ between a perpetual and a periodic inventory system, but that also means that cost of goods sold under the two systems will also differ. |
| 24. | False | All three cost components, direct materials, direct labor, and manufacturing overhead, form part of work in process. |
| 25. | True | |
| 26. | False | A physical count is carried out at the end of each period under the perpetual inventory system to confirm valuation of ending inventory. |
| 27. | False | Under the direct method, cash flow from operations is not found by adjusting net income. |
| 28. | False | A decrease in accounts payable is deducted from net income, and an increase is added to net income. |
| 29. | False | Since the average cost is calculated after every purchase under the perpetual system, the average cost can vary over the period and will differ from the average cost under the periodic system, which is calculated only once at the end of the period. |
| 30. | False | The physical flow of goods and the assumption made about cost flows are different. |

## Fill in the Blanks

31. raw materials, work in process, finished goods
32. opening inventories, purchases, closing inventories
33. LIFO conformity rule
34. lower-of-cost-or-market
35. gross profit
36. retail inventory
37. inventory turnover
38. average cost
39. LIFO reserve
40. LIFO liquidation
41. 300 units
42. $14
43. FIFO
44. LIFO
45. lower

## Problem 46

1.

| | |
|---|---|
| Sales | $300,000 |
| Gross profit % | 75% |
| **Cost of goods sold** | **$225,000** |
| Beginning inventory | $ 75,000 |
| *Plus* Purchases | 250,000 |
| Goods available for sale | 325,000 |
| *Less* Cost of goods sold | 225,000 |
| Ending inventory | 100,000 |
| *Less* Inventory recovered | 10,000 |
| Inventory lost in earthquake | 90,000 |
| *Less* Cash paid by insurance company | 80,000 |
| Loss on inventory after insurance recovery | $ 10,000 |

2.

| | Debit | Credit |
|---|---|---|
| Cash | 80,000 | |
| Loss on inventory | 10,000 | |
| Inventory | | 90,000 |

To record decline in value of inventory resulting from earthquake.

## Problem 47

1. TOYS "R" US uses the indirect method for preparing its cash flow statement, since cash flow from operations is found by adjusting net income from operations.

2. Inventories increased in 1998 and 2000, and decreased in 1999. The inventory balances can be found by adding the increase, or deducting the decrease, in inventory each year to, or from, the beginning inventory balance for that year.

| | |
|---|---|
| Balance - Inventory Account, January 30, 1997 | $1,000.0 |
| Plus: Increase in inventory to January 30, 1998 | 265.0 |
| Balance - Inventory Account, January 30, 1998 | 1,265.0 |
| Less: Decrease in inventory to January 29, 1999 | - 233.0 |
| Balance - Inventory Account, January 29, 1999 | 1,032.0 |
| Plus: Increase in inventory to January 28, 2000 | 192.0 |
| Balance - Inventory Account, January 28, 2000 | $1,224.0 |

## Problem 48

| 1. | Number of units | Cost per unit | Total cost |
|---|---|---|---|
| Beginning inventory | 1,000 | $40 | $40,000 |
| Purchases 3/31/00 | 600 | $43 | $25,800 |
| 5/27/00 | 800 | $49 | $39,200 |
| 8/26/00 | 700 | $50 | $35,000 |
| 10/19/00 | 1,000 | $56 | $56,000 |
| 12/15/00 | 900 | $60 | $54,000 |
| Total | 5,000 | | $250,000 |
| Less: Sales | 4,500 | | |
| Ending inventory | 500 | | |

| | Unit cost | Units | |
|---|---|---|---|
| **Average cost per unit** | | | $50 |
| Ending inventory | $50 | 500 | $25,000 |
| Cost of goods sold | $50 | 4,500 | $225,000 |

**LIFO**

| | | | |
|---|---|---|---|
| Ending inventory | $40 | 500 | $20,000 |
| Cost of goods sold | | 4,500 | $230,000 |
| ($250,000 - 20,000) | | | |

**FIFO**

| | | | |
|---|---|---|---|
| Ending inventory | $60 | 500 | $30,000 |
| Cost of goods sold | | 4,500 | $220,000 |
| ($250,000 - 30,000) | | | |

| 2. | Average cost | LIFO | FIFO |
|---|---|---|---|
| Sales | $ 270,000 | $ 270,000 | $ 270,000 |
| COGS | 225,000 | 230,000 | 220,000 |
| Gross margin | 45,000 | 40,000 | 50,000 |
| Expenses | 40,000 | 40,000 | 40,000 |
| Income before taxes | 5,000 | 10,000 | 0 |
| Tax payable (40%) | 2,000 | 4,000 | 0 |
| Income after taxes | $3,000 | $6,000 | $0 |

3.   Clare would pay the least taxes under LIFO.

4.   The effect would be to increase net income from $0 under LIFO to $6,000 under FIFO. In deciding whether or not to invest in the company, remember that this is an accounting rather than an economic change and that the fundamental economic situation of the company has not altered. A number of empirical studies have been done to see whether the stock prices of companies switching from LIFO to FIFO rise when the change is announced. The evidence is somewhat mixed, but there does not seem to be support for the view that investors are fooled by this type of accounting change.

## Critical Thinking Problem 49

1. In a period of rising prices, the inventory balance on the balance sheet will contain costs relating to periods when prices were substantially lower than current prices. When inventory levels drop, some of these low costs will be included in the cost of goods sold. As a result, reported income is higher than if LIFO liquidation had not taken place. Company X's 2002 tax liability would be higher than if the LIFO liquidation had not taken place.

2. Company X could have avoided a LIFO liquidation by ensuring that inventory levels did not drop over the year - in other words, by buying enough inventory to cover usage.

# Chapter 7

# Cash, Investments and Receivables

This chapter discusses accounting for cash, investments, and receivables. You have three main aims in this chapter. First, you should understand the nature of cash, and how it is accounted for and managed. Second, you should understand why and how companies invest, and the associated valuation and financial reporting issues. Third, you should address the various valuation and accounting issues associated with short-term receivables such as accounts receivable and notes receivable.

## Learning Objectives

**LO 1**   Identify and describe the various forms of cash reported on a balance sheet.

**LO 2**   Understand the various techniques that companies use to control cash.

**LO 3**   Understand the accounting for various types of investments that companies make.

**LO 4**   Understand how to account for accounts receivable, including bad debts.

**LO 5**   Understand how to account for interest-bearing notes receivable.

**LO 6**   Understand how to account for non-interest-bearing notes receivable.

**LO 7**   Explain various techniques that companies use to accelerate the inflow of cash from sales.

**LO 8**   Explain the effects of transactions involving liquid assets on the statement of cash flows.

## Key Textbook Exhibits

**Exhibit 7-3** provides an illustration of a bank reconciliation statement. *Self-Test:* What types of adjustments are made to the bank account balance? What types of adjustments are made to the book balance?

**Exhibit 7-4** summarizes the accounting and reporting requirements for each of the three categories of investments. *Self-Test:* Which types of securities can be held as current assets? Which types of securities are marked-to-market?

**Exhibits 7-5 and 7-6** illustrate the use of estimating uncollectible accounts using an aging schedule. *Self-Test:* How does the "percent uncollectible" change with the age of the debts.

**Exhibit 7-7** illustrates the relationships between the parties involved in credit card sales. *Self-Test:* In what way does the use of the credit card simplify the collection procedure for the seller? What, if any, is the disadvantage for the seller?

## Review of Key Concepts

**LO 1**  The cash figure shown in the balance sheet contains not only cash held by the company in the form of currency on hand and in checking, savings and money market accounts, but also **cash equivalents**. Cash equivalents are investments that are readily convertible to known amounts of cash and that have a maturity when acquired of less than three months; for example, commercial paper, treasury bills, and money market funds.

**LO 2**  At the end of each period, the company receives a statement from the bank for each of its accounts. The balance on the statement rarely matches the account balance maintained in the company's ledger because the bank and the company are not completely synchronized in their recording of transactions. As its name suggests, a **bank reconciliation** is carried out to explain the difference between the two figures. Two main types of adjustment which must be made in a bank reconciliation:

- **Transactions recorded by the company and not yet recorded by the bank.** For example, **outstanding checks** are checks that the company has issued and that have not yet been processed through the bank account. In addition, **deposits in transit** are deposits that the company made (usually just before the end of the accounting period) and that are not yet reflected in the bank account.

- **Transactions recorded by the bank and not yet recorded by the company.** For example, the bank enters service charges and interest on balances directly into the customer's account. Similarly, if the bank is acting as a collecting agent on behalf of the company, it will credit collections direct to the company's account.

Although it is possible to use several formats when preparing a bank reconciliation, the principle behind each is identical. The bank account balance must be increased by any deposits in transit and reduced by checks in transit; the book balance must be increased by any interest paid or collections made by the bank, and decreased by any charges or NSF checks (checks where the payee's account balance cannot cover the amount of the check). Mistakes can be made both by the bank and by the company. The bank reconciliation procedure is often the means through which these mistakes are found. Once the reconciliation is complete, entries are made in the accounts to record the adjustments made to the book balance.

### Sixty Second Quiz!

**Question:**     Why doesn't the company record adjustments made to the bank account balance in its accounts?

**Answer:**     Basically, the company is responsible only for maintaining its own set of accounts. The company is concerned with keeping the balance in its accounts consistent with the transactions it has processed during the period. The balance on the company's account in the bank records is the bank's responsibility, not the company's.

**LO 2**  A **petty cash fund** is used for small cash payments. An individual is given responsibility for maintaining the fund and is provided with an initial sum of money. Payments are made from this sum against receipts, and at the end of the period, the total of the receipts should equal the money paid out. The fund is replenished by the amount of the receipt total to bring it up to the original sum, and an adjustment is made both to record the replenishment and to recognize the various expenditures incurred.

**LO 3** Companies invest in other companies for two reasons: to invest spare cash, or for strategic reasons. As with individuals, companies may invest cash that is not needed immediately in securities of other companies. Such investments have the sole purpose of providing a return until the cash is needed. On the other hand, companies may have strategic reasons for wishing to gain control over, or influence, the companies in which they invest. The accounting treatment of each type of investment is different. According to current accounting standards, the proportion of the investee's stock that the company acquires determines the accounting treatment to use. The following table summarizes the current rules:

| Proportion of Stock In Investee Company | Influence of Investor Company on Investee Company | Accounting Treatment |
| --- | --- | --- |
| Less than 20% | No significant influence | Depends on type of investment, see below |
| Between 20% and 50% | Significant influence | Equity method |
| More than 50% | Control | Consolidated financial statements |

The accounting method used for investments of less than 20% in the investee company depends on which of three categories the investment falls into. **Held-to-maturity securities** are *bonds* that the investor has both the intention and ability to hold to maturity. **Trading securities** are *stocks or bonds* bought to sell again in the near future. **Available-for-sale securities** are securities, *either stocks or bonds,* not classified as held-to-maturity or trading securities.

**LO 3** A business's cash requirements are often seasonal, with certain times of the year requiring larger cash balances than others. Companies deal with cash shortages by borrowing on a short-term basis. Similarly, since cash balances are largely unproductive, companies usually try to invest any excess cash to earn interest or provide a return. Various vehicles for this type of short-term investment are available, but the most common are **certificates of deposit** (CDs), debt securities, and equity securities.

Since a penalty is paid for early withdrawal of a CD, the money invested in CDs may not be immediately available. So, whether CDs are classified as a cash equivalent or as a short-term investment depends on whether there are fewer than ninety days to the maturity date.

When an accounting period ends before a CD matures, the interest to the end of the accounting period must be accounted for. For example, assume that on December 1, 2000, Company X invests $6,000 excess cash in a 90-day CD at an annual rate of 5%. At this time, a CD asset account is created and cash is reduced by $6,000. At the company's financial year end on December 31, interest on the CD has been earned but not yet received. Since interest for 30 days has been earned, the amount of interest is:

$$5\% \times \$6,000 \times 30/360 \qquad = \qquad \$25$$

The $25 interest revenue will appear in the income statement for the year ended December 31, 2000. The effect on the accounting equation of the adjustment to record this is:

|  |  | Debit | Credit |
| --- | --- | --- | --- |
| 12/31/00 | Interest receivable | 25 | |
| | Interest revenue | | 25 |
| | Interest receivable on certificate of deposit | | |

On February 28, 2001, the principal and full 90 days of interest of $75 is received (5% x $6,000 x 90/360). The entry to record this is

|  |  | Debit | Credit |
|---|---|---|---|
| 2/28/01 | Cash | 6,075 | |
| | Interest receivable | | 25 |
| | Interest revenue | | 50 |
| | Short-term investment: CD | | 6,000 |
| | Repayment of interest and principal on certificate of deposit | | |

The interest receivable account is therefore closed and the interest revenue of $50 will be reported in the income statement for the year ended December 31, 2001. This series of entries ensures proper matching of interest revenue to the time period when it was earned.

**LO 3** By their nature, only bonds can be classified as **held-to-maturity securities**. Bonds can be bought at an amount different from the face value. In this case, the difference appears in either a premium or a discount account. This premium or discount is subsequently written off to the income statement over the life of the bonds. However, we will limit our discussion to the simpler case where the bond is bought at face value. The total price paid for the bonds is recorded in an investment account.

For example, assume that Corporation X buys 100, 10% bonds with a face value of $1,000 per bond on January 1 Year 1 from Corporation Y. Also assume that Corporation X intends to keep the bonds until they mature on December 31, Year 5, and that interest on the bonds is paid annually at the end of the year. The journal entry to record the bond purchase is:

|  |  | Debit | Credit |
|---|---|---|---|
| 1/1/1 | Investment in bonds | 100,000 | |
| | Cash | | 100,000 |
| | Purchase of bonds for cash | | |

When interest is received by Company X on December 31, Year 1, the journal entry to record the interest is:

|  |  | Debit | Credit |
|---|---|---|---|
| 12/31/1 | Cash | 10,000 | |
| | Interest income | | 10,000 |
| | Receipt of interest on bonds | | |

Now assume that Company X sells its bonds on January 1, Year 2 for $120,000, a change of plan resulting from a decision to acquire another company. Company X has made a $20,000 profit on its holding in the bonds, and this will appear on the income statement for Year 2. The journal entry to record the sale is:

|  |  | Debit | Credit |
|---|---|---|---|
| 1/1/2 | Cash | 120,000 | |
| | Investment in bonds | | 100,000 |
| | Gain on sale of bonds | | 20,000 |
| | Sale of bonds for cash | | |

**LO 3** **Trading securities** are bought with the intention of selling them in the near future. They are therefore reported as current assets. When they are bought, trading securities are recorded at cost. At the end of the accounting period, if the market price has changed, the investment account is adjusted so that the balance in the account equals the new market price. Any gain or loss is recognized in the income statement. For example, if Company X buys stock in Company C for $200,000 and at the end of the accounting

period the stock has a market value of $150,000, a loss of $50,000 will be recognized in the income statement. The investment account will be reduced by the same amount. This process is called the **mark-to-market approach.**

**LO 3**    **Available-for-sale** securities encompass any investment in stocks or bonds that does not qualify as trading securities, and bonds that are not intended to be held to maturity. They may be reported as either long-term or short-term assets. As with trading securities, available-for-sale securities must also be marked to market. However, instead of the gain or loss being reported in the income statement, it is entered into an unrealized gain or loss account, which appears as a part of stockholders' equity. For example, assume that Company X buys stock in Company A for $500,000 on July 25, 2001, and that the stock has a market value of $480,000 at the end of the accounting period on December 31, 2001. The investment account will be reduced $20,000 and a loss of $20,000 will be recognized in owners' equity, but not reported as a loss in the income statement. The journal entry to mark the available-for-sale stock to market is:

|  |  | Debit | Credit |
|---|---|---|---|
| 12/31/01 | Unrealized loss on available for sale securities | 20,000 |  |
|  | Investment in Company A |  | 20,000 |
|  | Adjustment of available-for-sale securities to fair value |  |  |

## Sixty Second Quiz!

**Question:**    Why is the difference between the book value and the current market price treated differently for trading securities and for available-for-sale securities?

**Answer:**    The argument hinges on the fact that available-for-sale investments are expected to be held for longer than trading securities. Trading securities are expected to be sold within the next year, available-for-sale investments are not. For trading securities, the current market price provides a good indication of what the final sale price will be. Therefore the gain or loss on these securities can be reliably estimated and reported in the income statement. Since it is uncertain when available-for-sale securities will be sold, the current market price does not offer similar insights into the ultimate gain or loss on these securities. However, the current market price is an important piece of information, and the best guide to the current value of these investments. The current market price of available-for-sale securities should be reported in the balance sheet along with the unrealized gain or loss.

**LO 4**    The balance of accounts receivable on the balance sheet represents the sum of many individual accounts. In order to better manage these individual accounts, a **subsidiary ledger** is often maintained to record separate transactions for each individual customer. In the general ledger, a **control account** summarizes the total transactions that take place in the subsidiary ledger.

**LO 4**    Companies can rarely collect all money owed to them by their customers and must account for amounts that are uncollectible. The two main methods for accounting for bad debts are the **direct write-off** and the **allowance** methods.

- The **direct write-off method** is carried out after a particular amount proves uncollectible. The account receivable involved is reduced by the uncollectible amount and the bad debt expense account is increased. Because the expense is recognized only after the account proves uncollectible, this method fails to provide proper matching of expenses and revenues in the time period in which the revenues are earned. Unless the amounts involved are immaterial, the direct write-off method is therefore unacceptable under GAAP.

- The **allowance method** in effect *predicts* how much of the accounts receivable balance will prove uncollectible and creates an allowance for doubtful accounts as a contra account to accounts receivable. The allowance method therefore better matches the revenues and costs in a period. Two main methods are used to estimate the amount of the allowance:

**Percentage of Net Credit Sales:** On the basis of past experience, the company estimates the percentage of net credit sales that will prove uncollectible. To illustrate, assume that net credit sales for a period are $100,000 and that the company estimates 2% of these will prove uncollectible. The estimate of uncollectible accounts for the current period is calculated as follows:

% of uncollectibles x net credit sales for the period  = 2% of $100,000
                                                       = $2,000

The following adjustment is made to record this:

|  | Debit | Credit |
|---|---|---|
| Bad debts expense | 2,000 | |
|     Allowance for doubtful accounts | | 2,000 |
| Increase in allowance for bad debts | | |

**Percentage of Accounts Receivable:** For this method, again on the basis of past experience, the company estimates what percentage of the closing accounts receivable balance will be uncollectible. To illustrate, assume that the accounts receivable balance is $2,500,000 and that the company estimates that 1% of these will prove uncollectible. The account balance for the contra allowance for doubtful accounts is calculated as follows:

% of uncollectibles x accounts receivable balance     = 1% of $2,500,000
                                                      = $25,000

The allowance account is increased to this amount and the difference increases bad debts expense. To continue the above example, if the current balance in the Allowance account is $24,000, the adjustment to increase the balance by the required amount is as follows:

|  | Debit | Credit |
|---|---|---|
| Bad debts expense | 1,000 | |
|     Allowance for doubtful accounts | | 1,000 |
| Increase in allowance for bad debts | | |

The percentage of accounts receivable method can be modified by classifying accounts receivable into different groups, according to how long they have been outstanding. This is known as an **aging schedule**. A different percentage is used for each group, with the percentage increasing as the period of the debt gets longer.

Under the allowance method, when a debt actually becomes uncollectible, both the customer's account and the allowance account are reduced by the amount of the uncollectible account. If an amount that has previously been written off is subsequently recovered, the entry is reversed. The customer's account and the allowance for doubtful account are both increased.

 A basic ratio, which gives users insights into how well a company manages its accounts receivables, is the accounts receivables turnover calculated as follows:

| Accounts receivables turnover | = | Net credit sales |
|---|---|---|
| | | Average accounts receivable |

## Sixty Second Quiz!

**Question**:     Company A has an accounts receivable turnover of 30 times a year; Company B has an accounts receivable turnover of 5 times per year. Is Company A six times as effective at managing its accounts receivable as Company B?

**Answer**:     Probably not. The two companies might be in very different industries. Even if they are in the same industry, Company A and Company B might have very different proportions of credit sales. However, even if the two companies are very similar, you cannot conclude that Company A is more effective at  handling its accounts receivable. The high turnover could be a signal that  Company A's credit policies are overly strict and that the company may be losing lucrative sales. It does appear that Company B should consider whether or not its credit department is operating effectively so that it is not losing the use of cash for long periods.

**LO 5,6** **Notes receivable** are promises to pay money in the future. There are two main types: **interest-bearing notes** and **non-interest-bearing notes** (or discounted notes).

- For an interest-bearing note, the interest payable is explicitly stated, and its accounting treatment for interest due but unpaid at the end of the accounting period is directly analogous to the example given above for a CD.

- For a non-interest-bearing note, the principal (the cash or value of goods received when the note was issued) is less than the maturity value (the cash that must be paid when the note matures). Although no interest rate is specifically stated on the note, interest is effectively paid since more money is paid at the end than is received at the beginning. Suppose, for example, that a note is received by Company A from a customer for goods with a net sales value of  $3,000. The note will mature in 3 months, and the maturity value is $3,150. The implicit interest in this agreement is $150 for three months, equivalent to $600 in a full year. The implicit *annual* interest rate is therefore $600 or  20% of $3,000. The journal entry to record the receipt of the note is as follows:

|  | Debit | Credit |
|---|---|---|
| Note receivable | 3,150 | |
| Sales revenue | | 3,000 |
| Discount on notes receivable | | 150 |
| To record receipt of note receivable | | |

The discount on notes receivable account is a contra account to the notes receivable account. As interest on the note is earned, this account is reduced and interest revenue is increased. If the accounting period ended one month after the note was received, the entry to record the interest earned on the note would be as follows:

|  | Debit | Credit |
|---|---|---|
| Discount on notes receivable | 50 | |
| Interest revenue | | 50 |
| Interest revenue on note receivable | | |

## Sixty Second Quiz!

**Question:** What would be the current balance on the notes receivable account in the balance sheet and how would the payment on the maturity of the note be recorded?

**Answer:** At this point, the notes receivable balance would be $3,150, with the contra account, discount on notes receivable, having a balance of $100. The net balance would therefore be $3,050. When the cash payment of $3,150 is received on maturity, the journal entry would be as follows:

|                                  | Debit | Credit |
|----------------------------------|-------|--------|
| Cash                             | 3,150 |        |
| Discount on notes receivable     | 100   |        |
| Notes receivable                 |       | 3,150  |
| Interest revenue                 |       | 100    |

**LO 7** Companies can speed up the flow of cash from sales in several ways. With **credit card sales**, the company receives payment directly from the credit card company and avoids the uncertainties and costs associated with multiple cash collections. However, the credit card company does charge a collection fee and so the system, while increasing the speed of cash collection, is not costless. Companies can also accelerate the receipt of cash by **discounting notes receivable**, either immediately after the note is received or after it has been outstanding, but before maturity. Again this method is not costless, since the amount received for the note will be less than the total amount that would have been received at maturity. When the note is discounted, cash is increased, notes receivable is reduced, and the difference between the principal and the amount received increases interest revenue.

**LO 8** If a company uses the direct method for its cash flow statement, the cash collected from customers is shown as a source of cash. When the company uses the indirect method, cash flow from operations is found by adjusting net income for increases or decreases in the accounts receivable balance. For example, if accounts receivable increase over the period, the sales figure exceeds the cash received from sales. To find cash flow from operations, the increase in accounts receivable must be deducted from net income.

# Review of Key Terms

| | |
|---|---|
| **Aging schedule** | A form used to categorize the various individual accounts receivable according to the length of time each has been outstanding. |
| **Allowance method** | A method of estimating bad debts on the basis of either the net credit sales of the period or the amount of accounts receivable at the end of the period. |
| **Available-for-sale securities** | Stocks and bonds that are not classified as either held-to-maturity or trading securities. |
| **Bank reconciliation** | A form used by the accountant to reconcile the balance shown on the bank statement for a particular account with the balance shown in the accounting records. |
| **Bank statement** | A document, provided by the bank, of all the activity for a particular account during the month. |
| **Cash equivalent** | Investments that are readily convertible to known amounts of cash and that have an original maturity to the investor of three months or less. |
| **Control account** | The general ledger account that is supported by a subsidiary ledger. |
| **Credit card draft** | A multiple-copy document used by a company that accepts a credit card for a sale. |
| **Credit memoranda** | Additions on a bank statement for such items as interest paid on the account and notes collected by the bank for the customer. |
| **Debit memoranda** | Deductions on a bank statement for such items as NSF checks and various service charges. |
| **Debt securities** | Bonds issued by corporations and governmental bodies as a form of borrowing. |
| **Deposit in transit** | A deposit recorded in the company's books but not yet reflected on the bank statement. |
| **Direct write-off method** | The recognition of bad debts expense at the point when an account is written off as uncollectible. |
| **Discounted note** | An alternative name for a non-interest-bearing promissory note. |
| **Discounting** | The process of selling a promissory note. |
| **Equity securities** | Securities issued by corporations as a form of ownership in the business. |
| **Held-to-maturity securities** | Investments in bonds of other companies in which the investor has the positive intent and the ability to hold the securities to maturity. |
| **Interest-bearing note** | A promissory note in which the interest rate is explicitly stated. |
| **Maker** | The party to a promissory note who agrees to repay the money at some future date. |
| **Non-interest-bearing note** | A promissory note in which interest is not explicitly stated but is implicit in the agreement. |

| | |
|---|---|
| **Note payable** | A liability resulting from the signing of a promissory note. |
| **Note receivable** | An asset resulting from the acceptance of a promissory note from another company. |
| **Outstanding check** | A check written by the company but presented to the bank for payment. |
| **Payee** | The party to a promissory note who will receive the money at some future date. |
| **Petty cash fund** | Money kept on hand for making minor disbursements in coin and currency rather than by writing checks. |
| **Promissory note** | A written promise to repay a definite sum of money on demand or at a fixed or determinable date in the future. |
| **Subsidiary ledger** | The detail for a number of individual items that collectively make up a single general ledger account. |
| **Trading securities** | Stocks and bonds of other companies bought and held for the purpose of selling them in the near term to generate profits on appreciation of their price. |

# Practice Test
# Questions and Problems

## Circle the alternative that best answers the question:

**LO 1**  1.  Which of the following would not be included in the cash balance in a balance sheet prepared on January 1, 2000?
a)  Coin and currency balances
b)  Balances in checking accounts
c)  Balances in petty cash accounts
d)  A CD maturing on May 1, 2000

*Use the following information to answer questions 2 through 5:*
Alpha bought 5% of Delta's stock for $2 per share. At the balance sheet date, one month later, the Delta stock is selling for $2.60 per share and has paid a dividend per share of $0.30.

**LO 3**  2.  If Alpha accounts for Delta stock as available-for-sale, the stock will be reported in the balance sheet at:
a)  $2.60 per share.
b)  $2 per share.
c)  $2.30 per share.
d)  $2.90 per share.

**LO 3**  3.  If Alpha accounts for Delta stock as available-for-sale, the entry in the income statement will be:
a)  unrealized gain of $0.90 per share.
b)  unrealized gain of $0.60 per share and dividend income of $0.30 per share.
c)  unrealized gain of $2.60 per share.
d)  dividend income of $0.30 per share.

LO 3   4.   If Alpha accounts for Delta stock as trading securities, the stock will be reported in the balance sheet at:
- a) $2.60 per share.
- b) $2 per share.
- c) $2.30 per share.
- d) $2.90 per share.

LO 3   5.   If Alpha accounts for Delta stock as trading securities, the entry in the income statement will be:
- a) unrealized gain of $0.90 per share.
- b) unrealized gain of $0.60 per share and dividend income of $0.30 per share.
- c) unrealized gain of $2.60 per share.
- d) dividend income of $0.30 per share.

LO 2   6.   In a bank reconciliation, bank charges are:
- a) added to the book balance.
- b) subtracted from the book balance.
- c) added to the bank balance.
- d) subtracted from the bank balance.

LO 4   7.   The face amount of accounts receivable for Company A is $50,000. It is estimated that 2% of these will prove uncollectible, that customers will take advantage of cash discounts of $1,000, and that sales of $2,000 will be returned. The net realizable value of accounts receivable is:
- a) $50,000
- b) $49,000
- c) $48,000
- d) $46,000

LO 4   8.   Under the direct write-off method, writing off an account as uncollectible will:
- a) increase both the current ratio and net income.
- b) decrease both the current ratio and net income.
- c) increase the current ratio and decreases net income.
- d) decrease the current ratio and increases net income.

LO 4   9.   Company B uses the percentage of sales method of accounting for doubtful accounts. Its allowance for doubtful accounts on January 1, 2000 was $6,000, and was $4,500 on December 31, 2000. During the year, sales were $500,000 and an allowance of 1% of sales was made for doubtful accounts. Accounts written off as uncollectible during 2000 amounted to:
- a) $1,500
- b) $4,500
- c) $5,000
- d) $6,500

LO 7   10.   If a company's collection period for accounts receivable is unacceptably long, which of the following statements is false?
- a) The company may need to borrow to meet its accounts payable.
- b) The company may offer cash discounts to increase the collection period.
- c) The company may discount its notes receivable to increase cash flow.
- d) Cash flow from operations may be lower than expected for the firm's sales.

**LO 3** 11. A company purchases 25% of the stock of the supplier of a key component in its manufacturing process. Which of the following is the most likely reason for the acquisition?
a) To obtain a return on idle cash
b) To control the activities of the supplier
c) To influence significantly the activities of the supplier
d) None of the above

**LO 3** 12. Zeta owns 80% of the stock of Alpha. Which of the following methods should Zeta use to account for its investment in Alpha?
a) Equity method
b) Fair value method
c) Consolidation
d) Amortized cost method

*Use the following information to answer question 13:*

On November 1, 2000, Zen Corporation invested $20,000 of excess cash in a 90-day certificate of deposit. The CD matures on January 31, 2001, and has an annual interest rate of 12%.

**LO 3** 13. The revenue recognized by Zen in the year to December 31, 2000, and the year to December 31, 2001, was:
a) 0, $600.
b) $200, $400.
c) $400, $200.
d) $600, 0.

**LO 7** 14. Soho Restaurant accepts Diners Club credit cards. During the week ended July 4, 2000, the total Diners Club credit card sales were $25,000. Diners Club pays the amount due to Soho on July 7 after deducting a 4% collection fee. The entry to record the receipt of cash from Diners Club on July 7 was:

a) Cash                                        25,000
    Accounts receivable - Diners Club              25,000

b) Cash                                        25,000
    Collection fee expense                          1,000
    Accounts receivable - Diners Club              24,000

c) Cash                                        24,000
    Collection fee expense                          1,000
    Accounts receivable - Diners Club              25,000

d) Cash                                        24,000
    Collection fee expense                          1,000
    Sales revenue                                  25,000

LO 4    15.   Which of the following statements is true?
a)   The direct write-off method can result in an understatement of the accounts receivable balance on the balance sheet.
b)   The main difference between the direct write-off method and the allowance method is the timing of the recognition of bad debt expense.
c)   Under the allowance method, when bad debts are written off, the allowance account is debited and bad debt expense is credited.
d)   The main difference between the percentage of net credit sales method and the percentage of accounts receivable method is the percentage used in calculating the allowance for doubtful debts.

## Indicate whether each of the following statements is true or false:

LO 2    16.   In a bank reconciliation, outstanding checks and deposits in transit are deducted from the bank statement balance.

LO 4    17.   Expenditures from the petty cash fund are recorded in the ledger only when the fund is replenished.

LO 8    18.   If accounts receivable decrease over the year, then sales are greater than cash collected from customers.

LO 4    19.   The direct write-off method for uncollectible accounts results in an understatement of current income and an overstatement of future income.

LO 4    20.   Under the allowance method, when an account is written off as uncollectible, the current ratio decreases.

LO 7    21.   A firm with a current ratio greater than one will increase its current ratio by discounting its non-current notes receivable.

LO 3    22.   Available for sale securities are always classified as current assets.

LO 4    23.   The link between a subsidiary ledger and the general ledger is provided by a control account.

LO 6    24.   As its name suggests, no interest is paid or earned on a non-interest-bearing note.

LO 2    25.   A bank reconciliation need be carried out only when errors are found in the ledger cash account.

LO 4    26.   Both the direct write-off method and the allowance method of accounting for bad debts expense are acceptable under GAAP.

LO 5    27.   For interest-bearing notes, interest earned but not yet collected is not recognized until the note matures.

LO 1    28.   Cash equivalents such as commercial paper, money market funds, and T-bills are included with cash on the balance sheet.

**LO 6**     29. Discounting a note receivable involves selling the note to a third party to accelerate the inflow of cash.

**LO 8**     30. Purchases and sales of short-term investments do not appear as a separate item on the statement of cash flows.

## Complete each of the following statements:

**LO 3**     31. _____ securities are purchased with the intention of selling them in the near future and are always classified as current assets.

**LO 3**     32. _____ are investments that are readily convertible to known amounts of cash and have a maturity when acquired of less than three months.

**LO 2**     33. _____ are checks for which the payee does not have sufficient money in his or her bank account to honor the check.

**LO 4**     34. The _____ method requires the company to estimate what proportion of its net sales will be uncollectible and to use this to identify the current period's adjustment to the allowance for doubtful accounts.

**LO 4**     35. Under the allowance method when individual accounts are recognized as uncollectible, the _____ account is debited and the _____ account is credited with the amount of the uncollectible debt.

**LO 4**     36. The ratio of net credit sales to average accounts receivable gives insights into how well a company manages its accounts receivable and is called _____.

**LO 6**     37. The _____ account is the contra account to notes receivable, in which the effective interest on a non-interest-bearing note is recorded.

**LO 8**     38. Under the indirect method for the cash flow statement, if a company's accounts receivable balance has decreased over the year, cash flow from operations is found by _____ the change in accounts receivable to net income.

**LO 4**     39. _____ is the procedure whereby accounts receivable are classified according to how long they have been outstanding.

**LO 3**     40. If a company's cash needs are seasonal, _____ are accommodated by short-term borrowing.

**LO 2**     41. A process whereby the bank statement balance and the book balance are reconciled is called a _____.

**LO 1**     42. _____ are issued by corporations as evidence of borrowing. _____ are issued by corporations as evidence of part ownership in the company, such as common stock and preferred stock.

**LO 2** 43. A fund that is set up to provide for minor cash disbursements and that is replenished to its starting balance on a regular basis is called a _____. Expenditure from the fund is recorded in the books at the time the fund is replenished.

**LO 5** 44. The amount of cash, or the fair value of the products or services, received by the maker when a promissory note is issued is the _____; the amount of cash to be paid by the maker to the payee on the maturity date of a promissory note is the _____.

**LO 5** 45. The length of time a promissory note is outstanding is known as the _____; the date that a promissory note is due is the _____.

## Answer each of the following problems:

**LO 2** 46. For the month ended December 31, 2000, the following information relating to the cash account of Delta Dentists is available:

a) According the bank statement, the balance on the checking account on December 31, 2000 is $140,326.

b) The cash account on the company books shows a balance of $148,072.

c) Delta made a deposit of $25,326 on December 31 which is not included in the bank statement.

d) The following checks were issued by Delta during December but have not yet appeared on the bank statement:

| Check No. | Amount |
|-----------|--------|
| 1147 | $7,350 |
| 1156 | 8,400 |
| 1270 | 1,526 |

e) The bank collected interest on notes receivable on behalf of the company. The bank statement shows that $500 was collected during December.

f) Two NSF checks were returned with the May statement. These were from customers Smith and Jones for $242 and $162, respectively.

g) Interest earned on the checking account was $256; $48 of bank charges were charged to the account.

h) It was discovered that a check for $250 written by Delta to Molar X-Rays was erroneously recorded in the Mortar Fillings account in the ledger.

**Required**

1. Prepare a bank reconciliation for Delta for the month of December and list some advantages to the company of preparing a bank reconciliation.

2. Prepare the journal entries recording any necessary changes to the company's bank account in its ledger.

**LO 5**  47.  Match Corporation accepted a nine-month interest-bearing note for $28,000 from Box Company on July 1, 2000, for sales of $25,000. Match Company prepares its accounts to December 31 each year.

**Required**

1. What is the effective rate of interest on the note?

2.  Give the journal entries recording the note over its life, assuming that the note is held to maturity and paid in full on the due date.

3.  What are the net balances for the note receivable on July 1, 2000 and on December 31, 2000?

4.  Show the journal entry on October 1, 2000, to record Match discounting the note on that day for $25,200.

**LO 3** 48. The following information appears on Alpha Corp.'s balance sheet for years ended December 31, 2000, and December 31, 1999.

| | December 31, 2000 | December 31, 1999 |
|---|---|---|
| 9-month certificates of deposit | $ 50 | $ 151 |
| IBM stock, acquired on 12/1/1999* | 0 | 265 |
| U.S. Treasury notes | 704 | 494 |
| Cash | 45 | 94 |
| Receivables less allowances | 947 | 803 |
| Inventories | 685 | 620 |

* When the company acquired the IBM stock, it intended to sell it in January, 2000. The company carried out its intention to sell the stock early in January 2000.

**Required**

1. Identify which items constitute cash equivalents, and suggest the order in which they should appear in the balance sheet.

2. Where should the non-cash equivalents appear on the balance sheet?

3. What is the amount and direction of change in the company's cash and cash equivalent balances over the year? Is the company as liquid at the end of the year as it was at the beginning? What additional information would you want to know to help you to judge whether or not the change was significant?

## Critical Thinking Problem

**LO 8** 49. The following table gives the cash flow statement of Compaq Computers for the years ended December 31, 1994, 1995, and 1996.

## CONSOLIDATED STATEMENT OF CASH FLO WS

| Year ended December 31, in millions | 1996 | 1995 | 1994 |
|---|---|---|---|
| **Cash flows from operating activities:** | | | |
| Cash received from customers | $17,939 | $13,910 | $9,986 |
| Cash paid to suppliers and employees | -13,639 | -12,437 | -9,778 |
| Interest and dividends received | 110 | 53 | 22 |
| Interest paid | -91 | -100 | -65 |
| Income taxes paid | -911 | -543 | -319 |
| Net cash provided by (used in) operating activities | 3,408 | 883 | -154 |
| **Cash flows from investing activities:** | | | |
| Purchases of property, plant and equipment, net | -342 | -391 | -357 |
| Purchases of short-term investments | -1,401 | | |
| Proceeds from short-term investments | 328 | | |
| Acquisition of businesses, net of cash acquired | -22 | -318 | |
| Other, net | -26 | 6 | -51 |
| Net cash used in investing activities | -1,463 | -703 | -408 |
| **Cash flows from financing activities:** | | | |
| Issuance of common stock pursuant to stock option plans | 112 | 79 | 100 |
| Issuance of long-term debt | | | 300 |
| Tax benefit associated with stock options | 91 | 60 | 53 |
| Net cash provided by financing activities | 203 | 139 | 453 |
| Effect of exchange rate changes on cash | 27 | -45 | -47 |
| Net increase (decrease) in cash and cash equivalents | 2,175 | 274 | -156 |
| Cash and cash equivalents at beginning of year | 745 | 471 | 627 |
| Cash and cash equivalents at end of year | $2,920 | $745 | $471 |
| **Reconciliation of net income to net cash provided by(used in) operating activities** | | | |
| Net income | $1,313 | $789 | $867 |
| Depreciation and amortization | 285 | 214 | 169 |
| Provision for bad debts | 155 | 43 | 36 |
| Purchased in-process technology | | 241 | |
| Deferred income taxes | -371 | -17 | -184 |
| Loss on disposal of assets | 5 | 2 | 2 |
| Exchange rate effect | 14 | 33 | 46 |
| Increase in accounts receivable | -210 | -863 | -926 |
| Decrease (increase) in inventories | 1,004 | -135 | -882 |
| Decrease (increase) in other current assets | 5 | -41 | -55 |
| Increase in accounts payable | 586 | 479 | 248 |
| Increase (decrease) in income taxes payable | 131 | -61 | 173 |
| Increase in other current liabilities | 491 | 199 | 352 |
| Net cash provided by (used in) operating activities | $3,408 | $883 | ($154) |

**Required**

Use the table to answer the following questions:

1. Does Compaq use the direct or indirect method for presentation of the cash flow statement?

2. How much cash was collected from customers each year?

3. By how much did accounts receivable increase in each of the three years?

4. If we were to assume that all accounts receivable were related to sales, what would the firm's revenues be in each of the three years?

## Solutions

### Multiple Choice

| | | | | |
|---|---|---|---|---|
| 1. | d | | 9. | d |
| 2. | a | | 10. | b |
| 3. | d | | 11. | c |
| 4. | a | | 12. | c |
| 5. | b | | 13. | c |
| 6. | b | | 14. | c |
| 7. | d | | 15. | b |
| 8. | b | | | |

### True/False

**COMMENT/EXPLANATION**

| | | |
|---|---|---|
| 16. | False | Outstanding checks are subtracted, and deposits in transit are added to, the balance shown in the bank account. |
| 17. | True | |
| 18. | False | When cash collected is greater than sales, the additional cash received reduces the balance on the accounts receivable account. |
| 19. | False | The direct write-off method results in uncollectible accounts receivable relating to the current period's sales being written off in the future. Therefore, the method results in an understatement of future income and an overstatement of current income. |
| 20. | False | When the allowance method is used, writing off uncollectible accounts reduces the allowance for doubtful accounts account and accounts receivable by the same amount. Current assets, and therefore the current ratio, are unaffected. |
| 21. | True | |
| 22. | False | Available-for-sale securities are marketable, but the intent of the company dictates whether or not they are classified as short-term or long-term. |
| 23. | True | |
| 24. | False | A non-interest-bearing note has an implicit rather than an explicit interest rate. |
| 25. | False | A bank reconciliation statement should be carried out irrespective of whether or not errors are found or suspected. |
| 26. | False | Only the allowance method is acceptable under GAAP. |
| 27. | False | Interest is recognized when earned, not received. |
| 28. | True | |
| 29. | True | |
| 30. | False | Purchases and sales of short-term securities are regarded as significant events and are therefore reported separately on the statement of cash flows. |

## Fill in the Blanks

| | | | | |
|---|---|---|---|---|
| 31. | trading | 39. | aging |
| 32. | cash equivalents | 40. | cash shortages |
| 33. | not sufficient funds | 41. | bank reconciliation |
| 34. | allowance | 42. | debt securities, equity securities |
| 35. | allowance for doubtful accounts, accounts receivable | 43. | petty cash fund |
| 36. | accounts receivable turnover | 44. | principal, maturity value |
| 37. | discounts on notes receivable | 45. | term, maturity date |
| 38. | adding | | |

## Problem 46

### Bank reconciliation December 31, 2000

| | | |
|---|---|---|
| Balance in bank statement | | $ 140,326 |
| Plus deposit in transit | | 25,326 |
| | | $165,652 |
| | | |
| Less Checks in transit | | |
| 1147 | $7,350 | |
| 1156 | 8,400 | |
| 1270 | 1,526 | |
| | | 17,276 |
| Adjusted balance | | $148,376 |
| | | |
| Balance in cash account | | $148,072 |
| Plus Interest collected on notes | 500 | |
| Interest on bank accounts | 256 | |
| | | 756 |
| | | 148,828 |
| Less NSF checks | 242 | |
| | 162 | |
| Charges | 48 | |
| | | 452 |
| Adjusted cash balance | | $148,376 |

Benefits to Delta of preparing a bank reconciliation include:

- increased control over cash
- the opportunity to find errors
- the opportunity to ascertain NSF checks and to amend credit policies accordingly
- the opportunity to assess actual cash available so that shortages and excesses can be dealt with

2.

**Journal entries**

| | | Debit | Credit |
|---|---|---|---|
| 12/31/00 | Cash | 500 | |
| |     Interest revenue | | 500 |
| | Interest collected on note by bank | | |

| | | Debit | Credit |
|---|---|---|---|
| 12/31/00 | Cash | 256 | |
| |     Interest revenue | | 256 |
| | Interest earned on checking account | | |

| | | Debit | Credit |
|---|---|---|---|
| 12/31/00 | Jones account | 242 | |
| | Smith account | 162 | |
| |     Cash | | 404 |
| | NSF checks | | |

| | | Debit | Credit |
|---|---|---|---|
| 12/31/00 | Bank charges expense | 48 | |
| |     Cash | | 48 |
| | Charges from bank | | |

| | | Debit | Credit |
|---|---|---|---|
| 12/31/00 | Morton Fillings | 250 | |
| |     Molar X-Rays | | 250 |
| | Correction of error in accounts payable | | |

## Problem 47

1. **Effective interest rate calculation**

| | | | | |
|---|---|---|---|---|
| Implicit interest | = | $28,000 - $25,000 | = | $3,000 |
| Period of note | | | = | 9 months |
| Interest for full year | = | $3,000 x $\frac{12}{9}$ | = | $4,000 |
| Effective annual interest rate | = | $\frac{\$4,000}{\$25,000}$ x 100% | = | 16% |

2. **Journal entries**

| | | Debit | Credit |
|---|---|---|---|
| 7/1/00 | Note receivable | 28,000 | |
| | Sales | | 25,000 |
| | Discount on note | | 3,000 |
| | Receipt of note receivable | | |

| | | Debit | Credit |
|---|---|---|---|
| 12/31/00 | Discount on note | 2,000 | |
| | Interest revenue | | 2,000 |
| | Interest earned on note receivable | | |

| | | Debit | Credit |
|---|---|---|---|
| 3/31/01 | Discount on note | 1,000 | |
| | Cash | 28,000 | |
| | Note receivable | | 28,000 |
| | Interest revenue | | 1,000 |
| | Receipt of note receivable | | |

3. **Balance sheet entries**

| | July 1, 2000 | December 31, 2000 |
|---|---|---|
| Note receivable | $28,000 | $28,000 |
| Less discount on note | (3,000) | (1,000) |
| Net book value | $25,000 | $27,000 |

4. If note is discounted on October 1, 2000:

| | | |
|---|---|---|
| Maturity value of note | = | $28,000 |
| Proceeds of discount | = | $25,200 |

**Journal entry**

| | | Debit | Credit |
|---|---|---|---|
| 10/1/00 | Cash | 25,200 | |
| | Discount on note | 3,000 | |
| | Note receivable | | 28,000 |
| | Interest revenue (28,000 - 25,200 - 3,000) | | 200 |
| | To record discounting of note receivable | | |

## Problem 48

1. Cash equivalents - possible order

| | December 31, 2000 | December 31, 1999 |
|---|---|---|
| Cash | $ 45 | $ 94 |
| U.S. Treasury notes | 704 | 494 |
| IBM stock | 0 | 265 |
| *Total* | *749* | *853* |

2. The following non-cash equivalents should appear on the balance sheet under current assets:

| | December 31, 2000 | December 31, 1999 |
|---|---|---|
| 9 month certificates of deposit | $ 50 | $ 151 |
| Receivables less allowances | 947 | 803 |
| Inventories | 685 | 620 |

3. The cash equivalents have reduced by $104, or 12.2%, over the year. The company is therefore not as liquid at the end of the year as it was at the beginning. The additional information that would be helpful is the level of sales (if the company's activities are lower, then the cash requirements may be lower), credit terms offered to customers and by suppliers, and whether other short-term sources of cash are available.

## Critical Thinking Problem 49

1. Compaq uses the direct method for its cash flow statement.

2. Cash received from customers:

| | 1996 | 1995 | 1994 |
|---|---|---|---|
| | $17,939 | $13,910 | $9,986 |

3. Increase in accounts receivable:

| | 1996 | 1995 | 1994 |
|---|---|---|---|
| | $210 | $863 | $926 |

4. If a company uses the direct method for its cash flow statement, the cash collected from customers is shown as a source of cash. If accounts receivable increase over the period, the sales figure exceeds the cash received from sales. To find the sales figure, the increase in accounts receivable is added to cash received from customers to obtain the following estimates for sales of the period:

| 1996 | 1995 | 1994 |
|---|---|---|
| $18,149 | $14,773 | $10,912 |

The actual sales reported on the income statement for those years were:

| 1996 | 1995 | 1994 |
|---|---|---|
| $18,109 | $14,755 | $10,866 |

The difference could be due to the fact that not all accounts receivable balances are related to sales transactions, but to other short-term receivables.

# Chapter 8

# Operating Assets: Property, Plant, and Equipment, Natural Resources, and Intangibles

This chapter explores the accounting issues associated with long-term assets. Both tangible and intangible assets are discussed in this chapter. Your goal is to understand the different accounting methods used for each type of asset.

## Learning Objectives

| | |
|---|---|
| **LO 1** | Understand balance sheet disclosures for operating assets. |
| **LO 2** | Determine the acquisition cost of an operating asset. |
| **LO 3** | Explain how to calculate the acquisition cost of assets purchased for a lump sum. |
| **LO 4** | Describe the impact of capitalizing interest as part of the acquisition cost of an asset. |
| **LO 5** | Compare depreciation methods and understand the factors affecting the choice of method. |
| **LO 6** | Understand the impact of a change in the estimate of the asset life or residual value. |
| **LO 7** | Determine which expenditures should be capitalized as asset costs and which should be treated as expenses. |
| **LO 8** | Analyze the effect of the disposal of an asset at a gain or loss. |
| **LO 9** | Understand the balance sheet presentation of intangible assets. |
| **LO 10** | Describe the proper amortization of intangible assets. |
| **LO 11** | Explain the impact that long-term assets have on the statement of cash flows. |

## Key Textbook Exhibits

**Exhibit 8-1** compares the straight-line and the double declining-balance methods. *Self-Test:* Does the double declining-balance method result in higher depreciation charges for every year of the asset's life? Does the double declining-balance method result in a lower book value for every year of the asset's life?

**Exhibit 8-2** presents the factors that affect a company's decision in choosing a depreciation method. *Self-Test:* Can a company choose one method for financial reporting purposes and another for tax purposes?

**Exhibit 8-3** indicates the results of a survey in which 600 companies were asked the depreciation method or methods used for their 1998 financial statements. *Self-Test:* Why do you think a vast majority of companies choose the straight-line method?

**Exhibit 8-5** provides descriptions of the most common intangible assets. *Self-Test:* Where on the financial statements are intangibles usually presented?

**Exhibit 8-8** illustrates the items discussed in this chapter and their effect on the statement of cash flows. *Self-Test:* Why is depreciation and amortization added back to net income to arrive at the amount of cash generated from operations?

## Review of Key Concepts

**LO 1** Operating assets are used to produce the goods and services the company sells, and are essential to the long-term viability of the company. There are two main types of operating assets: tangible assets that have physical form, such as land, buildings, machinery, and equipment; and intangible assets such as patents, goodwill, and trademarks. Accumulated depreciation is deducted from tangible assets to determine the net book value. Tangible and intangible accounts are presented below current assets on the balance sheet.

**LO 2** The first issue to be resolved in accounting for tangible assets (property, plant, and equipment) is how they should be valued. Under U.S. GAAP, historic cost is the basis of valuation for long-term assets. The historic cost, or acquisition cost, should include all costs normally necessary to acquire the asset and prepare it for its intended use. The purchase price, taxes, transportation charges, installation costs, and any necessary repairs or upgrades incurred at the time of the asset's purchase can also be included.

**LO 3** Sometimes assets are bought as a group at a price different from what would have been paid if the assets had been bought individually. When this happens, the acquisition cost of the group should be prorated to the individual items on the basis of their individual market prices. For example, if land and buildings are acquired together, the cost of the land should be separated from the cost of the building, using the respective market prices. This procedure is necessary because each asset may have a different economic life, and may therefore need to be written off over a different period. In the case of land and buildings, the building value decreases over time with depreciation whereas the land value stays the same.

**LO 4** When money is borrowed to acquire an asset, interest expense is incurred. The question arises of whether or not this interest should be included in the acquisition cost of the asset. Interest is normally regarded as part of the financing decision rather than as a part of the acquisition decision. As a result, interest is not normally included in the acquisition cost. However, there is one exception. When interest is used to finance the construction rather than the purchase of an asset, part of that interest can be included in the cost of the asset or **capitalized**. The proportion of interest that is capitalized is the interest on the average expenditure over the period. The logic resides in the idea that since construction takes place progressively over the period, the interest charges are also incurred progressively over that period. Therefore, the interest related to the construction is based on the average expenditure over the period.

The cost of land should be kept in a separate account because land has an unlimited life and is not depreciated. Improvements to land, which have limited life, should be accounted for separately from land and depreciated over their useful lives.

**LO 5** By their nature, long-term assets are used over more than one accounting period. The cost of an asset must therefore be spread over its useful life. The underlying principle is that cost allocation should closely match the decline in the asset's usefulness. The allocation process is called **depreciation.** In theory, a company should use a depreciation method that allocates the original cost of the asset to the periods benefited, and that allows the company to accurately match the expense to the revenue generated by the asset. Remember depreciation does not describe the increase or decrease in the market value of the asset.

### Sixty Second Quiz!

**Question**: Your brother buys a new car for $20,000 and comments that as soon as he drove it out of the car dealership, it depreciated by $2,000. Does he mean the same thing as an accountant does when he talks about depreciation?

**Answer**: No. He is implying that the car's value, or what he could get if he resold the car, has dropped by $2,000. Accountants are not attempting to find the market value of assets that they depreciate; rather, they are spreading the asset's cost over its useful life.

**LO 5** Since allocation of cost is a matter of judgment, several methods of depreciation have been developed. We consider three methods:

- The **straight-line method** assumes that the asset's usefulness declines uniformly over its life; thus an equal amount is written off the asset each year. The amount that is written off each year is calculated as follows:

$$\frac{\text{Acquisition cost - Residual value}}{\text{Useful life}}$$

- The **units-of-production** method allocates cost on the basis of how many units of production are produced by the asset in a particular accounting period. Depreciation expense for the period is found by multiplying the number of units produced in the period by the charge per unit. The charge per unit is calculated as follows:

$$\frac{\text{Acquisition cost - Residual value}}{\text{Estimated total number of units in asset's entire life}}$$

- **Double declining-balance** is one example of an **accelerated depreciation** method. It is used when more cost should be allocated to the early years of an asset's use and less to the later years. The double declining-balance method bases the depreciation on double the rate of depreciation under the straight-line method. This rate is applied to the net book value of the asset at the beginning of the year. Note that, when calculating the rate to be charged, residual value is ignored. For example, suppose a machine has a four-year life, an original cost of $10,000, and an estimated residual value of $1,000. The percentage straight-line depreciation rate is first calculated:

$$\frac{100\%}{4} = 25\%$$

The straight-line rate is then doubled to find the rate under the double declining-balance method:

$$2 \times 25\% \quad = \quad 50\%$$

The rate to be applied under the double declining-balance method is therefore 50%. The depreciation for this machine over its life is shown below. Note that Year 4's depreciation of $250 is not 50% of $1,250. It is a balancing figure resulting in an ending book value that equals the residual value of $1,000.

| Year | Rate | Book value beginning | Depreciation | Book value ending |
|------|------|----------------------|--------------|-------------------|
| 1 | 50% | $10,000 | $5,000 | $5,000 |
| 2 | 50% | 5,000 | 2,500 | 2,500 |
| 3 | 50% | 2,500 | 1,250 | 1,250 |
| 4 | 50% | 1,250 | 250 | 1,000 |

## Sixty Second Quiz!

**Question:** Which parameters of the above depreciation methods (acquisition cost, residual value, number of years of life, total number of units produced over the entire life) are known with certainty when the asset is purchased?

**Answer:** Only the acquisition cost is known with certainty when the asset is purchased. All of the other parameters must be estimated. Judgment plays a large part in determining depreciation charges and the resulting book values of long-term tangible assets.

**LO 5** Although the total depreciation written off over the life of the asset is identical under each method, the timing of the write-off over individual accounting periods varies greatly, resulting in substantially different reported income under each method. The double declining-balance method results in higher depreciation charges in the early years. This type of method is therefore called an accelerated method. These methods are appropriate when the usefulness of the asset declines substantially in the early years. The most commonly used method is straight-line, which produces the highest reported net income in the early years.

**LO 6** Since depreciation charges are based on estimates of acquisition cost, residual value, and asset life, it is possible that these estimates could be reevaluated and changed during the life of an asset. If that happens, depreciation already written off is not reassessed. Rather, the remaining book value at the time of the reevaluation is written off over the remaining life on the basis of the new estimates. For example, suppose a machine was bought for $100,000. When it was bought, the useful life was estimated to be 5 years, with no residual value. If straight-line depreciation is used, $20,000 is charged to depreciation each year. By the end of year 2, the net book value of the asset is $60,000. Now suppose that at the beginning of year 3 the company decides to replace the machine at the end of its fourth year of life, at which time, it can be sold for $5,000. New annual depreciation charges for years 3 and 4 are calculated as follows:

$$\frac{\text{Closing book value - New estimated residual value}}{\text{Remaining life}} \quad = \quad \frac{60,000 - 5,000}{2} \quad = \quad \$27,500$$

`LO 7` Whether expenditures are capitalized (added to the asset's cost) or expensed (charged immediately to income) can have a major impact on reported earnings. For example, suppose that major repairs costing $10,000 are carried out on an asset with an original cost of $25,000 and a book value of $10,000. If the repairs are expensed, then income will be reduced by the total amount of repairs in the year the repair is made. If, however, the costs of the repairs are capitalized, the impact on the income statement will be spread over the remaining life of the asset. As such, the capitalized cost is depreciated along with the remaining book value. In this case, the impact on the current income statement is much less dramatic. In general, if an expenditure increases the life of the asset or its productivity, it should be capitalized. Otherwise, it should be written off to the income statement as an expense in the period it is incurred.

`LO 8` When an asset is sold, the difference between the book value of the asset and the sale price should be recognized as a gain or a loss on sale. The gain or loss on sale is shown in the Other Income and Expense category of the income statement.

Natural resources, such as coalfields, oil wells, and timberlands, are assets that are carried in the Property, Plant, and Equipment category of the balance sheet. Originally, they are recorded at cost. The cost is then written off over the life of the asset using a method similar to the expensing of depreciation for other long-term assets. The process is usually referred to as **depletion**, and the calculation is based on the portion of the natural resource that was consumed during the current year.

`LO 9` Intangible assets are assets that have no physical form but still provide future economic benefits to the company. The most common types of intangibles are goodwill, patents trademarks, copyrights, and organization costs. The costs of research and development, however, are not capitalized under U.S. GAAP; rather, they are expensed during the period they are incurred. As with tangible assets, intangibles are presented in the balance sheet at historic cost minus amortization (where amortization is the word used for depreciation of an intangible). Therefore, the only intangibles that appear on the balance sheet are those that result from a purchase transaction.

## Sixty Second Quiz!

**Question**: The Coca Cola company did not purchase its famous trademark, which is easily its greatest asset. Would you expect to see it on the balance sheet as an intangible asset?

**Answer**: No. Only intangibles that are the result of a purchase transaction will appear on the balance sheet.

`LO 10` Intangibles should be amortized over their life in a way directly analogous to the depreciation of fixed assets. The main issue in amortizing intangibles is defining the period over which they should be amortized. In most cases, companies use the straight-line method of amortization. There are significant international differences in the amortization of intangibles; for example, goodwill is amortized over a maximum of 40 years under U.S. GAAP, but over a much shorter period in other countries.

Several ratios can be used to gain insight into the type and use of fixed assets. The average life and average age of long-term assets are both useful measures of how long the company can expect to use its assets. The asset turnover ratio is a measure of how productively the company uses its assets.

| | | |
|---|---|---|
| Average life | = | $\dfrac{\text{Historical cost of assets}}{\text{Depreciation expense}}$ |
| Average age | = | $\dfrac{\text{Accumulated depreciation}}{\text{Depreciation expense}}$ |
| Asset turnover | = | $\dfrac{\text{Net sales}}{\text{Average total assets}}$ |

**LO 11** In the statement of cash flows, the cash paid or received in the acquisition or sale of assets are shown under investing activities. When the indirect method is used, it is necessary to make two adjustments to net income in order to find cash from operations. First, since depreciation is a non-cash expense that has been deducted in calculating net income, it must be added back to net income in order to find cash from operations. Second, the gain or loss on sale has been added or deducted in the income statement in order to find net income. However, the proceeds from the sale of fixed assets (which includes the effect of the gain or loss) is reported under investing activities, and as a result the gain or loss must be deducted from (gain), or added back to (loss), net income to find cash flow from operations. The gain or loss adjustment to net income avoids the gain or loss being counted twice, once in the proceeds (investing) and once in the net income (operations).

## Review of Key Terms

| | |
|---|---|
| **Accelerated depreciation** | A term that refers to several methods by which a higher amount of depreciation is recorded in the early years of an asset's life and a lower amount is recorded in the later years. |
| **Acquisition cost** | An amount that includes all costs normally necessary to acquire an asset and prepare it for its intended use. |
| **Book value** | The original acquisition cost of an asset minus the amount of accumulated depreciation. |
| **Capital expenditure** | A cost that improves an operating asset and is added to the asset account. |
| **Capitalization of interest** | The process of treating the cost of interest on constructed assets as a part of the asset cost rather than as an expense. |
| **Change in estimate** | A change in the life of an asset or in its expected residual value. |
| **Depreciation** | The allocation of the original acquisition cost of an asset to the periods benefited by its use. |
| **Double declining-balance method** | A method by which depreciation is recorded at twice the straight-line rate but the depreciable balance is reduced in each period. |
| **Gain on sale of asset** | An account whose amount indicates how much the selling price on an asset's disposal exceeds its book value. |
| **Goodwill** | The amount indicating that the purchase price of a business exceeded the total fair market values of the identifiable net assets at the time the business was acquired. |
| **Intangible asset** | A long-term asset that has no physical properties, for example patents, copyrights, and goodwill. |
| **Land improvements** | Additions made to a piece of property such as paving or landscaping a parking lot. The costs are treated separately from land for purposes of recording depreciation. |
| **Loss on sale of asset** | An account whose amount indicates how much the book value of an asset exceeds the selling price received on the asset's disposal. |
| **Natural resources** | Assets that are consumed during their use, for example coal or oil. |
| **Organization costs** | Costs that are incurred at the initial formation of a corporation and are treated as an intangible asset. |
| **Research and development costs** | Expenditures incurred in the discovery of new knowledge and the translation of research into a design or plan for a new product. |
| **Revenue expenditure** | A cost that keeps an operating asset in its normal operating condition and is treated as an expense of the period. |
| **Straight-line method** | A method by which the same dollar amount of depreciation is recorded in each year of asset use. |
| **Units-of-production method** | A method by which depreciation is determined by the number of units the asset produces. |

# Practice Test
## Questions and Problems

### Circle the alternative that best answers the question:

**LO 4**   1.   Which of the following assets is not depreciated or amortized over its life?
   a) Land
   b) Goodwill
   c) Buildings
   d) Equipment

**LO 5**   2.   Which of the following statements about the accumulated depreciation account is true?
   a) It is a long-term liability.
   b) It provides a contra account to intangible assets.
   c) It provides a contra account to tangible assets so that their net book value approximates their market value.
   d) It represents the total depreciation charged over the life of the asset to which it relates, and reduces the book value of the asset.

*Use the following information to answer questions 3 through 6:*

On December 1, 2001, Company X bought from Company Y land with a warehouse on it for $800,000. Company Y showed the land and buildings on its balance sheet at $500,000. The fair market values of the land and building at the time of purchase were $700,000 and $300,000, respectively.

**LO 3**   3.   How much of the purchase price should Company X allocate to land?
   a) $700,000
   b) $500,000
   c) $300,000
   d) $560,000

**LO 3**   4.   What gain or loss would Company X record in its accounts for the purchase of the land?
   a) $140,000
   b) $200,000
   c) $100,000 loss
   d) Zero

**LO 8**   5.   What gain would Company Y show in its books for the sale of the land and building?
   a) $200,000
   b) $100,000
   c) $500,000
   d) $300,000

**LO 5** 6. Company X allocates the entire cost of the purchase to land. Normally it depreciates buildings over 20 years using the straight-line method with zero residual value. Because of its accounting treatment of the purchase, Company X's income for each of the next 20 years:

a) will be overstated by $12,000.

b) will be understated by $12,000.

c) will be overstated by $15,000.

d) will be understated by $15,000.

**LO 8** 7. A machine with a cost of $100,000 and accumulated depreciation of $80,000 was sold at a loss of $6,000. The cash received from the sale was:

a) $16,000.

b) $26,000.

c) $74,000.

d) $14,000.

**LO 8** 8. The net book value of equipment for Company Y was $150,000 on January 1, 2001, and $140,000 on December 31, 2001. During the year, depreciation expense for equipment was $20,000. Which of the following events is consistent with these facts?

a) Assets with a net book value of $10,000 were sold during the year; no assets were purchased.

b) Assets were purchased during the year for $30,000, and assets with a historic cost of $10,000 were sold during the year.

c) Assets with a net book value of $40,000 were sold during the year, and assets were purchased for $50,000.

d) Assets were purchased for $30,000 during the year; no assets were sold.

**LO 8** 9. On January 1, 2001, the balance in accumulated deprecation was $70,000. During the year, an asset with a historic cost of $20,000 was sold for $10,000 at a gain of $6,000. Depreciation expense on the remaining assets was charged on December 31 at $33,000. The balance on the accumulated depreciation account on December 31 was:

a) $103,000.

b) $ 87,000.

c) $ 83,000.

d) $ 93,000.

**LO 5** 10. A Company uses straight-line depreciation for its buildings, assuming a thirty-year life and zero residual value. The CEO points out that the buildings last much longer than 30 years, often 60 years, and asks what impact depreciating buildings over 60 years rather than 30 years would have on earnings per share. You reply that:

a) earnings per share will increase.

b) earnings per share will decrease.

c) there will be no effect on earnings per share..

**LO 9** 11. Which of the following is not an intangible asset?
  a) Patents
  b) Improvements to a building the company already owns
  c) Trademarks
  d) Goodwill arising as a result of an acquisition

**LO 8** 12. A machine was bought for $120,000 and was depreciated using the straight-line method. It was expected to have a ten-year life and $20,000 residual value. After six years, the machine is made obsolete by a new technological development, and the company decides to keep the machine for two more years and then sell it for scrap for $2,000. At the end of two years, the company carries out its plan and sells the machine for $2,000. The accounting treatment of this situation is:
  a) No change in depreciation expense for Years 1 through 6. Depreciation expense for Years 7 and 8 is $10,000 per year, and in addition, the company recognizes a loss on sale in Year 8 of $38,000.
  b) No change in depreciation expense for Years 1 through 6. Depreciation expense for Years 7 and 8 is $10,000 per year, and in addition, the company recognizes a loss on sale in Year 8 of $18,000.
  c) No change in depreciation expense for Years 1 through 6. Depreciation expense for Years 7 and 8 is $29,000 per year, and no additional loss on sale will be recognized in Year 8.
  d) The company restates its income for Years 1 through 6 to change the depreciation expense on the machine to $11,800 each year. Depreciation expense for Years 7 and 8 is also $11,800 per year, and no additional loss on sale will be recognized in Year 8.

**LO 5** 13. A company uses the double declining-balance method of depreciation. It purchases an asset for $40,000, which is expected to have a ten-year life and $4,000 residual value. Which of the following statements is true?
  a) The depreciation rate to be applied each year is 10%.
  b) The depreciation charge in the last year is calculated to bring the net book value to $4,000.
  c) By the end of three years, 60% of the original cost has been written off.
  d) Depreciation in the first year is 20% of $36,000.

**LO 9** 14. Which of the following statements is true?
  a) Goodwill, both as a result of an acquisition and internally generated, is the only intangible asset to appear on the balance sheet.
  b) The interest expense incurred when money is borrowed to buy an asset may be capitalized as part of the asset's cost.
  c) Accelerated methods are most appropriate when an asset's usefulness declines most in the later years of its life.
  d) If an expenditure increases an asset's productivity or life, its cost may be added to the cost of the asset and depreciated.

**LO 10** 15. Which of the following sets of ratios can be used to gain insights into a company's management of its fixed assets?
  a) Current ratio, quick ratio
  b) Inventory turnover ratio, accounts receivable turnover
  c) Debt to equity ratio, times interest earned
  d) Average age, asset turnover

## Indicate whether each of the following statements is true or false:

LO 9    16. All expenditures for research and development can be capitalized under U.S. GAAP.

LO 6    17. Long-lived assets can be revalued to market value during their life.

LO 5    18. An accelerated depreciation method results in increased cash flow to the company because of the tax shield provided by the method.

LO 5    19. The cost of land must be amortized over a period not exceeding forty years.

LO 1    20. Car manufacturers typically have a higher ratio of long-lived assets to total assets than advertising agencies.

LO 7    21. When a piece of machinery is bought, the cost of installing it in the factory must be expensed and cannot be added to the cost that is capitalized and depreciated.

LO 5    22. Accelerated methods of depreciation are most appropriate when the market value of the asset decreases most in the early years of the asset's life.

LO 5    23. Depreciation expense recognition results in a decreased profit margin.

LO 9    24. Not all intangible assets that have value to the company appear on the balance sheet; the balance sheet shows the cost of intangibles, not their market value.

LO 7    25. The cost of replacing a vehicle's engine is never capitalized, since it represents maintenance of an existing asset.

LO 5    26. If an asset has a ten-year life, and zero residual value, and the double declining-balance method of depreciation is used, its net book value at the end of five years will be less than half of its original cost.

LO 7    27. Improvements that significantly extend the asset's life are treated separately from the asset for the purposes of charging depreciation.

LO 5    28. Irrespective of the method used, the total depreciation charged over an asset's life should equal the difference between its original cost and its estimated residual value.

LO 8    29. An asset with a net book value of $3,000 and accumulated depreciation of $4,000 is sold for $8,000 at a loss of $1,000.

LO 9    30. According to GAAP, only goodwill arising as a consequence of an acquisition can be recognized as an asset and reported on the balance sheet.

## Complete each of the following statements:

**LO 10**   31.   _____ is calculated by dividing the property, plant, and equipment cost by depreciation expense. It indicates how long the company intends to keep its assets on average.

**LO 10**   32.   _____ is calculated by dividing accumulated depreciation by depreciation expense. It indicates how long, on average, the company has owned its long-term assets.

**LO 4**   33.   When interest costs for financing the construction of an asset are capitalized, the amount of interest is based on the _____ over the construction period.

**LO 10**   34.   _____ is a measure of how many dollars of assets are necessary for every dollar of sales.

**LO 11**   35.   When the indirect method of presentation is used for the statement of cash flows, depreciation expense is presented in the _____ section and acquisitions and sales of long-term assets appear in the _____ section.

**LO 2**   36.   The _____ of a long-term asset includes all the costs necessary to acquire the asset and prepare it for its intended use.

**LO 5**   37.   _____ is the allocation of the acquisition cost of a long-term asset over its expected life.

**LO 5**   38.   The _____ method of depreciation assumes that an asset's usefulness declines steadily over time.

**LO 9**   39.   _____ is calculated by deducting the market value of the individual net assets from the purchase price of an acquired business; it must be written off over not more than forty years.

**LO 10**   40.   _____ is the process of writing off intangibles over their lives.

**LO 5**   41.   An asset is acquired for $6,000 on January 1, Year 1. It is expected to have a five-year life and residual value of $1,000. The depreciation expense in Year 4 is _____ if the company uses straight-line depreciation.

**LO 5**   42.   An asset is acquired for $6,000 on January 1, Year 1. It is expected to have a five-year life and residual value of $1,000. The depreciation expense in Year 1 is _____ if the company uses the double declining-balance method of depreciation.

**LO 5** 43. An asset is acquired for $6,000 on January 1, Year 1. It is expected to have a five-year life and residual value of $1,000. The net book value of the asset at the beginning of Year 3 is _____ if the company uses the double declining-balance method of depreciation.

**LO 5,8** 44. An asset is acquired for $6,000 on January 1, Year 1. It is expected to have a five-year life and residual value of $1,000. The asset is fully depreciated to its expected residual value, and is sold at the end of Year 5 for _____ at a loss of $750.

**LO 5,8** 45. An asset is acquired for $6,000 on January 1, Year 1. It is expected to have a five-year life and residual value of $1,000. After two years, the asset is sold for $3,000, and the company uses the double declining-balance method of depreciation. The company makes a _____ of _____ on the sale of the asset.

## Answer each of the following problems:

**LO 5,6** 46. Company A is preparing its financial statements for the year ended December 31, 2000. The following information is available about Company A's long-term assets:

| Asset | Purchase date | Purchase price | Estimated life at date of purchase | Depreciation basis | Residual value | Improvements or Changes in estimate |
|-------|---------------|----------------|-------------------------------------|--------------------|-----------------|--------------------------------------|
| A | 7/1/98 | $130,000 | 6 years | Straight-line | $10,000 | |
| B | 1/1/99 | 60,000 | 3 years | Straight-line | 0 | On 1/1/00 expenditure of $30,000 was undertaken that increased the asset's life by 3 years |
| C | 1/1/99 | 150,000 | 10 years | Double declining-balance | 0 | |
| D | 1/1/99 | 150,000 | 5 years | Double declining-balance | 0 | |

In addition, on January 1, 2000, Company B was acquired for a total purchase price of $200,000. The net market value of Company B's individual assets was $120,000 at the time of the acquisition. Company A writes off goodwill over 40 years.

**Required**

1. Complete the following table:

| Asset | Acquisition cost on 12/31/00 | Depreciation or amortization expense for 2000 | Accumulated depreciation on 12/31/00 | Net book value on 12/31/00 |
|-------|------------------------------|-----------------------------------------------|--------------------------------------|----------------------------|
| A | | | | |
| B | | | | |
| C | | | | |
| D | | | | |
| E | | | | |
| Goodwill | | | | |

2. Asset A was sold for $50,000 on January 1, 2001. Calculate the gain or loss on sale, and give the journal entry to record the sale.

**LO 5** 47. Jerry Corporation purchased a molding machine for $100,000 on January 1, 2001. The company uses straight-line depreciation for financial reporting and an accelerated method for tax purposes. The machine has a four-year life and zero residual value. The accelerated method results in 50%, 30%, 15%, and 5% respectively being written off over Years 1 through 4. The tax rate is 40%.

**Required**

1. Complete the following table:

| Year | 1 | 2 | 3 | 4 | Total |
|------|---|---|---|---|-------|
| Book depreciation | | | | | |
| Tax depreciation | | | | | |
| Difference | | | | | |
| Increase (decrease) in tax paid under accelerated method | | | | | |

2. Explain why many companies choose accelerated methods of depreciation for tax purposes although the net effect over the life of the vehicle is zero.

## Critical Thinking Problem

**LO 11**  48.    The statement of cash flows for the Disney Company is provided below:

## CONSOLIDATED STATEMENT OF CASH FLO WS
(In millions)

| Year ended September 30 | 1999 | 1998 | 1997 |
|---|---|---|---|
| **Operating Activities:** | | | |
| Net Income | $1,300 | $1,850 | $1,966 |
| **Items not requiring cash outlays:** | | | |
| Amortization of film and television costs | 2,472 | 2,514 | 1,995 |
| Depreciation | 851 | 809 | 738 |
| Amortization of intangibles assets | 456 | 431 | 439 |
| Gain on sale of Starwave | (345) | | |
| Equity in Infoseek loss | 322 | | |
| Gain on sale of KCAL | | | (135) |
| Other | 80 | 31 | (15) |
| Changes in current assets and current liabilities | 452 | (520) | 111 |
| | 5,588 | 5,115 | 5,099 |
| **Investing Activities:** | | | |
| Film and television costs | (3,020) | (3,335) | (3,089) |
| Investments in theme parks, resorts and other property | (2,134) | (2,314) | (1,922) |
| Acquisitions (net of cash acquired) | (319) | (213) | (180) |
| Purchases of investments | (39) | (13) | (56) |
| Proceeds from sales of investments | 202 | 238 | 31 |
| Investment in and loan to E! Entertainment | | (28) | (321) |
| Proceeds from disposal of publishing operations | | | 1,214 |
| Proceeds from disposal of KCAL | | | 387 |
| | (5,310) | (5,665) | (3,936) |
| **Financing Activities:** | | | |
| Change in commercial paper borrowings | (451) | 308 | (2,088) |
| Other borrowings | 2,306 | 1,522 | 2,437 |
| Reduction of borrowings | (2,031) | (1,212) | (1,990) |
| Repurchases of common stock | (19) | (30) | (633) |
| Exercise of stock options and other | 204 | 184 | 180 |
| Dividends | | (412) | (342) |
| Proceeds from formation of REITs | | | 1,312 |
| | 9 | 360 | (1,124) |
| Increase (Decrease) in Cash and Cash equivalents | 287 | (190) | 39 |
| Cash and Cash Equivalents, Beginning of Year | 127 | 317 | 278 |
| Cash and Cash Equivalents, End of Year | $414 | $127 | $317 |

## Required
1.  How  much cash was used in the making of films in 1999, 1998, and 1997? How  much cash was invested in theme parks in those three years? Did Disney make any other major investments during those years?

2.  Disney received cash (proceeds) from the disposal of KCAL in 1997. Can you tell whether they made a gain or a loss from this transaction?

3.  Very little of the cash generated from operating activities is left over at year-end. For example, in 1999, $5.588 billion was generated from operations with only $414 million being on hand at year-end. What is Disney's management doing with all the cash generated from operating activities?

## Solutions

### Multiple Choice

| | | | | |
|---|---|---|---|---|
| 1. | a | | 9. | b |
| 2. | d | | 10. | a |
| 3. | d | | 11. | b |
| 4. | d | | 12. | c |
| 5. | d | | 13. | b |
| 6. | a | | 14. | d |
| 7. | d | | 15. | d |
| 8. | c | | | |

### True/False

**COMMENT/EXPLANATION**

| | | |
|---|---|---|
| 16. | False | Under U.S. GAAP, research and development expenditures are expensed when incurred. |
| 17. | False | Under U.S. GAAP, long-lived assets remain at historic cost. |
| 18. | True | |
| 19. | False | Land is not amortized over its life. |
| 20. | True | |
| 21. | False | Costs of installation may be capitalized. |
| 22. | False | Depreciation is a method of cost allocation, not of valuation. |
| 23. | True | |
| 24. | True | |
| 25. | False | Replacement of an engine could extend the vehicle's life and may therefore be regarded as capital expenditure. |
| 26. | True | |
| 27. | True | |
| 28. | True | |
| 29. | False | The asset is sold at a gain of $5,000. |
| 30. | True | |

## Fill in the Blanks

31. average life
32. average age
33. average accumulated expenditures
34. asset turnover
35. operating, investing
36. acquisition cost
37. depreciation
38. straight-line

39. goodwill
40. amortization
41. $1,000
42. $2,400
43. $1,296
44. $250
45. gain, $840

## Problem 46

1.

| Asset | Acquisition cost on 12/31/00 | Depreciation or amortization expense for 2000 | Accumulated depreciation on 12/31/00 | Net book value on 12/31/00 |
|-------|------------------------------|-----------------------------------------------|--------------------------------------|----------------------------|
| A | 130,000 | 20,000 | 50,000 | 80,000 |
| B | 90,000 | 14,000* | 34,000 | 56,000 |
| C | 150,000 | 24,000 (20% x 120,000) | 54,000 | 96,000 |
| D | 150,000 | 36,000 (40% x 90,000) | 96,000 | 54,000 |
| Goodwill | 80,000 | 2,000 | 2,000 | 78,000 |

\* Depreciation for 2000 is calculated as follows:

| | |
|---|---|
| Original cost | $60,000 |
| Depreciation in 1999 | 20,000 |
| Net book value 1/1/00 | 40,000 |
| Improvement | 30,000 |
| Total | 70,000 |
| Number of years of life | 5 years |
| Depreciation per year | $14,000 |

2. Loss on sale  =  $50,000 - $80,000  =  $30,000

| | Debit | Credit |
|---|-------|--------|
| Cash | 50,000 | |
| Accumulated depreciation | 50,000 | |
| Loss on sale | 30,000 | |
| Asset A | | 130,000 |

## Problem 47

1.

| Year | 1 | 2 | 3 | 4 | Total |
|------|-----|-----|-----|-----|-------|
| Book depreciation | 25,000 | 25,000 | 25,000 | 25,000 | 100,000 |
| Tax depreciation | 50,000 | 30,000 | 15,000 | 5,000 | 100,000 |
| Difference | 25,000 | 5,000 | (10,000) | (20,000) | 0 |
| Increase (decrease) in tax paid under accelerated method | (10,000) | (2,000) | 4,000 | 8,000 | 0 |

2. Many companies choose accelerated methods of depreciation for tax purposes even though the net effect over the life of the vehicle is zero because money has a time value. The company can use cash to provide a return, for example by investing in CDs, until it is needed.

## Critical Thinking Problem 48

1. The amounts invested are as indicated below:

|  | 1999 | 1998 | 1997 |
|---|------|------|------|
| Film and television costs | $ 3,020 | $ 3,335 | $3,089 |
| Investments in theme parks, resorts, and other property | 2,134 | 2,314 | 1,922 |

It is clear that Disney's biggest investment continues to be in the making of films, television programs, theme parks, and resorts. This is probably understandable since most of its other businesses, to a large extent, derive from their films. There were no other major purchases.

2. Yes, the operating section reflects a gain of $135 million from the sale of KCAL in 1997. This gain should also be reflected on Disney's income statement and the footnote should include a description of the transaction.

3. There are three major outflows of cash, film and television costs, theme parks and resort, and the repayment of borrowings. The repayment of borrowings is essentially offset with amounts borrowed during each year, with the net change in financing activities being relatively insignificant. It is clear however, that management is taking the roughly $5 billion cash generated by operations and reinvesting it in film, television, theme parks, and resorts. This is why the cash flow statement is so important. It tells you exactly where management is focusing their attention. Businesses do not run without cash. The question is: what is management doing with the cash they have?

# Chapter 9

# Current Liabilities, Contingent Liabilities, and the Time Value of Money

Liabilities are the debts and obligations of an enterprise. This chapter begins a detailed examination of liabilities and how they are identified, measured, and recorded. Your overall objective for this chapter is to understand the nature of current liabilities and the measurement issues associated with them.

## Learning Objectives

**LO 1**   Identify the components of the current liability category of the balance sheet.

**LO 2**   Examine how accruals affect the current liability category.

**LO 3**   Understand how changes in current liabilities affect the statement of cash flows.

**LO 4**   Determine when contingent liabilities should be presented on the balance sheet or disclosed in footnotes and how to calculate their amounts.

**LO 5**   Explain the difference between simple and compound interest.

**LO 6**   Calculate amounts using the future value and present value concepts.

**LO 7**   Apply the compound interest concepts to some common accounting situations.

**LO 8**   Understand the deductions and expenses for payroll accounting.

**LO 9**   Determine when compensated absences must be accrued as a liability.

## Key Textbook Exhibits

**Exhibit 9-1** illustrates the way that McDonald's presents its current liability section of the balance sheet. You should note the types of accounts presented as current liabilities. *Self-Test:* Should current liability accounts be presented in any specific order on the balance sheet?

**Exhibit 9-2** presents the current and quick ratios for the companies that are used as examples in the chapter. *Self-Test:* Why are these ratios important to investors, creditors, and other financial statement users?

**Exhibit 9-3** illustrates the placement of current liabilities on the statement of cash flows (using the indirect method) and their effect. *Self-Test:* Would there ever be a situation where "notes payable" would be presented in the operating activities section of the statement of cash flows?

**Exhibit 9-8** indicates some of the personal and accounting decisions affected by the time value of money concept. *Self-Test:* You will notice the accounts shown at the bottom of Exhibit 9-8 are of a long-term nature. Do we consider the time value of money when accounting for current assets and liabilities?

**Table 9-1** gives **future value factors** for different interest rates and periods. Note how the factors increase with both the interest rate and the number of periods. This is consistent with the idea that the longer you leave money invested, and the higher the interest rate, the more money you will have at the end.

**Table 9-2** gives **present value factors** for different interest rates and periods. Note that the higher the interest rate and number of periods, the lower the present value factor. Intuitively, the longer you have to wait for a payment, and the higher the interest you can earn, the less value the payment will have to you now.

## Review of Key Concepts

**LO 1** **Current liabilities** is one of the two categories of liabilities (current and long-term) presented in the balance sheet. Current liabilities are usually identified as those obligations that the firm must satisfy within one year or the normal operating cycle, which ever is longer. A liability that is expected to be paid more than a year from the balance sheet date is normally classified as a **long-term liability.**

**LO 1** Current liabilities on the balance sheet are usually shown in the order they have to be paid, starting with the liability that is expected to be paid first and ending with the liability that is expected to be paid last. They are also shown at face value, ignoring the time value of money.

**LO 1** Users of the company's financial statements, particularly potential suppliers and creditors, are concerned about the amount and nature of current liabilities. Current liabilities provide an invaluable insight into the short-term obligations of the company. The ability to meet these obligations is indicated by the relationship between current assets and current liabilities. A useful summary measure of the ability to meet short-term obligations through normal operations is the **current ratio**. Some users prefer to use the **quick ratio** as a measure of liquidity, since it represents the ability to immediately satisfy current liabilities.

| | | |
|---|---|---|
| Current ratio | = | $\dfrac{\text{Current Assets}}{\text{Current Liabilities}}$ |
| Quick ratio | = | $\dfrac{\text{Current Assets - Inventory}}{\text{Current Liabilities}}$ |

**LO 1** Some of most common current liability accounts appearing on the balance sheet are **accounts payable, notes payable, current maturities of long-term debt, taxes payable,** and **other accrued liabilities**.

**Accounts payable** arise when inventory, goods, or services are bought on credit as part of the normal operations of the business. The amount recorded is normally the gross amount of the invoice, ignoring any prompt payment discount. Invoice terms can be stated as 3/15, net 30. In other words, a 3% discount is available if payment occurs within 15 days; otherwise the full amount must be paid within 30 days. Generally, it is to the company's benefit to take advantage of discounts when they are available.

**Notes payable** are formal contracts requiring the company to pay both a sum of money, and interest on that money by a specified time in the future. They often arise from acquiring a cash loan from a bank or creditor, and can also arise through dealings with a supplier. Notes that are payable within a year of the balance sheet date are classified as current liabilities. The note can be accounted for in two ways depending on whether interest is paid on the note's due date, or in advance of that date. To illustrate, assume that Zeta Corporation receives a six-month loan from its bank on January 1, Year 1. The face amount of the loan is $5,000 that must be repaid on July 1, Year 1. Interest on the note is 10% per annum.

First, assume that interest is paid on the note's due date. The journal entry recording the issue of the note is:

|  | Debit | Credit |
|---|---|---|
| Cash | 5,000 | |
| Notes payable | | 5,000 |

The journal entry recording the repayment of the note with interest is:

|  | Debit | Credit |
|---|---|---|
| Notes payable | 5,000 | |
| Interest expense | 250 | |
| Cash | | 5,250 |

Now assume that interest on the note is deducted in advance, and the cash received from the bank on January 1, Year 1, is $4,750, which equals the face value of the note of $5,000, minus the interest on the note of $250. The journal entry on January 1, Year 1 is:

|  | Debit | Credit |
|---|---|---|
| Cash | 4,750 | |
| Discount on note payable | 250 | |
| Notes payable | | 5,000 |

When the note is repaid on July 1, two adjustments must be made. First, the repayment of the note must be recorded:

|  | Debit | Credit |
|---|---|---|
| Notes payable | 5,000 | |
| Cash | | 5,000 |

In addition, the discount on the note is transferred to interest expense over the life of the note. The journal entry is:

|  | Debit | Credit |
|---|---|---|
| Interest expense | 250 | |
| Discount on notes payable | | 250 |

The Discount on Notes Payable is a contra liability that represents interest deducted from a loan in advance and should be treated as a reduction of Notes Payable in the long-term liabilities section of the balance sheet.

## Sixty Second Quiz!

**Question:** Which type of note has the higher effective interest rate and why?

**Answer:** When the interest is paid at the end of the loan period, the borrower has the use of the total amount borrowed throughout the period of the loan ($5,000 in the case of Zeta). When the interest is paid at the beginning of the loan period, the borrower only has the use of the loan amount minus interest for the period of the loan ($4,750 for Zeta). The interest rate, effectively paid, is therefore higher in the second case than the first.

**Current Maturities of Long-Term Debt** represent the portion of a long-term liability that will be paid within one year. For example, if a company obtained a $100,000 loan this year with $20,000 due each year for the next five years, the liability section of the balance sheet would be presented as follows:

**Current liabilities:**
Current maturities of long-term debt          20,000

**Long-term debt:**
Notes payable          80,000

The Current Maturities of Long-Term Debt account should include only the amount of principal to be paid. Interest due on the loan should be accounted for separately in the Interest Payable account

**LO 2**    **Taxes payable** represent obligations of the company to pay taxes of various types. There is often a delay between realizing the earnings on which the tax is to be paid and actually paying the cash sum due. Taxes must therefore be accrued and recorded as an expense when they are incurred, not when they are paid. In analyzing the performance of a company, the effect of tax changes should be separated from changes in operating performance.

**Other accrued liabilities** includes any other amount that has been incurred due to the passage of time, but has not been paid as of the balance sheet date. Examples include: Salaries, Wages Payable, and Interest Payable.

**LO 3**    The change in the balance of each current liability is reflected in the statement of cash flows, usually in the operating activities category. If a current liability has decreased, then cash has been used to pay the liability and should appear as a deduction on the cash flow statement. If a current liability has increased, then an expense has been recognized that has not been paid and should appear as an addition on the cash flow statement. Where a current liability is not part of the normal operations of the company (i.e. notes payable), then the change in that item will be found in the financing category of the cash flow statement.

**LO 4**    **Contingent liabilities** are liabilities that are not certain to be realized. Examples include potential damages under lawsuits and obligations under warranties and guarantees. The accounting treatment of contingent liabilities depends on the accountant's judgment as to the likelihood of the potential liability. If the liability is judged to be probable, and if the amount can be reasonably estimated, then the liability should be accrued and presented on the balance sheet. If the liability is judged not to be probable, but reasonably possible, then the liability should be disclosed in the footnotes to the financial statements but not reported in the balance sheet. Unlike contingent liabilities, **contingent assets** are not recorded until the gain actually occurs. This is consistent with the doctrine of conservatism.

**LO 5** Money has a time value. In other words, people prefer a payment at the present time rather than in the future because an amount received can be invested to earn interest. The time value of money affects many personal and accounting decisions (see Exhibit 9-8).

Interest payments can be calculated in one of two ways:

- In a **simple interest** calculation, interest is earned only on the principal or capital sum.

- In a **compound interest** calculation, interest is earned both on the principal and on any interest previously earned. With compound interest, the more frequently interest is calculated, the higher the effective interest rate. In calculating future and present values, we assume compound interest.

## Sixty Second Quiz!

**Question**: Suppose you are offered two loans: you pay simple interest on one and compound interest on the other. The capital sum, interest rate, and length of the loan are equal under both loans. Which loan would you prefer?

**Answer**: You would prefer the simple interest loan, since the amount of interest paid under compounding is substantially higher because you pay interest on both the principal and on any interest earned.

**LO 6** The **future value** of a sum of money refers to how much the sum will amount to in the future, if we can invest at a specified rate of interest. In calculating future value, we need to specify

1. the sum invested (p)
2. the interest rate (i)
3. the number of periods compounding (n)

The formula to calculate future value is:

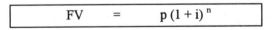

$$FV = p(1+i)^n$$

To illustrate, suppose that you invest \$5,000 in a savings account that pays 4% annually. The total amount you will have in your account at the end of five years is

$$FV = 5,000(1+0.04)^5$$
$$= \$6,083$$

**LO 6** In the same way that we can calculate the future value, we can calculate the **present value** of a sum of money at a specified time in the future. The present value of a sum of money is how much we need to invest now to have that sum in the future. Again, we need to specify three things:

1. the amount in the future (payment)
2. the interest rate (i)
3. the number of periods (n)

The formula to calculate present value is:

$$PV = payment(1+i)^{-n}$$

To illustrate, suppose that you wish to have $10,000 savings in ten years time in an account that pays 8% interest each year. How much do you have to put in the account now to have $10,000 in ten years?

$$PV = 10,000 (1 + 0.08)^{-10}$$
$$= \$4,632$$

**LO 6,7** An **annuity** is a series of equal payments made at equal intervals. Since many business contracts involve this type of payment scheme, shortcuts in handling future and present values of annuities have been derived. In calculating future and present values of annuities, it is possible, but time-consuming and tedious, to calculate individually the future or present value of each payment. To shorten this process, tables have been developed that give future value and present value factors for annuities of different lengths and at different interest rates. Tables 9-3 and 9-4 give future value and present value annuity factors. Annuities are particularly helpful when using compound interest concepts to solve for other unknowns, such as the effective interest rate on a series of payments.

## Sixty Second Quiz!

**Question:** Suppose you wish to invest $1,000 four times a year for three years in a savings scheme, with the first payment being made in three months' time. The interest rate is 8% compounded four times a year. Which factor should you use in calculating the future value of this set of payments?

**Answer:** The number of periods is 12, four times per year for three years. The interest rate per quarter year is 8% / 4 = 2%, and the relevant factor from Table 9-3 is therefore 13.412. The future value of this series of payments is therefore $1,000 x 13.412 or $13,412.

**LO 8,9** The appendix introduces the calculations and accounting entries necessary when payroll is recorded. When preparing the amount to be paid to each employee, the gross wages (including any overtime payment) is first calculated. Net pay is calculated from this by deducting:

1. Income tax,
2. FICA (Federal Insurance Contributions Act or, more commonly, social securities tax), and
3. Voluntary deductions (health insurance, pension contributions, union dues, etc.).

Taxes on employers must also be calculated and charged as Payroll Tax Expense, and include:

1. FICA (the employer normally has to pay an additional amount equal to that deducted from the employee) and
2. Unemployment tax.

**Compensated absences** are absences from employment for which it is expected that employees will be paid, such as vacation days and sick days. As a result of a FASB ruling, most employers are required to record a liability and an expense for vacation days when earned. Sick days however, are not recorded until employees are actually absent. Compensated absences are another example of the use of the matching principle, since they are an attempt to match costs with the revenues generated from those costs.

## Review of Key Terms

| | |
|---|---|
| **Accounts payable** | Amounts owed for the purchase of inventory, goods, or services acquired in the normal course of business. |
| **Accrued liability** | A liability that has been incurred but has not been paid by the date of the balance sheet. |
| **Annuity** | A series of equally spaced payments of equal amount. |
| **Compensated absences** | An absence from employment, such as sick days and vacation days, for which it is expected that employees will be paid. |
| **Compound interest** | Interest that is calculated on the principal plus interest already earned. |
| **Contingent asset** | A sum of money or asset that the company may receive that depends on an existing condition where the outcome of the condition is not known with certainty. |
| **Contingent liability** | A liability that involves an existing condition where the outcome of the condition is not known with certainty and is dependent on some future event. |
| **Current liability** | An amount of money owed by the enterprise that will be paid within one year, or during the next operating cycle. |
| **Current maturities of long-term debt** | The portion of long-term liability that will be paid within one year of the balance sheet date. |
| **Discount on notes payable** | A contra liability account that represents interest deducted in advance on a loan or a note. |
| **Estimated liability** | A contingent liability that is accrued and recorded on the balance sheet. |
| **Future value of a single amount** | The amount that will be accumulated in the future from a single sum that is invested now and that accrues interest until the future time. |
| **Future value of an annuity** | The amount that will be accumulated in the future when a series of payments is invested and accrues interest until that time. |
| **Gross wages** | The amount of an employee's wages before deductions. |
| **Net pay** | The amount of an employee's paycheck after deductions. |
| **Notes payable** | Amounts owed that are represented by a formal contractual agreement and usually involve the payment of interest. |
| **Present value of a single amount** | The amount of money now that is equivalent to the single sum to be received in the future. |
| **Present value of an annuity** | The amount needed now to be equivalent to a series of equally spaced payments in the future. |
| **Simple interest** | Interest that is calculated on the principal amount only. |
| **Time value of money** | The concept that indicates that people prefer a sum of money paid immediately to the same sum paid in the future. |

# Practice Test
# Questions and Problems

## Circle the alternative that best answers the question:

**LO 1**  1.  For users of financial statements, the current liability classification in the balance sheet is important because it is closely tied to the concept of:
a)  materiality.
b)  liquidity.
c)  profitability.
d)  leverage.

**LO 1**  2.  Alpha Company has current assets of $100,000 and current liabilities of $40,000. How much inventory could it purchase on account and achieve its minimum desired current ratio of 2:1?
a)  $10,000
b)  $20,000
c)  $40,000
d)  It cannot purchase any inventory on account and achieve its minimum desired current ratio.

**LO 1**  3.  Beta Company has current assets of $80,000 and current liabilities of $60,000. How much of its short-term notes payable could it pay in cash and achieve its minimum desired current ratio of 2:1?
a)  $10,000
b)  $20,000
c)  $40,000
d)  It cannot repay any of its short-term notes payable and achieve its minimum desired current ratio.

**LO 1**  4.  In the liabilities section of the balance sheet:
a)  only current liabilities are adjusted for the time value of money.
b)  only long-term liabilities are adjusted for the time value of money.
c)  both current liabilities and long-term liabilities are stated at their face value.
d)  both current liabilities and long-term liabilities are stated at their present value.

**LO 2**  5.  An invoice received from a supplier for $5,000 on January 1, with terms 3/15, net 30 means that the company should pay:
a)  $5,000 between January 4 and January 16.
b)  $4,850 before the end of January.
c)  $4,250 before January 4.
d)  either $4,850 before January 16 or $5,000 before the end of the month.

LO 3  6. In the statement of cash flows, an increase in short-term notes payable would be shown as:
a) an increase in cash in the operating activities category.
b) a decrease in cash in the operating activities category.
c) an increase in cash in the financing category.
d) a decrease in cash in the financing category.
e) an increase in cash in the investing category.
f) a decrease in cash in the investing category.

LO 3  7. In the statement of cash flows, a decrease in accounts payable would be shown as:
a) an increase in cash in the operating activities category.
b) a decrease in cash in the operating activities category.
c) an increase in cash in the financing category.
d) a decrease in cash in the financing category.
e) an increase in cash in the investing category.
f) a decrease in cash in the investing category.

LO 4  8. Omega Company is involved in two unrelated lawsuits, one as the plaintiff and one as the defendant. As a result of these two lawsuits, the company has therefore both a contingent asset and a contingent liability. How should Omega record these on its balance sheet?
a) Omega should record both the contingent liability and the contingent asset separately on the balance sheet.
b) Omega should record both the contingent liability and the contingent asset on the balance sheet by offsetting the liability against the asset.
c) Omega must record the contingent asset if the realization of the asset is probable and the amount can be reasonably estimated, but must not record the contingent liability on the balance sheet.
d) Omega must not record the contingent asset, but must record the contingent liability on the balance sheet, if the liability is probable and the amount can be reasonably estimated.

LO 6  9. You are due to receive a fixed $100,000 in three years from a rich uncle. If interest rates increase:
a) the present value of the $100,000 decreases.
b) the present value of the $100,000 increases.
c) the present value of the $100,000 is not affected by a change in interest rate.

LO 6  10. You are due to receive a fixed $100,000 in three years from a rich uncle. If interest rates increase:
a) the future value of the $100,000 decreases.
b) the future value of the $100,000 increases.
c) the future value of the $100,000 is not affected by a change in interest rate.

*Use the following information to answer questions 11 through 13:*
You have $1,000 to invest and have been offered the following interest rates:
Option I - Nominal rate of 10%, compounded twice a year,
Option II - Nominal rate of 12%, compounded annually, or
Option III - Nominal rate of 8%, compounded four times a year.

**LO 6** 11. You decide to choose Option I. How much will you have in your account at the end of five years?
a) $1,629
b) $12,578
c) $1,762
d) $1,611

**LO 6** 12. You decide to choose Option II. How much will you have in your account at the end of five years?
a) $6,353
b) $1,486
c) $1,791
d) $1,762

**LO 6** 13. You decide to choose Option III. How much will you have in your account at the end of five years?
a) $16,351
b) $1,486
c) $6,353
d) $1,469

**LO 6** 14. You are required to pay $5,000 for college fees for each of the next four years, and a friendly uncle has offered to give you enough money now to cover these future payments. How much must he give you now, if you can invest at 10% per year, compounded annually?
a) $40,555
b) $20,000
c) $15,850
d) $13,660

**LO 6** 15. You are required to pay $5,000 for college fees for each of the next four years, and a not-so-friendly uncle has offered to give $14,275 towards your college fees. What is the annual interest rate that you would need to earn to allow you to invest the money and meet the four payments?
a) 10%
b) 18%
c) 12%
d) 15%

## Indicate whether each of the following statements is true or false:

**LO 4** 16. If a contingent liability is both probable and measurable, it should be disclosed in the footnotes to the accounts rather than reported in the balance sheet.

**LO 6** 17. If the interest rate were zero, then the present value of an annuity would equal the sum of the individual payments.

**LO 5** 18. The effective interest on a note payable is lower if the interest is deducted in advance than if it is paid at the same time as the capital is repaid.

**LO 4** 19. A contingent asset should always be reported in the balance sheet.

**LO 6** 20. The more often interest is compounded, the lower the effective interest rate.

**LO 1** 21. The current ratio is found by dividing the company's cash by its current liabilities.

**LO 3** 22. If a company increases its current liabilities by buying a piece of machinery for a short-term note payable, its quick ratio will increase.

**LO 1** 23. An invoice with terms 3/10, net 30 means that a 3% discount can be taken up to and including thirty days after invoice date.

**LO 1** 24. The time value of money is ignored when valuing current liabilities for the balance sheet.

**LO 2** 25. Current liabilities are presented in the balance sheet according to the date the liability was incurred.

**LO 6** 26. We wish to have $110 in one year's time and can invest in an account that provides an annual interest rate of 10% compounded quarterly. We therefore need to invest a minimum of $100 now.

**LO 8** 27. The amount to be paid to each employee is found by deducting the taxes paid by the employer, such as unemployment taxes and employer's portion of FICA, from the gross wages the employee earns.

**LO 6** 28. If we invest $1,000 now in an account that pays a nominal 12% each year compounded annually, we will have the same as if we invested in an account that pays 12% each year, compounded quarterly.

**LO 5** 29. If we use simple interest, interest is earned only on the principal sum and not on interim interest earned.

**LO 9** 30. As a result of a FASB ruling, sick days to which employees are entitled must be recorded as a liability and an expense although they were not used by the employee.

## Complete each of the following statements:

**LO 1**  31.  _____ are distinguished from long-term liabilities because they are normally due to be paid within one year of the balance sheet date.

**LO 4**  32.  A liability under a warranty agreement is an example of a _____ liability.

**LO 6**  33.  The higher the interest rate, the _____ is the present value of a sum of money received in the future.

**LO 5**  34.  Interest that is calculated on both the capital sum and any previously accumulated interest is called _____ interest.

**LO 5**  35.  The idea that a sum of money received now is worth more than the same sum received in the future is called the _____ of money.

**LO 9**  36.  FASB calls absences from employment for which it is expected that employees will be paid (such as sick days and vacation days) _____.

**LO 1**  37.  Amounts owed for the purchase of goods or services during the normal operations of the business appears in the balance sheet under the heading of _____.

**LO 6**  38.  A series of equal payments at regular intervals is called an _____.

**LO 2**  39.  Obligations to pay taxes of various types appear in the balance sheet as _____.

**LO 8**  40.  To find an employee's _____, it is necessary to deduct taxes, FICA, and any voluntary deductions from his or her _____.

**LO 2**  41.  An _____ is a liability that has been incurred but has not been paid by the date of the balance sheet.

**LO 1**  42.  _____ is a contra liability account that represents interest deducted in advance on a loan or a note.

**LO 1**  43.  The portion of long-term liability that will be paid within one year of the balance sheet date is called the _____.

**LO 5**  44.  If an account pays an annual rate of 12% compounded quarterly, the interest received per quarter is _____.

**LO 5**  45.  In a _____ calculation, interest is earned only on the principal or capital sum. In a _____ calculation, interest is earned both on the principal and on any interest previously earned.

## Answer each of the following problems:

**LO 4,6** 46.     The Clydesdale Company is a retailer of domestic appliances. As a sales promotion, the company offers to buy back in ten years, at the original price, any washing machine purchased from it. Assume that you are interested in buying a washing machine that costs $300 and that the interest rate is 9%. You can obtain the same washing machine for $250 from a discount warehouse.

**Required**

1. What is the present value of the offer by Clydesdale, assuming you are certain to take up its buy-back offer in eight years?

2. How low could the probability of your taking up the offer be, before the discount warehouse price for the washing machine is competitive with Clydesdale's offer?

3. Clydesdale estimates that only 2% of people buying washing machines will take up the buy-back in eight years. If it sells 100,000 washing machines under this promotion, how should it record its liability under these buy-back agreements?

LO 1,2 47.        Show the journal entries for the following transactions for Home Buy Company:

a)   Inventory is purchased on account for $1,500 on June 10, 2000.

b)   The terms of the purchase are 2/10, net 30. The inventory is paid for on June 12, 2000.

c)   A twelve-month note is issued by Home Buy to West Fargo Bank on July 1, 2000. The face value of the note is $4,000, and interest (of 7% per annum) is payable at the time the note is issued.

d)   A six-month note payable is issued by Home Buy to a supplier for inventory on October 1, 2000. The face amount of the note is $1,000 and interest (of 10% per annum) is payable at the same time as the principal is repaid on March 31, 2001.

e)   On December 31, 2000, the interest on the $4,000 note (c above) is accrued for reporting in the balance sheet.

f)   On December 31, 2000, the interest on the $1,000 note (d above) is accrued for reporting in the balance sheet.

g)   The portion of long-term debt that becomes current on December 31, 2000, is $2,000.

h)   Home Buy estimates its liabilities under warranties for the coming year to be $7,000. No provision has yet been made for this in the balance sheet on December 31, 2000.

i) Repayment is made on the current portion of long-term debt on January 31, 2001.

j) During 2001, repair costs for Home Buy under warranties amount to $6,500, all of which were paid in cash.

**LO 2**  48. PJ Corporation manufactures and sells computer peripherals. The company recently introduced a new laser printer which sells for $1,000 and comes with a three-year parts and labor warranty. The company offers this unusually long guarantee because it expects that, due to their revolutionary design, these printers will be substantially more reliable than previous models. The company expects only 1% of the printers to be returned for repair in each year of the three-year warranty period, and that labor and parts replacement will cost an average of $20 for each machine. During 2001, the first year that the printer was sold, 500 printers were sold.

**Required**

1. Show the journal entry to record PJ Corporation's liability under the warranty agreement for the new printers at the end of 2001.

2. During 2002, the number of new printers returned for repairs were 50 and actual repair costs averaged $100 per machine. Show the journal entry to record the costs of repair under warranty, assuming all expenses were paid in cash.

3. Because of the higher than expected repair costs under warranty, the company investigated the new printers and discovered that a key microchip was subject to failure. These chips were replaced in all new printers sold during 2002, but it was not possible to retrofit the printers sold in 2001. The company estimates that an additional 100 of the printers sold during 2001 will require repairs at an average cost of $100. Show the journal entry to record the liability under the remaining warranty agreement for the first batch of 500 new printers.

## Critical Thinking Problem

**LO 1,3** 49.    The accounts payable balance for Ben & Jerry's Corporation on December 31, 2000 is $1,400,000. It is expected that half of these accounts payable will be paid within thirty days of the balance sheet date, and the remainder will be paid within sixty days of the balance sheet date. Annual short-term interest rates at the balance sheet date are approximately 12%.

**Required**

1.    What is the present value of the payments that Ben & Jerry's will make to its creditors over the next two months? You may assume that two payments are made: the first, one month from the balance sheet date, and the second, two months from the balance sheet date.

2.    Do you think that the accounts payable account should be adjusted for the difference between the present value and the actual cash payments? Why or why not?

## Solutions

### Multiple Choice

| | | | |
|---|---|---|---|
| 1. | b | 9. | a |
| 2. | b | 10. | c |
| 3. | c | 11. | a |
| 4. | b | 12. | d |
| 5. | d | 13. | b |
| 6. | c | 14. | c |
| 7. | b | 15. | d |
| 8. | d | | |

*Explanation of Question 2*

Let $x be the amount of inventory the company purchases on account. Then the current assets of $100,000 increase by the amount of the inventory to 100,000 + x, and the current liabilities of $40,000 increase by the new accounts payable to 40,000 + x.

Current ratio is current assets divided by current liabilities.

i.e. (100,000 + x) / (40,000 + x).

This ratio must be greater than or equal to two.

We solve (100,000 + x) / (40,000 + x) $\geq$ 2 for x.

Therefore, x = 20,000.

*Explanation of Question 3*

Let $x be the amount of cash the company uses to redeem notes payable. Then the current assets of $80,000 decrease by the amount of cash to 80,000 - x, and the current liabilities of $60,000 decrease by the retired notes payable to 60,000 - x.

Current ratio is current assets divided by current liabilities.

i.e. (80,000 - x) / (60,000 - x).

This ratio must be greater than or equal to two.

We solve (80,000 - x) / (60,000 - x) $\geq$ 2 for x.

Therefore x = 40,000.

## True/False

### COMMENT/EXPLANATION

16.      False      If a contingent liability is both probable and measurable, it is reported in the balance sheet.

17.      True

18.      False      If interest is deducted in advance on a note payable, less money is available during the period of the loan, and therefore the effective interest rate is higher.

19.      False      A contingent asset should not be reported on the balance sheet until it is realized.

20.      False      The more often compounding takes place, the higher the interest rate that is effectively paid or charged.

21.      False      The current ratio is the current assets divided by the current liabilities; the quick ratio is the cash or cash equivalents divided by the current liabilities.

22.      False      The transaction has no effect on cash, but increases current liabilities. The quick ratio, equal to cash divided by current liabilities, therefore decreases.

23.      False      3/10, net 30 means that a 3% discount can be taken up to 10 days from the invoice date and the net amount must be paid within 30 days of the invoice date.

24.      True      Only long-term liabilities are adjusted for the time value of money in the balance sheet.

25.      False      Current liabilities are presented in the balance sheet according to the date the liability is likely to be paid.

26.      False      Quarterly compounding would require an investment of less than $100 now.

27.      False      Employee's expenses are deducted to get net pay, not employer's.

28.      False      The more often interest is compounded in a period, the higher the effective interest rate, although the nominal rate does not change.

29.      True

30.      False      Only vacation days need be accounted for.

## Fill in the Blanks

31. current liabilities
32. contingent liability
33. lower
34. compound
35. time value
36. compensated absences
37. accounts payable
38. annuity

39. taxes payable
40. net pay, gross wages
41. accrued liability
42. discount on notes payable
43. current maturities of long-term debt
44. 3%
45. simple interest, compound interest

## Problem 46

1. 

| | |
|---|---|
| Original cost of machine | $300 |
| Present value factor (10 years, 9%) | 0.42241 |
| Present value of future payment | $126.72 |

The offer to buy-back the washing machine is worth $127 if you are certain to take up the offer. The discount warehouse offers a discount of ($300 - $250) = $50.

2. Your probability of taking up the offer could go as low as ($50/$127) = 39.37% before the discount warehouse price is competitive with Clydesdale's offer.

3. Whether Clydesdale reports the liability on the balance sheet or discloses it in the notes to the accounts depends on how much confidence it has in their estimated take up rate of 2%. Given that it is unlikely to have had experience with this type of offer, it would appear unlikely that its estimate is other than a guestimate. The argument would therefore be strong for disclosing the liability in the notes. If however, the company has some evidence for, and confidence in, the 2% estimate, it would record the liability at the present value of the likely cash flow in year eight. In this case, the liability would be long-term.

i.e. 2% of 100,000 machines at $300 times the present value interest factor for ten years at 9% (0.42241)

i.e. 2% x 100,000 x $300 x 0.42241 = $253,446.

## Problem 47

**a) 6/10/00**

| | Debit | Credit |
|---|---|---|
| Inventory | 1,500 | |
| Accounts payable | | 1,500 |

**b) 6/12/00**

| | Debit | Credit |
|---|---|---|
| Accounts payable | 1,500 | |
| Purchase discount | | 30 |
| Cash | | 1,470 |

**c) 7/1/00**

| | Debit | Credit |
|---|---|---|
| Cash | 3,720 | |
| Discount on notes payable | 280 | |
| Notes payable | | 4,000 |

**d) 10/1/00**

| | Debit | Credit |
|---|---|---|
| Inventory | 1,000 | |
| Notes payable | | 1,000 |

**e) 12/31/00**

| | Debit | Credit |
|---|---|---|
| Interest expense | 140 | |
| Discount on notes payable | | 140 |

**f) 12/31/00**

| | Debit | Credit |
|---|---|---|
| Interest expense | 25 | |
| Interest payable | | 25 |

**g) 12/31/00**

| | Debit | Credit |
|---|---|---|
| Long-term debt | 2,000 | |
| Current maturities of long-term debt | | 2,000 |

**h) 12/31/00**

| | Debit | Credit |
|---|---|---|
| Warranty expense | 7,000 | |
| Liability under warranty | | 7,000 |

**i) 1/31/01**

| | Debit | Credit |
|---|---|---|
| Current maturities of long-term debt | 2,000 | |
| Cash | | 2,000 |

**j) 12/31/01**

| | Debit | Credit |
|---|---|---|
| Liability under warranty | 6,500 | |
| Cash | | 6,500 |

## Problem 48

1. In 2001, the company estimates 1% of the 500 printers will be returned for repair at a cost of $20 each. The total contingent liability for these printers is $100. The effect of recognizing this liability is:

| | Debit | Credit |
|---|---|---|
| Warranty expense | 100 | |
| Liability under warranty | | 100 |

2. Total repair costs in 2001 were 50 x $100 or $5,000. The effect of recognizing these expenses is:

| | Debit | Credit |
|---|---|---|
| Liability under warranty | 100 | |
| Warranty expense | 4,900 | |
| Cash | | 5,000 |

3.  At the end of 2001, the company reevaluates its likely warranty expense as 100 printers at $100 per printer i.e. $10,000. The company should increase its contingent liability by this amount. The journal entry is:

|                            | Debit  | Credit |
|----------------------------|--------|--------|
| Warranty expense           | 10,000 |        |
| Liability under warranty   |        | 10,000 |

## Critical Thinking Problem 49

1.  The interest rate per month is the annual interest rate divided by 12, or 1%. The relevant present value factors are, therefore, 0.9901 for one month and 0.9803 for two months. The present value of the two payments is:
    ($700,000 x 0.9901) + ($700,000 x 0.9803) = $1,379,280

2.  The difference between the present value and the accounts payable balance is $20,720 or about 1.5%. Because this difference is not material, the accounts payable balance would not be adjusted for the time value of money.

# Chapter 10
# Long-Term Liabilities

This chapter explores the long-term liability section of the balance sheet. The first part of the chapter considers accounting for bonds, and the second part discusses other long-term liabilities such as leases, pensions, and deferred taxes. Your overall objective is to understand the financial and accounting issues associated with long-term liabilities so that you can interpret financial reports containing these items.

## Learning Objectives

| | |
|---|---|
| LO 1 | Identify the components of the long-term liability category of the balance sheet. |
| LO 2 | Define the important characteristics of bonds payable. |
| LO 3 | Determine the issue price of a bond using compound interest techniques. |
| LO 4 | Understand the effect on the balance sheet of issuance of bonds. |
| LO 5 | Find the amortization of premium or discount using effective interest amortization. |
| LO 6 | Find the gain or loss on retirement of bonds. |
| LO 7 | Determine whether a lease agreement must be reported as a liability on the balance sheet. |
| LO 8 | Explain the effects that transactions involving long-term liabilities have on the statement of cash flows. |
| LO 9 | Explain deferred taxes and calculate the deferred tax liability. |
| LO 10 | Understand the meaning of a pension obligation and the effect of pensions on the long-term liability category of the balance sheet. |

## Key Textbook Exhibits

**Exhibit 10-1** indicates that long-term debt is one portion of the long-term liability category of the balance sheet. *Self-Test:* What are some other accounts generally presented in the long-term liability section of the balance sheet?

**Exhibit 10-2** illustrates a bond certificate. *Self-Test:* What items are generally found on the face of the certificate? Which of these items are used in the accounting for the bond?

**Exhibit 10-4** illustrates the effective interest method of amortizing bond discount. Notice how the amount of cash interest and the amount of interest expense differ and how the effective interest rate is constant over the life of the bond. *Self-Test:* What's the rationale for interest expense being greater than the amount of cash paid for interest? Does the difference ever get paid to the bondholder?

**Exhibit 10-5** illustrates the effective interest method of amortizing a bond premium. Notice how the amount of cash interest and the amount of interest expense differ and how the effective interest rate is constant over the life of the bond. *Self-Test:* Why does the bond issuer have to pay interest in an amount greater than the amount recorded as interest expense on the income statement?

**Exhibit 10-7** illustrates the amortization of a lease using the effective interest method. Note how it parallels the amortization of bond discount in Exhibit 10-4. *Self-Test:* Does the lease obligation represent an actual loan made by the company?

**Exhibit 10-8** indicates the impact that long-term liabilities have on a company's cash flow and their placement on the cash flow statement. Most long-term liabilities are related to a firm's financing activities. *Self-Test:* Why is the change in the deferred tax account reflected in the Operating Activities category of the statement of cash flows?

## Review of Key Concepts

**LO 1** All obligations of the company that will not be satisfied within one year are classified as long-term liabilities. Although many different items fall into this category, we concentrate on bonds or notes, leases, deferred taxes, and pension obligations.

**LO 2,3** Bonds are securities that are traded on stock markets and that represent a liability of the company to repay long-term borrowing. Bonds must have the following items defined and specified on the bond certificate:

- **Due date or maturity date:** the point in time when the bond must be repaid.

- **Face value or par value:** the amount of money the firm must repay on the maturity date, typically $1,000.

- **Face rate or nominal rate:** the interest rate paid each interest period. The amount of interest is calculated by applying the face rate to the face value of the bond.

- **Collateral:** secured bonds have assets that can be claimed by the bondholders if the company defaults. Examples include the company's land, buildings, and inventory. Debenture bonds are not backed by collateral.

**Convertible bonds** can be converted into common stock at a future time. **Callable bonds** may be retired before their specified due date.

**LO 3** Since bonds are traded on securities markets, the price that the company can sell its bonds for will depend on the return provided by other similarly risky investments. For example, if companies with similar risk are offering bond interest of 10% (**the market rate of interest**), and Company A is selling bonds offering interest of 12%, the demand for Company A's bonds will be considerable and their price will rise relative to other bonds. Similarly, if Company B is selling bonds offering 8%, which is less than the market rate of interest of 10%, Company B's bond prices will be lower than those of other comparable bonds. Using discounted cash flow techniques, we can value the bonds and confirm these relationships. For example, suppose that the bonds of both Company A and Company B mature in three years' time. The cash flows from a $1,000 bond are:

| | Cash Flow Year 1 Interest | Cash Flow Year 2 Interest | Cash Flow Year 3 Interest | Cash Flow Year 3 Capital |
|---|---|---|---|---|
| Company A | 120 | 120 | 120 | 1,000 |
| Company B | 80 | 80 | 80 | 1,000 |

Assuming that Company A and Company B are equally risky, it is clear that Company A's bonds should have a higher value, since the cash flows are higher at each date. To find the present values of the two bonds, we must discount at the market rate of interest because we wish to compare the bonds with what the market is offering. Discounting at the market rate of interest, the present values of the bonds are:

Company A:
| | |
|---|---|
| Interest = $120 x 2.487 (factor from Table 9-4 for 3 periods, 10%) | $299 |
| Principal = $1,000 x .751 (factor from Table 9-2 for 3 periods, 10%) | 751 |
| | $1,050 |

Company B:
| | |
|---|---|
| Interest = $80 x 2.487 (factor from Table 9-4 for 3 periods, 10%) | $199 |
| Principal = $1,000 x .751 (factor from Table 9-2 for 3 periods, 10%) | 751 |
| | $950 |

Confirming our intuition, Company A could sell its $1,000 bond for $1,050, at a **premium** and Company B could sell its $1,000 bond for $950, at a **discount**.

**LO 4** When bonds are issued at face value, the accounting treatment is straightforward. The asset category (cash) and the liability category (bonds payable) of the balance sheet are both increased by the amount of cash received. When the bond is issued at a premium or a discount, the cash received is either greater or less than the amount that will be paid at the maturity of the bond. We will use the above examples of Company A and Company B to illustrate the different accounting treatments.

**Issue at a premium**

When Company A issues a $1,000 bond for $1,050, the difference between the face value (the company's liability under the bond) and the market value of the bond is called a **premium on bonds payable**. The premium on bonds payable is shown as an addition to bonds payable in the balance sheet. The effect of the issue on the financial statements is:

| | Debit | Credit |
|---|---|---|
| Cash | 1,050 | |
| Bonds payable | | 1,000 |
| Premium on bonds payable | | 50 |

**Issue at a discount**

When Company B issues a $1,000 bond for $950, the difference between the face value of the bond and the market value is called a **discount on bonds payable**. The discount on bonds payable is shown as a contra liability to bonds payable in the balance sheet.

| | Debit | Credit |
|---|---|---|
| Cash | 950 | |
| Discount on bonds payable | 50 | |
| Bonds payable | | 1,000 |

**LO 5** When bonds are issued at a discount or premium, the discount or premium account must be written off over the life of the bonds. Each year, the interest expense of the bond is increased or decreased by the amount written off the discount or premium accounts. The effective interest paid on the bond is different from the nominal interest paid. Transferring an amount from the discount or premium account to interest expense is called **amortization**. The effective interest method is commonly used to calculate the appropriate amortization of the discount or premium.

The effective interest rate of a bond is defined as the annual interest expense over the carrying value, where carrying value is the face value, plus the unamortized premium or less the unamortized discount. Since the amount owed under the bond is constant over all periods, the effective interest rate of the bond should also be constant over all periods. The effective interest rate method amortizes the discount or premium by an amount that ensures that the effective interest rate is constant.

To illustrate for Company A:

| | Cash Interest (a) | Interest Expense (b) | Premium Amortized (c) = (a) - (b) | Carrying Value (d) | Effective Interest Rate (e) = (b) / (d) |
|---|---|---|---|---|---|
| Rate | 12% | 10% | | 1,000 + 50 = 1,050 | |
| Year 1 | 120 | 10% of 1,050 = 105 | 120 - 105 = 15 | 1050 - 15 = 1,035 | 105/1,050 = 10% |
| Year 2 | 120 | 10% of 1,035 =103.50 | 120 - 103.50 = 16.5 | 1035 - 16.5 = 1,018.5 | 103.5/1,035 = 10% |
| Year 3 | 120 | 10% of 1,018.5 = 101.85 | 120 - 101.85 = 18.15 | 1018.5 - 18.15 = 1,000.35 | 101.85/1,018.5 =10% |

The effective interest rate method results in a reduction of the carrying value of the bonds to their face value while ensuring that the effective interest on the bonds is constant. Note that again we are progressively reducing the interest expense each year by a proportion of the premium that was received at the beginning.

## Sixty Second Quiz!

**Question:** Can you repeat the effective interest rate calculations for Company B? What are the interest expense and carrying values each year? What is the effect on interest expense of reducing the discount account each year?

**Answer:** Interest expense is $95 for Year 1, $96.50 for Year 2, and $98.15 for Year 3. The carrying value is $965 at the end of Year 1, $981.50 at the end of Year 2, and $999.65 at the end of Year 3. The effect of reducing the discount over the life of the bonds is to increase the interest expense each year.

**LO 6** When bonds are retired early, they are normally repaid at more than their face value. The amount repaid may be higher or lower than the carrying value. The company may therefore either sustain a loss or realize a gain on the redemption of the bonds. The gain or loss on redemption is reported in the income statement as an extraordinary item.

**LO 7** A **lease** is a contract in which the **lessee** is granted the right to use an asset in exchange for making payments to its owner, the **lessor**. In accounting for leases, the fundamental issue that must be resolved is whether the lease is a rental agreement or effectively a purchase. If the lease is simply an agreement to rent the asset, and the rights and responsibilities of ownership do not pass to the lessee, then the lease is accounted for as an **operating lease**. If the lease effectively transfers ownership rights to the lessee, then the lease is accounted for as a **capital lease**.

Under U.S. GAAP, capital leases must meet one or more of four criteria. These criteria involve: transfer of ownership at the end of the lease period, bargain purchase option, the percentage of the asset life that the lease spans, and the present value of the lease payments in relation to the market value of the asset. If a lease satisfies one of the criteria for capital leases, it is deemed, in effect, to transfer ownership rights to the lessee. The lessee records the present value of the lease payments as an asset (leased assets) and as a liability (obligations under leases) at the inception of the lease. The asset is depreciated like any other long-term asset over the life of the lease. The obligation under leases is progressively reduced over the life of the lease using the effective interest method. Note that the account balances in leased assets, and obligations under leases, are unlikely to be equal during the life of the lease, since depreciation will not match the amortization of the obligation.

The effective interest method of amortizing a lease obligation results in the lease payment being separated into two components: interest for the year, and reduction of lease obligation.

The lessee accounts for operating leases by recording the cash payment under the lease each year. No liability or asset is recorded for these leases. However, FASB requires a footnote disclosing the amount of future lease obligations under operating leases.

Three ratios are useful in assessing the company's reliance on debt finance and its ability to service that debt:

| | | |
|---|---|---|
| Debt-to-Equity Ratio | = | $\dfrac{\text{Total Liabilities}}{\text{Total Stockholders' Equity}}$ |
| Times Interest Earned | = | $\dfrac{\text{Income Before Interest and Taxes}}{\text{Interest Expense}}$ |
| Debt Service Coverage | = | $\dfrac{\text{Cash Flow from Operations Before Interest and Taxes}}{\text{Interest and Principal Payments}}$ |

**LO 8** Most changes in long-term liabilities are reflected in the financing section of the statement of cash flows. An exception involves the change in the deferred tax account which is reflected in the Operating Activities category of the statement of cash flows, as it is related to an operating item, income tax expense.

**LO 9** The calculation of net income for financial reporting often differs from the net income calculated for tax purposes. Permanent differences arise when an item is included for tax purposes but never included for book purposes, or vice versa. For example, the interest from tax-exempt bonds is included in reported income (income statement) but not in taxable income. Temporary differences occur when there is a timing difference between when an item affects book and tax income calculations. For example, the calculation of depreciation expense is often based on the straight-line method for financial reporting purposes and on an accelerated method for tax purposes. The total depreciation expense for book and tax purpose over the life of the asset is the same, but the depreciation expense for tax is greater in the early years. The deferred tax account, which often appears as a long-term liability in the balance sheet, is used to reconcile temporary differences between book accounting and tax reporting.

To illustrate accounting for deferred tax, assume that Company C buys an asset for $60,000 in Year 1 and uses straight-line depreciation with zero residual value and a four-year life. Under the Modified Accelerated Cost Recovery System allowed by the IRS, the amounts that can be written off for years 1 through 4 are 33.33%, 44.45%, 14.81%, and 7.41%, respectively. The following table illustrates the calculation of deferred taxes for this asset:

| Year | Tax Depreciation | Book Depreciation | Difference | Tax Impact @ 40% Impact on Deferred Tax Account | Deferred Tax Account Balance |
|-------|-------|-------|-------|-------|-------|
| 1 | 20,000 | 15,000 | 5,000 | 2,000 increase | 2,000 |
| 2 | 26,670 | 15,000 | 11,670 | 4,668 increase | 6,668 |
| 3 | 8,885 | 15,000 | -6,115 | -2,446 decrease | 4,222 |
| 4 | 4,445 | 15,000 | -10,555 | -4,222 decrease | 0 |
| **Total** | **60,000** | **60,000** | **0** | **0** | |

In the early years of the asset's life, the tax depreciation is greater than the book depreciation resulting in a deferred tax liability. The amount increases both the deferred tax account and the tax expense for the year. In the later years, the book depreciation is greater than the tax depreciation. The difference reduces both the balance in the deferred tax account and the tax expense in the income statement. The above table illustrates the temporary nature of this type of deferred tax, since the tax impact is zero over the life of the asset.

**LO 10** In accounting for pensions, two issues must be resolved. **Pension expense** on the income statement must reflect the **accrued pension cost** over the period, not just the cash paid to the pension fund (funding payment). The difference between the two is transferred to the accrued pension cost account.

The accrued pension cost appears either as an asset or a liability in the balance sheet and represents the accumulated difference between pension expense and total funding payments. As well as accrued pension cost shown in the balance sheet, the company must provide additional footnote information. The accumulated benefit obligation (ABO) is a measure of the obligation to employees if they were to retire at their current salary; the projected benefit obligation (PBO) calculates the pension obligation on the assumption of future salary increases. These are both compared to the value of the assets in the pension plan to indicate whether or not the plan is underfunded.

In addition to pensions, there are other postretirement benefits paid to employees. For example, many firms promise to pay a portion of retirees' health care costs. Postretirement costs must be accrued as an expense during the period that the employee helps the firm generate revenues.

## Review of Key Terms

| | |
|---|---|
| **Accrued pension cost** | An account that represents the difference between the amount of pension recorded as an expense and the amount of the funding payment made to the pension fund. |
| **Accumulated benefit obligation** | A measure of the amount owed to employees for pensions if the employees retired at their existing salary levels. |
| **Bond issue price** | The total of the present value of the cash flows produced by a bond. It is calculated as the present value of the annuity of interest payments plus the present value of the principal. |
| **Callable bonds** | Bonds that may be redeemed or retired before their specified due date. |
| **Capital lease** | A lease that meets one or more of the four FASB criteria and is recorded as an asset by the lessee. |
| **Carrying value** | The face value of a bond plus the amount of unamortized premium or minus the amount of unamortized discount. |
| **Debenture bonds** | Bonds that are backed by the general creditworthiness of the issuer and are not backed by specific collateral. |
| **Deferred tax** | The account used to reconcile the difference between the amount recorded as income tax expense and the amount that is payable as income tax. |
| **Discount** | The excess of the face value of bonds over the issue price. It occurs when the market rate on the bonds exceeds the face rate. |
| **Effective interest method of amortization** | The process of transferring a portion of premium or discount to interest expense. This method transfers an amount resulting in a constant effective interest rate. |
| **Face rate of interest** | The interest stated on the bond certificate. It is also called the nominal or coupon rate. |
| **Face value** | The principal amount of the bond as stated on the bond certificate. |
| **Funding payment** | A payment made by the employer to the pension fund or its trustee. |
| **Gain or loss on redemption** | The difference between the carrying value and the redemption price at the time bonds are redeemed. This amount is recorded as an income statement account. |
| **Long-term liability** | An obligation that will not be satisfied within one year. |
| **Market rate of interest** | The interest rate that bondholders could obtain by investing in other bonds that are similar to the issuing firm's bonds. |
| **Operating lease** | A lease that does not meet any of the four FASB criteria and is not recorded by the lessee on the balance sheet. |
| **Pension** | An obligation to pay retired employees as compensation for service performed while employed. |
| **Permanent difference** | A difference between the accounting for tax purposes and the accounting for financial reporting purposes. This type of difference occurs when an item affects one set of calculations but never affects the other set. |

| Premium | The excess of the issue price over the face value of bonds. It occurs when the face rate on the bonds exceeds the market rate. |
| --- | --- |
| Projected benefit obligation | A measure of the amount owed to employees for pensions that incorporates an estimate of the future salary increases that employees will receive. |
| Serial bonds | Bonds that do not all have the same due date. A portion of the bonds come due each time period. |
| Temporary difference | A difference between the accounting for tax purposes and the accounting for financial reporting purposes. This type of difference affects both book and tax calculations but not in the same time period. |

## Practice Test
## Questions and Problems

## Circle the alternative that best answers the question:

**LO 4**   1.   If a bond covenant specifies that the ratio of long-term debt to stockholders' equity must not exceed 0.75:1 and the ratio is currently standing at 0.70:1, which of the following actions will result in a risk that the bond covenant is violated?
a) Pay a cash dividend to stockholders
b) Issue stock for cash
c) Issue stock to employees for service rendered
d) Retire callable bonds

**LO 3**   2.   If a bond is issued at a premium, then the interest expense each year:
a) is greater than the cash payment for interest.
b) is less than the cash payment for interest.
c) equals the cash payment for interest.
d) cannot be determined without details of the bond issue.

*Use the following information to answer questions 3 through 7:*
On January 1, 2000, Omega Corporation issued a three-year, $1,000 bond with a nominal interest rate of 9%. At the time, the market rate of interest was 9%. Omega uses the effective interest rate method to account for the premium or discount on bonds.

**LO 4**   3.   The company's issue price for the bond would be:
a) $1,000.
b) $1,300.
c) $1,025.
d) $700.

**LO 4**   4.   The present value of the bond is:
a) $1,000.
b) $1,300.
c) $1,025.
d) $700.

LO 4    5.    The total interest expense recognized over the life of the bond is:
     a)    $300.
     b)    $275.
     c)    $25.
     d)    $270.

LO 4    6.    At the end of 2000, the carrying value of the bond was:
     a)    $1,000.
     b)    $1,300.
     c)    $1,025.
     d)    $700.

LO 4    7.    The effective annual interest rate on the bond is:
     a)    9%.
     b)    more than 9%.
     c)    less than 9%.

*Use the following information to answer questions 8 through 11:*

On January 1, 2001, Company T leased equipment under a five-year lease with payments of $10,000 on each December 31 of the lease period. The present value of the lease payments is $37,908, using a discount rate of 10%. Assume the equipment is depreciated straight-line over 5 years with zero salvage value.

LO 7    8.    If the lease is considered a capital lease, depreciation expense and interest expense for 2001 are:
     a)    $3,791 and $7,582.
     b)    $7,582 and $0.
     c)    $7,582 and $3,791.
     d)    $7,582 and $10,000.

LO 7    9.    If the lease is considered a capital lease, the balance sheet value of the leased asset and the lease obligation on January 1, 2001 are:
     a)    $50,000.
     b)    $0.
     c)    $37,908.
     d)    $10,000.

LO 7    10.    If the lease is considered an operating lease, which of the following expenses are recognized in the 2001 income statement?
     a)    Depreciation $7,582 and interest $3,791
     b)    Depreciation $10,000 and interest $10,000
     c)    Depreciation $10,000 and interest $0
     d)    Rental under lease $10,000

LO 7    11.    If the lease is considered an operating lease the amount shown on the December 31, 2001 balance sheet for leased assets is:
     a)    $50,000.
     b)    $40,000.
     c)    $10,000.
     d)    $0.

**LO 10** 12. The accrued pension cost is:

a) the amount of benefits payable to employees under the pension scheme if they were to retire at their current salaries.

b) the amount of benefits payable to employees under the pension scheme if it is assumed that they earn future salary increases.

c) the cash payment made each year into the pension fund.

d) the difference between pension expense and the cash payment into the pension fund.

**LO 3** 13. A company issues bonds on January 1, 2000, and they are publicly traded. Which of the following factors does not affect the market price of the bond on July 30, 2001?

a) Current market interest rate

b) Nominal interest rate of bond

c) Original issue price of bond

d) Maturity date of bond

**LO 3** 14. Bonds are issued on January 1, 2001, at an issue price of $1,232. They have a ten-year life, $1,000 face value, and a nominal interest rate of 8%. The market rate of interest at the time of the bond issue is:

a) more than 8%.

b) less than 8%.

c) 8%.

**LO 7** 15. Companies P and Q are identical in all respects except that P has long-term liabilities of $1 million, on which it pays 10% interest, and stockholders' equity of $1 million; whereas Q has no long-term liabilities and stockholders' equity of $2 million. Which of the following statements is true?

a) P's quick ratio is higher than Q's.

b) P's debt/equity ratio is higher than Q's.

c) P's debt service coverage is higher than Q's.

d) P's current ratio is higher than Q's.

## Indicate whether each of the following statements is true or false:

**LO 7** 16. A company has a debt covenant requiring that the ratio of debt to equity not exceed 0.5:1; the ratio is currently 0.4:1. The company would probably prefer to acquire property under an operating lease rather than a capital lease.

**LO 4** 17. If the market rate of interest is less than the face rate of bonds, then the bonds must be issued at a discount.

**LO 2** 18. Convertible bonds allow the company to convert the bonds into equity if it wishes.

**LO 2** 19. Serial bonds are often preferred by growing companies because the companies do not need to repay the principal all at one time but rather can spread the payment of principal over a period.

**LO 3** 20. A bond that did not pay interest, but only repaid the principal at some future date, would have a present value equal to the principal.

**LO 5** 21. The effective-interest method of bond amortization results in the effective interest rate on the bond being constant over the entire life of the bond.

**LO 6** 22. If bonds are retired early, the company must pay more than the principal and it therefore incurs a loss on redemption.

**LO 7** 23. To determine whether a lease is a capital lease, ascertain whether the lease is effectively an installment sale rather than a rental.

**LO 9** 24. A deferred tax liability arises because of both permanent and temporary differences between income reported for financial purposes and that reported for tax purposes.

**LO 10** 25. The accrued pension cost is a liability that represents the amount by which a pension fund's assets are exceeded by the potential claims on those assets.

**LO 9** 26. Alpha Corporation uses straight-line depreciation for its financial reporting and an accelerated method for its tax calculation. The balance in Alpha's deferred tax account reflects all the temporary differences between accounting methods chosen for tax and book purposes.

**LO 9** 27. Alpha Corporation uses straight-line depreciation for its financial reporting and an accelerated method for its tax calculation. The amount in Alpha's income statement for "tax expense" is the cash paid in taxes for the year.

**LO 9** 28. Alpha Corporation uses straight-line depreciation for its financial reporting and an accelerated method for its tax calculation. A credit balance on the deferred tax account indicates that Alpha has underpaid its taxes for the current year.

**LO 10** 29. The cash a company pays as a funding payment to its pension scheme is not the same as pension expense.

**LO 3** 30. The market rate of interest is the interest rate that bondholders could obtain by investing in other bonds that are similar to the issuing firm's bonds.

## Complete each of the following statements:

**LO 10** 31. The_____ benefit obligation is a measure of the amount of pension benefits payable to employees if they were to retire at their current salary levels.

**LO 10** 32. A pension plan is _____ if the plan assets exceed the obligations under the plan.

**LO 8** 33. Changes in the deferred tax account appear in the _____ section of the statement of cash flows.

**LO 2** 34. _____ are the assets that back bonds and that can be used by bondholders to satisfy interest and capital payments if the bond issue defaults.

**LO 2** 35. _____ bonds are bonds that may be retired before their due date by the issuer; _____ bonds can be retired before their due date by the bondholder.

**LO 3** 36. The _____ equals the present value of the future cash flows from the bond, discounted at the market rate of interest.

**LO 4** 37. Bonds are issued at a _____ if the issue price exceeds the face value.

**LO 5** 38. The _____ of a bond is found by deducting unamortized discount or adding unamortized premium to the face value of the bond.

**LO 5** 39. Amortizing bond discount or premium using the _____ method ensures that interest expense equals a constant percentage of carrying value over the life of the bond.

**LO 7** 40. The _____ ratio is a measure of how adequately the cash flow from operations covers interest and principal repayments on a bond.

**LO 9** 41. _____ is the difference between the accounting for tax purposes and the accounting for financial reporting purposes. This type of difference occurs when an item affects one set of calculations but never affects the other set.

**LO 9** 42. The account used to reconcile the difference between the amount recorded as income tax expense and the amount that is payable as income tax is called the _____.

**LO 6** 43. _____ is the difference between the carrying value and the redemption price at the time bonds are redeemed. This amount is recorded as an income statement account.

LO 10    44.    _____ is an account that represents the difference between the amount of pension recorded as an expense and the amount of the funding payment made to the pension fund.

LO 10    45.    _____ is a measure of the amount owed to employees for pensions that incorporates an estimate of the future salary increases that employees will receive.

## Answer each of the following problems:

LO 3    46.    On January 1, 2000, Alpha Company issued bonds with a face value of $100,000, a period to maturity of five years, and a nominal interest rate of 10% payable annually on December 31.

**Required**

1.  Without doing any calculations, indicate whether the company could issue the bonds at, above, or below face value in each of the following circumstances:

    a)  The market rate of interest is 10%.

    b)  The market rate of interest is 15%.

    c)  The market rate of interest is 6%.

2.  Support your intuition in the question above by calculating the present value of the bond for each of a), b), and c).

**LO 2,3** 47.    Beta Company issues bonds with a face value of $50,000, a three-year period to maturity, and a nominal interest rate of 10%. Interest is paid annually in arrear, and the market rate of interest at the time of the issue is 9%.

**Required**

1.  Ignoring any issue costs, calculate the proceeds of the bond issue.

2.  Show the effect of the bond issue on the accounting equation.

3.  Complete the following table using the effective interest rate method of bond amortization:

| Date | Cash Interest | Premium Amortized | Interest Expense | Unamortized Premium | Carrying Value | Interest Expense as % of Carrying Value |
|------|------|------|------|------|------|------|
| 1/1/Year 1 | | | | | | |
| 12/31/Year 1 | | | | | | |
| 12/31/Year 2 | | | | | | |
| 12/31/Year 3 | | | | | | |

LO 7,9  48    The following information has been extracted from the financial statement and notes of Computers R Us for the year ended January 30, 2001:

**Summary Balance Sheet on January 30, 2001**

| | |
|---|---|
| Current assets | $2,384,508 |
| Property and equipment | 2,803,550 |
| Other assets | 134,794 |
| Total assets | $5,322,852 |
| | |
| Current liabilities | $1,587,649 |
| Deferred income taxes | 175,430 |
| Long-term debt | 660,488 |
| Obligations under capital leases | 10,264 |
| Stockholders' equity | 2,889,021 |
| Total liabilities and stockholders' equity | $5,322,852 |

Minimum rental payments for operating leases are provided in the notes as follows:

| | |
|---|---|
| 2002 | $  160,287 |
| 2003 | 159,088 |
| 2004 | 159,233 |
| 2005 | 158,151 |
| 2006 | 157,299 |
| 2007 and later | 2,285,913 |

**Required**

1. Assuming a 10% discount rate and that all payments for 2007 and later are actually made in 2007, calculate the present value of the payments under operating leases.

2. Assume now that the operating leases were capital leases and that the present value of the leases would be included as both an asset and a liability in the balance sheet. Restate the summary balance sheet on that assumption.

3. Calculate the debt-to-equity ratio for both the original and restated summary balance sheets.

4. Use your calculations to explain why many companies prefer to record the assets that they lease from another company as operating rather than capital leases.

## Critical Thinking Problem

**LO 10** 49. The footnotes to the financial statements of Company A for the year ended December 31, 2000, provide the following information about the company's pension plan:

| | |
|---|---|
| Accumulated benefit obligation | $445 million |
| Projected benefit obligation | $560 million |
| Plan assets at fair value | $780 million |

**Required**

1. Explain the difference between accumulated benefit obligation and projected benefit obligation.

2. Does either the projected benefit obligation or the accumulated benefit obligation take into account additional obligations deriving from existing employees' projected additional years of service?

3. If you were an employee of Company A, would you feel confident that the company would be able to pay your pension when you retired?

# Solutions

## Multiple Choice

| | | | | |
|---|---|---|---|---|
| 1. | a | | 9. | c |
| 2. | b | | 10. | d |
| 3. | a | | 11. | d |
| 4. | a | | 12. | d |
| 5. | d | | 13. | c |
| 6. | a | | 14. | b |
| 7. | a | | 15. | b |
| 8. | c | | | |

## True/False

### COMMENT/EXPLANATION

| | | |
|---|---|---|
| 16. | True | |
| 17. | False | The bonds would be issued at a premium, since they are returning a higher interest rate then comparable bonds. |
| 18. | False | Convertible bonds allow the investor to convert the bonds into equity. |
| 19. | True | |
| 20. | False | The present value of a sum of money in the future is worth less than if the sum were to be received now. |
| 21. | True | |
| 22. | False | Whether a gain or loss is recognized on early redemption depends on *both* the price at which the company redeems the bonds (redemption price) and the carrying value of the bond. If the carrying value is above the redemption price, a gain will be recognized. |
| 23. | True | |
| 24. | False | Deferred tax liability results only when there are temporary differences between income reported for financial and tax purposes. |
| 25. | False | The Accrued Pension Cost appears either as an asset or a liability in the balance sheet and represents the accumulated difference between pension expense and total funding payments. |
| 26. | True | |
| 27. | False | Tax expense is the amount the company would have paid if tax accounting and book accounting were identical. |
| 28. | False | A credit balance indicates a temporary difference between tax and book accounting. |
| 29. | True | |
| 30. | True | |

## Fill in the Blanks

| | | | |
|---|---|---|---|
| 31. | accumulated | 39. | effective interest |
| 32. | overfunded | 40. | debt service coverage |
| 33. | operating | 41. | permanent difference |
| 34. | collateral | 42. | deferred tax |
| 35. | callable, redeemable | 43. | gain or loss on redemption |
| 36. | bond issue price | 44. | accrued pension cost |
| 37. | premium | 45. | projected benefit obligation |
| 38. | carrying value | | |

## Problem 46

1.

   a) at face value
   b) below face value
   c) above face value

2.

| Year | Cash Payment | Discount Factor 10% | Present Value | Discount Factor 15% | Present Value | Discount Factor 6% | Present Value |
|---|---|---|---|---|---|---|---|
| 1 | $10,000 | 0.909 | $9,090 | 0.870 | $8,700 | 0.943 | $9,430 |
| 2 | $10,000 | 0.826 | $8,260 | 0.756 | $7,560 | 0.890 | $8,900 |
| 3 | $10,000 | 0.751 | $7,510 | 0.658 | $6,580 | 0.840 | $8,400 |
| 4 | $10,000 | 0.683 | $6,830 | 0.572 | $5,720 | 0.792 | $7,920 |
| 5 | $110,000 | 0.621 | $68,310 | 0.497 | $54,670 | 0.747 | $82,170 |
| | Proceeds from issue a) | | $100,000 | b) | $83,230 | c) | $116,820 |

## Problem 47

1.

| | Interest rate | 9% | |
|---|---|---|---|
| Year | Cash Flow | Discount Factor | Present Value |
| 1 | 5,000 | 0.92 | $4,587 |
| 2 | 5,000 | 0.84 | $4,208 |
| 3 | 55,000 | 0.77 | $42,470 |
| | Issue price | | $51,266 |
| | Premium | | $1,266 |

2.

| | Debit | Credit |
|---|---|---|
| Cash | 51,266 | |
| Bonds payable | | 50,000 |
| Premium on bonds payable | | 1,266 |
| Issuance of bonds at a premium | | |

3.

| Date | Cash Interest | Premium Amortized | Interest Expense | Unamortized Premium | Carrying Value | Interest Expense as % of Carrying Value |
|---|---|---|---|---|---|---|
| 1/1/Year 1 | | | | | 51,266 | |
| 12/31/Year 1 | 5,000 | 386 | 4,614 | 880 | 50,880 | 9.00% |
| 12/31/Year 2 | 5,000 | 421 | 4,579 | 459 | 50,459 | 9.00% |
| 12/31/Year 3 | 5,000 | 459 | 4,541 | 0 | 50,000 | 9.00% |

## Problem 48

1.

| | Discount rate | 10% | |
|---|---|---|---|
| | *Lease Payments* | *Discount Factor* | *Present value* |
| 2002 | $160,287 | 0.91 | $145,715 |
| 2003 | $159,088 | 0.83 | $131,478 |
| 2004 | $159,233 | 0.75 | $119,634 |
| 2005 | $158,151 | 0.68 | $108,019 |
| 2006 | $157,299 | 0.62 | $97,670 |
| 2007 and later | $2,285,913 | 0.56 | $1,290,338 |
| | | Total | $1,892,855 |

2. and 3.

**Summary Balance Sheet on January 30, 2001**

| | Unadjusted Balances | Effect of Capitalizing leases | Adjusted Balances |
|---|---|---|---|
| Current assets | $2,384,508 | | $2,384,508 |
| Property and equipment | 2,803,550 | +$1,892,855 | 4,696,405 |
| Other assets | 134,794 | | 134,794 |
| Total assets | $5,322,852 | | $7,215,707 |
| | | | |
| Current liabilities | $1,587,649 | | $1,587,649 |
| Deferred income taxes | 175,430 | | 175,430 |
| Long term debt | 660,488 | | 660,488 |
| Obligations under capital leases | 10,264 | +$1,892,855 | 1,903,119 |
| Stockholders equity | 2,889,021 | | 2,889,021 |
| Total liabilities and stockholders' equity | $5,322,852 | | $7,215,707 |
| | | | |
| Debt-to-equity ratio | .84 | | 1.50 |

4.  It is apparent from the above table that capitalizing the leases significantly impacts the debt-to-equity ratio of Computers R Us. If you were asked to lend the company money or wanted to buy its bonds, the adjusted debt-to-equity ratio would be more relevant. Clearly, the company has long-term commitments under leases that do not appear in the balance sheet and yet are likely to impact significantly the availability of cash to pay interest and dividends. The capitalization of leases in this case provides significant insights into the company's capital structure.

## Critical Thinking Problem 49

1.  The accumulated benefit obligation (ABO) is a measure of the obligation to employees if they were to retire at their current salary; the projected benefit obligation (PBO) calculates the pension obligation on the assumption of future salary increases.

2.  Neither the ABO nor the PBO allow for possible additional years of service by existing employees and therefore neither represents a true economic measure of the pension obligation.

3.  Since the plan assets currently exceed both the ABO and the PBO, an employee could be reasonably confident about receiving his or her pension. However, the company must continue to make the necessary funding payments to the pension fund for this situation to continue.

# Chapter 11
# Stockholders' Equity

This chapter examines stock, the second main source of financing for a corporation. You have two overall aims in this chapter. First, you should understand the different components of stockholders' equity. Second, you should be able to account for stock transactions, including the issue and repurchase of stock and the various forms of dividend transactions.

## Learning Objectives

**LO 1**    Identify the components of the Stockholders' Equity category of the balance sheet and the accounts found in each component.

**LO 2**    Understand the characteristics of common and preferred stock and the differences between the classes of stock.

**LO 3**    Determine the financial statement impact when stock is issued for cash or for other consideration.

**LO 4**    Describe the financial statement impact of stock treated as treasury stock.

**LO 5**    Compute the amount of cash dividends when a firm has issued both preferred and common stock.

**LO 6**    Understand the difference between cash and stock dividends and the effect of stock dividends.

**LO 7**    Determine the difference between stock dividends and stock splits.

**LO 8**    Understand the statement of stockholders' equity and comprehensive income.

**LO 9**    Understand how investors use ratios to evaluate owners' equity.

**LO 10**    Explain the effects that transactions involving stockholders' equity have on the statement of cash flows.

**LO 11**    Describe the important differences between the sole proprietorship and partnership forms of organization versus the corporate form.

## Key Textbook Exhibit

**Exhibit 11-1** illustrates the relative advantages and disadvantages of stock versus debt financing. *Self-Test:* Which of the two forms of financing provides the higher return to investors? Which form is more advantageous to the issuing company from a tax perspective?

**Exhibit 11-6** is Hewlett-Packard's Statement of Stockholders' Equity for 1998. *Self-Test:* Did Hewlett-Packard pay out more in dividends than it earned in 1998?

**Exhibit 11-7** illustrates the relationship between the income statement and the statement of comprehensive income. *Self-Test:* Which of the additional items on the statement of comprehensive income have we discussed in this text?

## Review of Key Concepts

**LO 1** The stockholders' equity category of the balance sheet represents the stockholders' interest in the corporation. It contains two principal components: **contributed capital** and **retained earnings**. Contributed capital represents the consideration, normally cash, that the corporation has received for the issue of stock. In determining contributed capital, several key parameters must be defined.

- **Number of shares.** Three separate numbers must be identified. **Authorized shares** represent the maximum number of shares that the corporation may issue. This is determined when the company is incorporated and is usually set high enough to allow for the future growth. **Issued shares** represent the number of shares that have been sold or transferred to stockholders. **Outstanding shares** are shares that are actually in the hands of stockholders. The difference between numbers of shares issued and outstanding derives from shares that the company has itself repurchased as treasury stock.

- **Par value and additional paid-in capital.** **Par value** causes many students confusion but simply represents the arbitrary face value of the stock set by the corporation. Since corporations can face legal obstacles if they attempt to issue stock at a price below par value, the par value is usually set low. However, par value does not influence the price at which the company can sell its stock. When a company sells its stock at a price above par value, the difference between par value and issue price is called **additional paid-in capital**. This appears as a credit balance in the stockholders' equity section of the balance sheet.

As its name suggests, the **retained earnings** balance is the total earnings of the company since its inception, minus any dividends (including stock dividends) that the company has paid. Note that a large balance in the retained earnings account does not indicate that the same amount of cash is available to pay dividends.

## Sixty Second Quiz!

**Question**: Suppose Company A wishes to issue common stock. Is the amount of money that Company A can raise influenced by whether the par value per share is 10 cents or 50 cents?

**Answer**: No! The same amount of money can be raised in both cases.

**LO 2** There are two principal types of stock: **preferred stock** and **common stock.** The difference between the two types of stock typically relates to dividend payments. For preferred stock, dividends are a fixed and stated percentage of the stock's par value. In addition, dividends on preferred stock must be paid before dividends are paid on common stock. Preferred stock can be **cumulative** (any dividend unpaid in previous years must be paid before any dividend on common shares is paid), **participating** (preferred stockholders may share in further distributions after preferred and common dividend have been paid), **convertible** (can be converted to common shares by the shareholder), or **callable** (can be retired by the company after they have been issued). Since the dividend on preferred stock is more stable and predictable than that on a share of common stock, preferred stock is arguably more like a bond than common stock. For that reason, in analyzing company accounts, many analysts regard preferred stock as debt rather than equity.

**LO 3** Stock can be issued for cash, for noncash consideration, and on a subscription basis.

- When stock is issued for **cash**, it is often issued for more than its par value. For example, suppose Corporation A issues 100,000 common shares with a par value per share of 10 cents, for 25 cents each. The total cash received is $25,000, but the par value of the shares issued is $10,000. The difference between the total cash and the par value is reported in a special account called **Additional Paid-In Capital**, which appears as part of stockholders' equity.

- When **noncash consideration** is received in return for the issue of stock, the key problem is determining the value of the transaction. The general rule is that the transaction should be recorded at fair market value. Market value can be found from either the value of the consideration given (stock) or the value of the consideration received (assets). Suppose, for example, that instead of cash, Corporation A had received a manufacturing plant and machinery in exchange for its 100,000 preferred shares. The shares are not traded on the market. Although the par value of the stock will remain at $10,000, the additional paid-in capital will depend on the value of the plant and machinery. How easy it is to value the plant and machinery depends on how active the market for that type of plant and machinery is. In some cases, it will not be possible to identify a market price and some surrogate will have to be used, such as an appraisal by an independent valuer.

**LO 4** Companies repurchase their own shares for many reasons: to prevent a takeover, to increase the stock's market price, and to provide stock that can be used for employee stock bonuses. When stock is repurchased it may or may not be canceled or **retired**. Stock that is repurchased but not retired is called **treasury stock**.

Treasury stock appears as a contra in the stockholders' equity section of the balance sheet and can be recorded using either the par value method or the cost method. To illustrate the more commonly used cost method, suppose Corporation B repurchases 10,000 shares of stock for 50 cents per share on January 15, 2001. When the stock is repurchased, the journal entry recording the repurchase is:

|  | Debit | Credit |
|---|---|---|
| 1/15/01  Treasury stock | 5,000 | |
| Cash | | 5,000 |

The treasury stock balance of $5,000 appears as a contra to the stockholder's equity in the balance sheet. If the company subsequently reissues the stock, the accounting treatment depends on whether or not it is reissued at above or below the repurchase cost. If the stock is reissued above the repurchase price, the additional consideration is recorded in additional paid-in capital. If the stock is reissued at less than the repurchase price, the difference between the sales price and the repurchase price is deducted from additional paid-in capital or from retained earnings if no additional paid-in capital is available.

When treasury stock is retired, the relevant balances in both the treasury stock account and the additional paid-in capital account must be eliminated. When the total of the related par value and additional paid-in capital is less than the consideration paid for the retired stock, the difference reduces the retained earnings account. When the original issue price is higher than the repurchase price of the stock, the difference is reported in the paid-in capital from the stock retirement account.

## Sixty Second Quiz!

**Question:** Initially, Company A and Company B have the identical number of authorized, issued, and outstanding shares. Both repurchase identical numbers of their own shares. Company A retires its repurchased stock, but Company B holds the stock as treasury stock. Does the issued stock of both companies remain the same?

**Answer:** No! Company A's issued shares will be lower than Company B's.

**LO 5** When companies declare a cash dividend, a liability called **dividend payable** is created by reducing retained earnings on the day that the dividend is declared. When the dividend is actually paid, the dividend payable account is eliminated, and the cash account is reduced by the amount of the dividend.

The allocation of dividend to preferred and common stockholders depends on the terms of the preferred stock. Holders of **noncumulative preferred shares** are entitled only to the current year's preferred dividend, even if there are unpaid arrears of preferred dividend from previous years. Before any dividend is paid to the common stockholders, holders of **cumulative preferred shares** must be paid any arrears of dividend in addition to the current year's dividend. In addition to arrears and current year's dividends, holders of **cumulative and participating preferred shares** may be paid additional dividends if the dividend on the common stock reaches a stated percentage.

**LO 6** **Stock dividends** occur when companies issue additional shares of stock to existing stockholders. They provide an alternative to the traditional cash dividend. The principle advantages of stock dividends are that:

- they preserve the company's cash,
- they can reduce the stock price making the stock more accessible to a wider range of investors, and
- they can have tax benefits to recipients, since they do not represent taxable income.

Normally, stock dividends involve reducing the retained earnings account by the amount of the stock dividend. Note that stock dividends do not affect the assets, liabilities, or total amount of stockholders' equity. Rather, they simply increase the number of shares of stock. Relatively small stock dividends are recorded at the market value of the stock on the declaration day. As with cash dividends, the value of the stocks issued in excess of par increases additional paid-in capital. With larger stock dividends, the stock dividend is recorded at par value rather than at market value. When the dividend is declared, a stockholders' equity account, called common stock dividend distributable, is created. When the distribution actually takes place, that account is closed to the common stock account.

**LO 7** **Stock splits** occur when the company reduces its par value per share. Companies carry out stock splits for reasons similar to those for stock dividends. In a stock split, the stock's market price is reduced, making it more marketable. Stock splits, however, require no accounting entries, since the total par value of the shares outstanding does not change.

**LO 9** A relatively recent development in GAAP is that the FASB has allowed certain gains and losses to be recorded directly into the stockholders' equity section of the balance sheet rather than being reported in the income statement. One example is unrealized holding gains and losses on securities, which were discussed in Chapter 7. **Comprehensive income** refers to the increase in net assets resulting from all transactions during the period, except for investments by, and dividends paid to, owners.

Comprehensive income is found by adjusting net income for the items that are directly reported in stockholders' equity, such as unrealized gains or losses on securities and gains or losses on foreign currency translation.

**LO 9** In analyzing stockholders' equity in a corporation, two different measures are useful: **book value per share** and **market value per share**. Book value per share of common stock represents the rights that each share of common stock has in the net assets of the company. In this calculation, the rights of the preferred stockholders must be deducted. The market value per share is the price at which the share is currently trading on the stock exchange. Note that the book value per share is different from the market value per share. Since book value is based on the historic cost of assets, of the two measures, market value per share gives the better indication of the future financial performance of the company.

**LO 10** The cash inflow from the sale of stock and the cash outflow from stock repurchases appear in the financing section of the statement of cash flows. Similarly, since dividends represent a cost of financing the business, dividend payments also appear as a cash outflow in the financing section of the cash flow statement. Note that dividends appear on the statement of cash flows when they have been paid as opposed to when they are declared.

**LO 11** The following table summarizes the main differences between the three forms of organization:

| | Sole Proprietorship | Partnership | Corporation |
|---|---|---|---|
| Ease of transfer of ownership | Difficult: Owner must find a buyer to buy the whole business, and, when ownership is transferred, the original entity ceases to exist. | Difficult: When one partner leaves, the partnership is dissolved and a new one must be formed. | Easy: Usually shares are traded on a Stock Exchange and the sale of stock is a simple transaction. The corporation as an entity continues in existence even although its shares change hands. |
| Personal liability of owners | Owner has unlimited liability for business debts. | Partners have unlimited liability for business debts. | Stockholders' liability is limited to the value of their stock. |
| Ease of raising additional capital | Limited by resources of owner. | Limited by resources of partners. | Corporations can raise additional capital by selling more stock. This can be done without much difficulty |
| Separation of ownership and entity | Separate accounting entity. | Separate accounting entity. | Separate legal, tax, and accounting entity |

# Review of Key Terms

| | |
|---|---|
| **Additional paid-in capital** | The amount received for the issuance of stock in excess of the par value of the stock. |
| **Authorized shares** | The maximum number of shares a corporation may issue as indicated in the corporate charter. |
| **Book value per share** | Total stockholders' equity divided by the number of shares of common stock outstanding. |
| **Callable feature** | Allows the issuing firm to eliminate a class of stock by paying the stockholders a fixed amount. |
| **Comprehensive income** | The amount that reflects the total change in net assets from all sources except investments or withdrawals by the owners of the company. |
| **Convertible feature** | Allows preferred stock to be returned to the corporation in exchange for common stock. |
| **Cumulative feature** | The holders of this stock have a right to dividends in arrears before the current year's dividend is distributed. |
| **Dividend payout ratio** | The annual dividend amount divided by the annual net income. |
| **Issued shares** | The number of shares sold or distributed to stockholders. |
| **Market value per share** | The selling price of the stock as indicated by the most recent stock transactions. |
| **Outstanding shares** | The number of shares issued less the number of shares held as treasury stock. |
| **Par value** | An arbitrary amount stated on the face of the stock certificate that represents the legal capital of the firm. |
| **Participating feature** | Stock that has a provision allowing the stockholders to share in the distribution of an abnormally large dividend on a percentage basis. |
| **Partnership** | A business owned by two or more individuals and with the characteristic of unlimited liability. |
| **Partnership agreement** | A document that specifies how much each owner should invest, the salary of each owner, and how profits are to be shared. |
| **Retained earnings** | Net income that has been made by the corporation but not paid out as dividends. |
| **Retirement of stock** | When the stock of a corporation is repurchased with no intention to reissue at a later date. |
| **Sole proprietorship** | A business with a single owner. |

| Statement of stockholders' equity | A statement that reflects the differences between beginning and ending balances for all accounts in the Stockholders' Equity category. |
| Stock dividend | Declaration and issue of additional shares of its own stock by a corporation to existing stockholders. |
| Stock split | Creation of additional shares of stock with a reduction of the par value per share of the stock. |
| Treasury stock | Stock issued by the firm and then repurchased but not retired. |

## Practice Test
## Questions and Problems

### Circle the alternative that best answers the question:

*Use the following information to answer questions 1 through 4:*
Corporation A has 1 million authorized common shares of par value $0.10. It has 250,000 issued shares and 10,000 shares in treasury. Answer each question independently.

**LO 1** 1. The number of outstanding shares of Corporation A is:
a) 1 million
b) 250,000
c) 240,000
d) 990,000

**LO 6** 2. If the company declares a 20% stock dividend, the number of outstanding shares after the stock dividend is:
a) 351,000
b) 288,000
c) 12 million
d) Cannot say unless the details of the treasury stock purchase are known.

**LO 7** 3. If the company has a 3-for-1 stock split, the number of outstanding shares after the stock split is:
a) 2,970,000
b) 720,000
c) 3 million
d) 750,000

**LO 1** 4. The par value of 10 cents is which of the following?
a) The minimum price at which the stock can trade
b) The maximum dividend that can be paid on the stock
c) An arbitrary value that represents the face value of the stock
d) The maximum price at which the stock can be issued

*Use the following information to answer questions 5 through 10:*

The following appears in the stockholders' equity section of Corporation B's balance sheet at the beginning of Year 3:

Preferred Stock

10,000, 10% nonparticipating, cumulative shares

| | | |
|---|---|---|
| $10 par value shares | 100,000 | |
| Additional paid-in capital | 50,000 | |
| | | 150,000 |

Common Stock

Authorized 10 million shares, 10 cents par value

| | | |
|---|---|---|
| Issued 5 million shares | 500,000 | |
| Additional paid-in capital | 300,000 | |
| | | 800,000 |
| Retained earnings | | 250,000 |
| Total stockholders' equity before treasury stock | | 1,200,000 |
| Less treasury stock: 150,000 shares at cost | | (130,000) |
| Total stockholders' equity | | $1,070,000 |

Corporation B has paid *no* dividends for the last two years because of a temporary downturn in business. For year 3, the company has net earnings of $450,000. The company's board of directors intends to pay a total dividend to both common and preferred stock of $400,000.

 5. For year 3, dividends per share for preferred stockholders will be:
   a) $1
   b) $10
   c) $3
   d) $30

LO 5 6. For year 3, the total dividend available to common stockholders is:
   a) $400,000
   b) $450,000
   c) $420,000
   d) $370,000

LO 1 7. The common stock was initially sold for an average of:
   a) 13 cents per share
   b) 10 cents per share
   c) 16 cents per share
   d) 8 cents per share

LO 5 8. After the dividends for year 3 have been paid, the balance on the retained earnings account will be:
   a) $250,000
   b) $300,000
   c) $200,000
   d) Cannot tell from available information

LO 7 9. Company B makes a 2-for-1 stock split at the end of year 3 after the dividends have been paid. The number of common shares outstanding after the split is:
   a) 20 million
   b) 10 million
   c) 9.9 million
   d) 9.7 million

**LO 7** 10. Company B makes a 2-for-1 stock split at the end of year 3, after the dividends have been paid. The book value per common share *after* the split is:

   a) 11.5 cents

   b) 11.0 cents

   c) 9.5 cents

   d) 10 cents

**LO 4** 11. Alpha Inc. has 3,000 shares in treasury for which it paid $8,000, and which have a total par value of $3,000. The shares were originally issued for $5,000. Which of the following statements is true?

   a) The treasury stock appears on the balance sheet as marketable securities.

   b) If Alpha reissues the stock at $10,000, it must deduct $2,000 from additional paid-in capital.

   c) If Alpha retires the stock, it will reduce retained earnings by $3,000.

   d) Alpha may only reissue the stock to its employees for the payment of stock bonuses.

**LO 11** 12. Which of the following statements is true?

   a) The corporate form of enterprise provides more financial protection for its owners than either sole proprietorships or partnerships.

   b) Transfer of ownership is equally easy with sole proprietorships, partnerships, and corporations.

   c) Corporations are more restricted in their ability to raise capital than partnerships or sole proprietorships because they must sell their stock through a stock exchange.

   d) Corporations, partnerships, and sole proprietorships are all legally separate entities from their owners.

*Use the following information to answer questions 13 through 15:*

Jura Juice Company has three partners: Grumpy, Sneezy, and Happy. The partnership agreement provides for the following distribution to partners:

|  | **Grumpy** | **Sneezy** | **Happy** |
|---|---|---|---|
| Annual salary | $50,000 | $50,000 | $100,000 |
| Interest on invested capital before distribution of profits for the year. | ? | ? | ? |
| Distribution of remaining income | 25% | 25% | 50% |
| Capital balance on December 31, 2001 |  |  |  |
| - before distribution for year | $500,000 | $600,000 | $1,000,000 |
| - after distribution for year | $615,000 | $720,000 | $1,230,000 |

All partners receive the same rate of interest on their invested capital balance at the start of the year. Happy's share of remaining income was $80,000 for the year.

**LO 11** 13. Sneezy receives total interest and salary for the year to December 31, 2001, of $53,000. The interest paid on invested capital is:

   a) 10%.

   b) 5%.

   c) 7.5%.

   d) 12.5%.

LO 11  14.  The remaining income (after salaries and interest on capital) that was distributed to all three partners for 2001 was:
a) $460,000.
b) $160,000.
c) $80,000.
d) $200,000.

LO 11  15.  The total income that was distributed to partners for 2001 was:
a) $160,000.
b) $200,000.
c) $465,000.
d) $80,000.

## Indicate whether each of the following statements is true or false:

LO 1  16.  When a company has repurchased but not yet retired its own stock, the number of issued and outstanding shares will differ.

LO 1  17.  Par value is the price at which stock was originally issued.

LO 2  18.  Preferred stockholders have the right to receive their dividends before any dividend is paid on common stock.

LO 1  19.  Additional paid-in capital is the difference between par value and the stock's current market value.

LO 1  20.  As long as a company's net earnings are positive, its retained earnings balance will increase.

LO 4  21.  The difference between the authorized and issued shares is identified as treasury stock on the balance sheet.

LO 9  22.  The book value per share is the minimum price at which the company's shares should trade on the stock market.

LO 2  23.  The Acme Corporation had net earnings of $15,000 in Year 5. The company has 10,000, 10% cumulative, preferred shares with a par value of $20 per share. The dividend payable to the preferred stockholders is $15,000 for Year 5.

LO 2  24.  Cumulative preferred stock confers the right to share in earnings after a stated level of common stock dividend has been paid.

LO 10  25.  When dividends are declared, they are reported both in the Income Statement and as a cash flow in the Statement of Cash Flows.

LO 6  26.  Both stock and cash dividends reduce stockholders' equity.

LO 7  27.  Stock splits require no accounting entries, and they reduce market and par value per share.

LO 9　28. Market value per share gives a better insight into the likely future financial performance of the company than book value per share.

LO 4　29. When a company repurchases its stock, its authorized share capital is reduced.

LO 2　30. A company that has been in business for several years wishes to raise $1 million by issuing common stock. The par value of its common stock is 10 cents per share, so it will issue 10 million shares to raise the required amount.

## Complete each of the following statements:

LO 9　31. _____ represents the rights that each share of common stock has in the net assets of the company.

LO 10　32. Dividend payments appear as a cash _____ in the _____ section of the cash flow statement.

LO 7　33. In a _____, the number of shares outstanding is increased and the par value per share is decreased.

LO 7　34. In a _____, retained earnings are used to distribute additional stock to shareholders.

LO 2　35. Preferred stock that confers the right to receive arrears of dividends is called _____.

LO 3　36. In a _____, an investor agrees to buy a specified number of shares at a specified price but to pay for them at some future date.

LO 1　37. _____ represents the total number of shares the company has sold, including those it has subsequently repurchased but not retired.

LO 9　38. The _____ is the price at which the stock is currently selling.

LO 6　39. The _____ is calculated as the annual dividend divided by annual net income.

LO 4　40. _____ is stock that has been repurchased by the firm but not retired.

*Use the following information to answer questions 41 through 45:*
The following information has been extracted from the Santa Maria Corporation's financial statements for the year ended December 31, 2001.

|  | **December 31, 2001** | **December 31, 2000** |
| --- | --- | --- |
| Common stock: issued and outstanding, 10 cents par value | $ 200,000 | $ 150,000 |
| Additional paid in capital | 100,000 | 50,000 |
| Preferred stock: 5%, $10 par value | 10,000 | 10,000 |
| Retained earnings | 800,000 | 700,000 |
| Total dividend paid and payable on both common and preferred stock | 50,000 | 20,000 |

**LO 3**    41. During 2001, the company issued _____ shares of common stock, with a par value of _____, at an issue price of _____.

**LO 3**    42. Total proceeds from the issue of common stock were _____.

**LO 5**    43. The total dividend paid and payable on preferred stock during 2001 was _____.

**LO 5**    44. The total dividend paid and payable on common stock during 2001 was _____.

**LO 5**    45. Net income for 2001 was _____.

## Answer each of the following problems:

**LO 1,4**   46. The stockholders' equity section of the February 1, 2001, balance sheet of Alphanumeric Corporation appears as follows:

| | |
|---|---:|
| Additional paid-in capital - preferred | $ 45,000 |
| Non cumulative preferred stock, $10 par value, ? shares issued | 25,000 |
| Additional paid-in capital - common | 384,803 |
| Retained earnings | 2,092,329 |
| Common stock, 10 cents par value, 550,000 shares authorized, 297,940 shares issued | 29,794 |
| Treasury stock - common, 8,641 shares at cost | 127,717 |

**Required**

1. Calculate the number of shares of preferred stock issued.

2. Calculate the number of shares of common stock outstanding.

3.   Calculate the average per-share sales price of the preferred stock when issued.

4.   Calculate the average per-share sales price of the common stock when issued.

5. Calculate the cost of the treasury stock per share.

6. Prepare in good form the stockholders' equity section of Alphanumeric's balance sheet.

LO 2,4  47.  The following list of accounts appears in Omega Corporation's trial balance on August 31, 2000. All of the accounts have their normal balances. Omega is authorized to issue 2,000,000 shares of common stock and 4,000 shares of preferred stock. The preferred stock is cumulative, nonparticipating. The treasury stock represents 5,000 shares at cost.

| | |
|---|---:|
| Common stock, 50 cents par | $ 200,000 |
| Additional paid-in capital - common | 50,000 |
| Preferred stock, $5 par, 3% | 20,000 |
| Retained earnings | 430,000 |
| Treasury stock (common) | 10,000 |
| Dividends paid (for first quarter) | $15,000 |
| Dividends payable (for second quarter) | 12,000 |

Required

1. Prepare the owners' equity section of the balance sheet for Omega.

2. Explain why some of the listed accounts do not appear in the owners' equity section.

LO 3,4 48. Horatio Company, in its first year of operations, reported net earnings for the year of $420,000. It also undertook the following transactions during the year:
   a) Authorized share capital is 2 million common shares, 50 cents par value.
   b) Issued 200,000 common shares at $2 each.
   c) Issued 20,000 common shares in return for machinery and a building. The machinery has a market value of $5,000, but the value of the building is indeterminate. At the time of the stock issue, the market value of the common stock was $3.00.
   d) Declared a 3-for-1 stock split. After the split, the stock price was $4 per share.
   e) Declared and paid a dividend of $0.10 per share.

**Required**
1. Complete the following table, indicating the effect of each transaction on the accounting equation.

| | Assets | = | Liabilities | + Stockholders' Equity |
|---|---|---|---|---|
| a) | | | | |
| b) | | | | |
| c) | | | | |
| d) | | | | |
| e) | | | | |
| f) | | | | |

2. Prepare the owners' equity section of the balance sheet.

3. Calculate the dividend yield, earnings per share, and dividend payout ratio after the split has taken place.

## Critical Thinking Problem

**LO 7**    49.    Tiree Corporation declared a 10% stock dividend on January 1, Year 1. At that time, the company had issued 200,000 common shares of stock with a par value of $1 per share. Prior to the stock dividend, the market price of the company's stock was $10.

**Required**

1.    How many shares did the company issue in its stock dividend?

2.    Show the journal entry recording the stock dividend when it was declared.

3.    Assuming nothing else changed, what would the stock price be immediately after the stock dividend was paid.

4.    Mr. Mull owns 100 shares of Tiree's common stock. He is concerned that although he has more stock in the corporation after the stock dividend, each share is worth less than before the dividend and that overall he is worse off after he has received the dividend. Is he correct? Why?

5.    In the light of your answer to Mr. Mull, can you think of why Tiree would choose to make a stock dividend?

## Solutions

### Multiple Choice

| | | | | |
|---|---|---|---|---|
| 1. | c | | 9. | d |
| 2. | b | | 10. | d |
| 3. | b | | 11. | c |
| 4. | c | | 12. | a |
| 5. | c | | 13. | b |
| 6. | d | | 14. | b |
| 7. | c | | 15. | c |
| 8. | b | | | |

### True/False

**COMMENT/EXPLANATION**

16. True

17. False — Par value is the arbitrary face value of the stock.

18. True

19. False — Additional paid-in capital is the difference between par value and the stock's original issue price.

20. False — Retained earnings is increased by net income and decreased by cash dividends and net losses. Even if the company has positive net income, if dividends are greater than net income, retained earnings can decline.

21. False — Treasury stock is stock that the company has repurchased.

22. False — Since the stock market price reflects future cash flow from the stock, it may be lower than book value per share, which reflects the historic cost of the company's assets.

23. False — Since the preferred stock is cumulative, the preferred stockholders are entitled to their full $20,000 dividend for Year 5. If Acme cannot meet its obligation to the preferred stockholders in Year 5, in future years, it must pay the arrears of dividend on preferred stock before paying any dividends to common stockholders.

24. False — Cumulative preferred stock means that any preferred dividend unpaid in previous years must be paid before any dividend on common shares is paid; participating preferred stock means that preferred stockholders may share in further distributions after preferred and common dividends have been paid.

25. False — Dividends are reported in the statement of cash flows only when they have been paid. Dividends are never reported on the income statement.

26. False — Only cash dividends reduce stockholders' equity.

27. True

28. True

29. False — The company's authorized share capital is unaffected by stock transactions.

30.      False      The number of shares the company will issue is determined by the market price of the share, not their par value.

## Fill in the Blanks

| | | | |
|---|---|---|---|
| 31. | book value per share of common stock | 39. | dividend payout ratio |
| 32. | outflow, financing | 40. | treasury stock |
| 33. | stock split | 41. | 500,000, 10 cents, 20 cents |
| 34. | stock dividend | 42. | $100,000 |
| 35. | cumulative | 43. | $500 |
| 36. | subscription agreement | 44. | $49,500 |
| 37. | issued stock | 45. | $150,000 |
| 38. | market value per share | | |

## Problem 46

1. $25000/$10 = 2,500 shares

2. 297,940 - 8,641 = 289,299

3. $(45,000 + 25,000)/2,500 = $28

4. $(384,803 + 29,794)/297,940 = $1.39

5. $127,717/8,641 = $14.72

6.

| Preferred Stock | | |
|---|---|---|
| 2,500, 5% nonparticipating, cumulative shares | | |
| $10 par value shares | $ 25,000 | |
| Additional paid-in capital | 45,000 | |
| | | $ 70,000 |

| Common Stock | | |
|---|---|---|
| Authorized 550,000 shares, 10 cents par value | | |
| Issued 297,940 shares | 29,794 | |
| Additional paid-in capital | 384,803 | |
| | | 414,597 |
| Retained earnings | | 2,092,329 |
| Total stockholders' equity before treasury stock | | 2,576,926 |
| Less treasury stock: 8,641 shares at cost | | (127,717) |
| Total stockholders' equity | | $2,449,209 |

## Problem 47

1.  <u>Preferred Stock</u>
    4,000, 3% nonparticipating, cumulative shares
    $5 par value shares                                                                    $  20,000

    <u>Common Stock</u>
    Authorized 2,000,000 shares, 50 cents par value
    Issued 400,000 shares                                           $  200,000
    Additional paid-in capital                                          50,000
                                                                                            250,000
    Retained earnings                                                                       430,000
    Total stockholders' equity before treasury stock                                        700,000
    Less treasury stock:  5,000 shares at cost                                             (10,000)
    Total stockholders' equity                                                             $690,000

2.  Neither dividends paid nor payable appears in the owners' equity section, since these
    balances have already been deducted from retained earnings.

## Problem 48

1.

|     | Assets     | = | Liabilities | + Stockholders' Equity |
|-----|------------|---|-------------|------------------------|
| a)  | 0          |   | 0           | 0                      |
| b)  | + 400,000  |   | 0           | + 400,000              |
| c)  | +  60,000  |   | 0           | +  60,000              |
| d)  | 0          |   | 0           | 0                      |
| e)  | (66,000)   |   | 0           | (66,000)               |

2.  <u>Common Stock</u>
    Authorized 6 million shares, 16.7 cents par value
    Issued 660,000 shares                                           110,000
    Additional paid-in capital                                      350,000
                                                                    460,000
    Retained earnings                                               354,000
    Total stockholders' equity                                     $814,000

3.  Dividend yield          =       Dividend per share/ Market price per share
                            =       10 cents / $4
                            =       2.5%
    Earnings per share      =       Net income/number of shares
                            =       $420,000 / 660,000
                            =       64 cents
    Dividend payout         =       Dividends per share/Earnings per share
                            =       10 cents / 64 cents
                            =       15.6%

## Critical Thinking Problem 49

1. The company issued an additional 20,000 common shares, each with a par value of $1 and a market value of $10. After the stock dividend, the company has 220,000 issued shares with a par value of $1.

2.

|  | Debit | Credit |
|---|---|---|
| Retained earnings | 200,000 | |
|     Common stock dividend distributable | | 20,000 |
|     Additional paid-in capital | | 180,000 |

3. The total market value of the company's stock before the stock dividend is:

    200,000 shares @ $10 per share = $2,000,000.

Since no other changes have taken place, the total market value of the company's stock must be unchanged after the stock dividend. Since the company now has 220,000 shares, the value of each share after the stock dividend is:

$$\frac{\$2,000,000}{220,000 \text{ shares}} = \$9.09 \text{ per share.}$$

4. The value of Mr. Mull's 100 shares before the stock dividend is:

    100 x $10  =  $1,000.

After the stock dividend, Mr. Mull has 200 shares, which have a value of:

    110 x $9.09  =  $1,000.

The stock dividend has not increased Mr. Mull's wealth, and there has been no economic exchange between the company and Mr. Mull.

5. Stock dividends can be used as a substitute for cash dividends when a company is short of cash. As we have seen in Part 4, stock dividends do not transfer wealth from the company to the stockholder. This argument is therefore weak. It can also be argued that stock dividends are a way of reducing the price of the stock and making it more marketable. However, stock dividends are usually smaller than the example in this problem and have a relatively small effect on stock price. It is also claimed that stock dividends provide a way of capitalizing retained earnings, but doing this can put constraints on future cash dividends. Overall, the arguments for making a stock dividend are fairly weak, and as a result, stock dividends are often interpreted as a sign of financial weakness.

# Chapter 12

# The Statement of Cash Flows

The Statement of Cash Flows is the last major financial statement to be considered in detail. In previous chapters you have looked at the impact of different elements of the income statement and balance sheet on the cash flow statement. This chapter considers the cash flow statement in detail and identifies how the statement can be prepared. Your objective in this chapter is to understand the components and presentation of the cash flow statement and how the statement can be derived from information contained in the balance sheet and income statement.

## Learning Objectives

**LO 1** Explain the purpose of a statement of cash flows.

**LO 2** Explain what cash equivalents are and how they are treated on the statement of cash flows.

**LO 3** Describe operating, investing, and financing activities and give examples of each.

**LO 4** Describe the difference between the direct and indirect methods of computing cash flows from operating activities.

**LO 5** Use T accounts to prepare a statement of cash flows, using the direct method to determine cash flow from operating activities.

**LO 6** Use T accounts to prepare a statement of cash flows, using the indirect method to determine cash flow from operating activities.

**LO 7** Use a worksheet to prepare a statement of cash flows, using the indirect method to determine cash flow from operating activities.

## Key Textbook Exhibits

**Exhibit 12-5** illustrates the format of the statement of cash flows. Note the classification of cash flows into operating, investing, and financing activities. *Self-Test:* Try to think of at least two examples of cash flow activity that would be reported in each of these three categories.

**Exhibit 12-6** classifies various activities according to whether they would appear as operating, investing, or financing activities and describes their effect on cash flow. *Self-Test:* What do all the examples of financing activities have in common? Hint: cash flows from investing activities originate from non-current assets.

**Exhibit 12-19** illustrates the use of a worksheet to prepare the statement of cash flows. *Self-Test:* Do the T account approach and the worksheet approach result in the same amounts being reported on the statement of cash flows?

## Review of Key Concepts

**LO 1** The **Statement of Cash Flows** provides valuable information to supplement the information provided in the income statement and balance sheet. The cash flow statement not only reports the change in the entity's cash balance over the period but it also provides an explanation. Current accounting practice requires that cash flows be classified according to whether they relate to **operating, investing, or financing activities** of the entity.

**LO 2** The cash flow statement must report not only changes in the actual cash balances but also changes in cash equivalents. A cash equivalent is any item that can be readily converted into a known amount of cash and have a maturity to the investor of three months or less (e.g. commercial paper, money market funds, and treasury bills).

## Sixty Second Quiz!

**Question:** Assume that on November 1, Year 5, Company X accepts a note receivable that is due to mature on December 31, Year 5. Is the note a cash equivalent?

**Answer:** Yes! The note is readily convertible to a known amount of cash, and it has a maturity to the investor (Company X) of less than three months.

**LO 3** Cash flows must be classified according to whether they are operating, investing, or financing activities.

- **Operating activities** are those activities necessary to acquire, produce, and sell products and services. Examples include a house builder buying timber, a bank processing loan applications, or an insurance company paying sales commissions to its sales force.

- **Investing activities** are those activities that relate to the acquisition and disposal of long-term assets. Examples include the purchase of plant and equipment, and the sale of stocks or bonds held as investments.

- **Financing activities** are those activities resulting in changes in the debt or equity of the company. Examples include the issue of stocks or bonds, the repayment of bonds, and the repurchase of the company's own stock.

**LO 4** When reporting cash flows from operations, either the **direct** or the **indirect** method can be used. With the direct method, the cash flows from individual operating activities are reported on the statement of cash flows. With the indirect method, the net income figure from the income statement is adjusted from an accrual basis to a cash basis. To illustrate the two methods, assume that Company Z begins operations on January 1, Year 1, and on that day, the owner provides cash of $100,000 to the business in return for 100,000 shares of $1 par value stock. The company's balance sheet and income statement at the end of Year 1 are as follows:

**Income statement for year ended December 31, Year 1**

| | |
|---|---|
| Sales | $1,500,000 |
| Expenses | 900,000 |
| Income before tax | 600,000 |
| Taxes | 200,000 |
| Net income | $400,000 |

**Balance Sheet on December 31, Year 1**

| | | | |
|---|---|---|---|
| Cash | $ 50,000 | Accounts payable | $ 70,000 |
| Accounts receivable | 100,000 | **Stockholders' Equity** | |
| Land | 420,000 | Common stock at $1 par | 100,000 |
| | | Retained earnings | 400,000 |
| | $570,000 | | $570,000 |

## Sixty Second Quiz!

**Question:** Net income, which is all derived from operating activities, is shown as $400,000. Can we conclude that we have also generated cash of $400,000 from operations?

**Answer:** No! Since we have both accounts receivable and accounts payable on the balance sheet, we must have made both credit sales and credit purchases; therefore, our cash flows from operations is unlikely to equal our net income. As illustrated below, the changes in accounts receivable and accounts payable are used to find the cash flows from operations in both the direct and indirect methods.

**Direct method**

Since we have an accounts receivable balance, not all of our sales were for cash. We find the cash from customers by subtracting accounts receivable from total sales (i.e. $1,500,000 - $100,000 = $1,400,000). Similarly, since we have an accounts payable balance, not all of our expenses were paid in cash. We find the cash outflow for purchases by subtracting accounts payable from expenses (i.e. $900,000 - $70,000 = $830,000). Since there is no tax payable on the balance sheet, the tax expense must equal the cash paid. These calculations allow us to prepare the following statement of cash flow using the direct method:

**Statement of Cash Flow - Direct Method**

| | |
|---|---|
| *Cash flows from operating activities* | |
| Cash collected from customers | $1,400,000 |
| Less cash payments for operating expenses | -830,000 |
| Less cash payments for taxes | - 200,000 |
| Net cash inflow from operating activities | $370,000 |
| | |
| *Cash flows from investing activities* | |
| Purchase of land | - 420,000 |
| | |
| *Cash flows from financing activities* | |
| Issuance of capital stock | 100,000 |
| Net increase in cash | 50,000 |
| Cash balance at beginning of period | 0 |
| Cash balance at end of period | $50,000 |

**Indirect method**

This method reconciles the net income from operations to the amount of cash provided by operations. The net income of $400,000 was derived from sales of $1,500,000. However, cash was not received for all the sales of $1,500,000 because the accounts receivable balance of $100,000 represents sales the have not yet been collected in cash. Therefore, $100,000 is subtracted from net income to adjust for non-cash sales. Similarly, expenses of $900,000 were not all paid in cash because the accounts payable balance of $70,000 represents expenses that have not yet used cash. Therefore, $70,000 is added back to net income. As before, tax paid and tax expense are identical. The statement of cash flows using the indirect method is as follows:

### Statement of Cash Flow - Indirect Method

*Cash flows from operating activities*

| | |
|---|---:|
| Net income | $400,000 |
| Increase in accounts receivable | - 100,000 |
| Increase in accounts payable | 70,000 |
| Net cash inflow from operating activities | $370,000 |

*Cash flows from investing activities*

| | |
|---|---:|
| Purchase of land | - 420,000 |

*Cash flows from financing activities*

| | |
|---|---:|
| Issuance of capital stock | 100,000 |
| Net increase in cash | 50,000 |
| Cash balance at beginning of period | 0 |
| Cash balance at end of period | $50,000 |

Note that the calculation of cash flows from operating activities is different in the two methods; yet both methods result in identical figures for cash flows from operations. Also note that the cash flow statements produced under both methods are identical, apart from the derivation of cash flows from operating activities.

**LO 4** When a company enters into a significant noncash transaction, accounting standards require that it be reported either in a separate schedule or in a footnote to the cash flow statement. For example, if a stockholder was issued a large block of shares in return for giving the company a valuable such as land, this transaction would not appear in the statement of cash flows since cash was not exchanged. However, the company is required to report the transaction in a footnote or in a separate schedule.

**LO 5** A standard procedure for preparing a statement of cash flows can be developed for both the direct and indirect methods. For the direct method, the following four steps are taken:

1. Set up three schedules to record cash flows from each of operating, investing, and financing activities.
2. Determine the cash flows from operating activities. This requires analyzing each item on the income statement and the current asset and current liability accounts. As cash flows are determined in this analysis, they are entered on the schedule of Cash Flows from Operating Activities.
3. Determine the cash flows from investing activities. This requires analyzing the long-term asset accounts and any additional information provided. As cash flows are determined in this analysis, they are entered on the schedule of Cash Flows from Investing Activities.
4. Determine the cash flows from financing activities. This requires analyzing the long-term liability and stockholders' equity accounts. As cash flows are determined in this analysis, they are entered on the schedule of Cash Flows from Financing Activities.

To illustrate this method, assume that at the end of Year 2, Company Z's income statement and balance sheet are as follows:

**Income statement for year ended December 31, Year 2**

| | |
|---|---|
| Sales | 2,000,000 |
| Expenses | 1,260,000 |
| | 740,000 |
| Gain on sale of land | 60,000 |
| Income before tax | 800,000 |
| Taxes | 300,000 |
| Net income | $500,000 |

**Balance Sheet on December 31, Year 2**

| | | | |
|---|---|---|---|
| Cash | $ 100,000 | Accounts payable | $ 90,000 |
| Accounts receivable | 80,000 | *Stockholders' Equity* | |
| Equipment (at cost) | 200,000 | Common stock at $1 par | 150,000 |
| Land | 400,000 | Retained earnings | 540,000 |
| | $780,000 | | $780,000 |

The following information is available for Year 2:
a) Land that had originally cost $20,000 was sold for $80,000.
b) Stock was issued for cash.
c) A cash dividend was declared and paid.

**Step 1:  Set up three master T accounts to record cash flows from each of operating, investing, and financing activities.** Note that these accounts are initially empty.

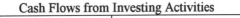
Cash Flows from Operating Activities

Cash Flows from Investing Activities

Cash Flows from Financing Activities

**Step 2:  Determine the cash flows from operating activities.**
We analyze each item on the income statement and its related balance sheet account balance, to find the associated cash flow.

a) Sales revenue and accounts receivable are clearly related. We reconstruct the T account for accounts receivable to find the cash received from customers:

| Accounts Receivable | | | |
|---|---|---|---|
| Jan.1,Year 2 | 100,000 | | |
| Sales | 2,000,000 | ? | Cash collections |
| | | | |
| Dec. 31, Year 2 | 80,000 | | |

Sales as reported on the income statement were $2,000,000. In addition, accounts receivable reduced over the year by $20,000. Company Z must have made $20,000 less in sales than it collected from customers. Cash received from customers must be ($100,000 + $2,000,000 - $80,000) = $2,020,000. This is shown as an inflow of cash in the schedule of Cash Flows from Operating Activities (debit side).

b) Expenses and accounts payable are also related. The T account for accounts payable is as follows:

| Accounts Payable | | | |
|---|---|---|---|
| | | 70,000 | Jan. 1,Year 2 |
| Cash payments | ? | 1,260,000 | Expenses |
| | | | |
| | | 90,000 | Dec. 31, Year 2 |

Expenses as reported on the income statement were $1,260,000. In addition, accounts payable increased over the year by $20,000. Company Z must have paid $20,000 less to its suppliers than it incurred in expenses. Cash paid to suppliers must be ($70,000 + $1,260,000 - $90,000) = $1,240,000. This is shown as an outflow of cash in the schedule of Cash Flows from Operating Activities (credit side).

c) The cash received from the sale of land is reported in the cash flow from investing activities section of the cash flow statement. We therefore ignore the gain when finding the cash flow from operating activities.

d) The last item on the income statement is tax expense. There is no tax payable on either balance sheet so we can conclude that the tax expense was equal to the cash outflow for taxes. $300,000 appears as an outflow of cash in the schedule of Cash Flows from Operating Activities.

The master T account appears as follows:

| Cash Flows from Operating Activities | | | |
|---|---|---|---|
| Cash receipts: | | Cash payments: | |
| (a) from customers | 2,020,000 | (b) to suppliers | 1,240,000 |
| | | (d) for taxes | 300,000 |

**Step 3: Determine the cash flows from investing activities.**

Next, we find the cash flows from investing activities. There are two main types: cash outflows from the purchase of long-term assets, and cash inflows from the sale of long-term assets.

a) Equipment with a book value of $200,000 appears for the first time in Year 2's balance sheet and must have been purchased in Year 2. Since it appears at cost, we can conclude that the company paid $200,000 for it. The T account for equipment appears as follows:

| Equipment | | |
|---|---|---|
| Jan. 1, Year 2 | 0 | |
| Cash payment | ? | |
| | | |
| Dec. 31, Year 2 | 200,000 | |

The cash outflow of $200,000 appears as an outflow of cash in the schedule of Cash Flows from Investing Activities (credit side).

b) We are told that land with an original cost of $20,000 was sold for $80,000 during the year. The T account for land appears as follows:

| Land | | | |
|---|---|---|---|
| Jan. 1, Year 2 | 420,000 | | |
| Acquisitions | ? | 20,000 | Disposals |
| | | | |
| Dec. 31, Year 2 | 400,000 | | |

The difference between the opening and closing balances on the Land account is equal to $20,000, so no acquisitions of land have taken place. We can reconstruct the journal entry recording the sale of land:

| | Debit | Credit |
|---|---|---|
| Cash | 80,000 | |
| Land – original cost | | 20,000 |
| Gain on sale | | 60,000 |
| Sale of land | | |

The cash inflow from the sale is $80,000 and is recorded in the schedule of Cash Flows from Investing Activities (debit side).

The master T account appears as follows:

| Cash Flows from Investing Activities | | | |
|---|---|---|---|
| (b) Sale of land | 80,000 | (a) Purchase of equipment | 200,000 |

**Step 4: Determine the cash flows from financing activities.**
The cash flows from financing activities are found by considering the changes in long-term liability and stockholders' equity accounts.

a) By comparing the balance sheets at the beginning and end of Year 2, we see that capital stock has increased by $50,000. Reconstructing the capital stock account:

| Capital Stock | | | |
|---|---|---|---|
| | | 100,000 | Jan. 1, Year 2 |
| | | ? | Issue of stock |
| | | | |
| | | 150,000 | Dec. 31, Year 2 |

We can deduce that the company has issued stock for cash of $50,000. This is recorded as a cash inflow in the schedule of Cash Flows from Investing Activities (debit side).

b) We are told that the company has paid a cash dividend, but we are not told how much was distributed. We also note that no statement of retained earnings is presented and that the dividend has not been deducted from the net income in the income statement. Reconstruct the retained earnings account:

| Retained Earnings | | | |
|---|---|---|---|
| | | 400,000 | Jan. 1, Year 2 |
| Dividend | ? | 500,000 | Net income, Year 2 |
| | | 540,000 | Dec. 31, Year 2 |

The opening balance on the Retained Earnings account is $400,000. The closing balance is $540,000 and net income for the year is $500,000. The dividend paid must have been ($400,000 + $500,000 - $540,000) = $360,000. This appears as a cash outflow in the schedule of Cash Flows from Investing Activities (credit side).

The master T account appears as follows:

| Cash Flows from Financing Activities | | | |
|---|---|---|---|
| (a) Stock issue | 50,000 | (b) Dividends paid | 360,000 |

 **LO 5** The statement of cash flows can then be prepared from the three master T accounts above.

**Statement of Cash Flows for the year ended December 31, Year 2**

**Cash flows from operating activities**
| | |
|---|---|
| Cash receipts from customers | $2,020,000 |
| Cash payments to suppliers | (1,240,000) |
| Cash payments for taxes | (300,000) |
| Net cash provided by operating activities | 480,000 |

**Cash flows from investing activities**
| | |
|---|---|
| Sale of land | 80,000 |
| Purchase of equipment | (200,000) |
| Net cash used by investing activities | (120,000) |

**Cash flows from financing activities**
| | |
|---|---|
| Stock issue | 50,000 |
| Dividends paid | (360,000) |
| Net cash used by financing activities | (310,000) |

| | |
|---|---|
| Net increase in cash | 50,000 |
| Cash balance, December 31, Year 1 | 50,000 |
| Cash balance, December 31, Year 2 | $100,000 |

Although the above example is relatively straightforward, it illustrates the principles involved in preparing the statement. A more sophisticated example appears in the text and in the first problem in this chapter of the study guide.

**LO 6** We can adapt the above method to find the cash flows from operating activities using the indirect method. Using the example of Company Z above, the procedure starts with the net income reported for Year 2 of $500,000 and adjusts for cash flow differences.

a) Accounts receivable decreased over Year 2 by $20,000. In other words, the company received more cash than its net sales figure would suggest. The net income figure understates the cash inflow from sales, and the $20,000 reduction in accounts receivable must be added to net income to find cash flow from operations.

b) Accounts payable increased by $20,000 over Year 2. This implies that the cash paid to creditors was less than what the expenses figure in the income statement would suggest. The net income figure overstates the cash outflow for expenses, and understates the cash flow from operations. The $20,000 increase in accounts payable must be added to net income to find cash flow from operations.

c) As before, the gain on the sale of land of $60,000 is reported in cash flow from investing activities and must be deducted from net income to find cash flow from operations.

The cash flow from operations under the indirect method is:

**Cash flows from operating activities**

| | |
|---|---|
| Net income | $500,000 |
| Decrease in accounts receivable | 20,000 |
| Increase in accounts payable | 20,000 |
| Gain on sale | (60,000) |
| Net cash used by operating activities | $(480,000) |

Many students find the indirect method counter-intuitive and have difficulty with the direction of the adjustments. In practice, the vast majority of firms use the indirect method so you need to understand the indirect method. To help you, the following table is reproduced from the text. It provides a list of the most common adjustments to net income under the indirect method. However, by far the most effective way to deal with this type of problem is to get as much practice as you can. You should work through the problems in this study guide, as well as the problems in the text.

| Additions to net income | Deductions from net income |
|---|---|
| Decrease in accounts receivable | Increase in accounts receivable |
| Decrease in inventory | Increase in inventory |
| Decrease in prepayments | Increase in prepayments |
| Increase in accounts payable | Decrease in accounts payable |
| Increase in accrued liabilities | Decrease in accrued liabilities |
| Losses on sales of long-term assets | Gains on sales of long-term assets |
| Losses on retirements of bonds | Gains on retirements of bonds |
| Depreciation, amortization, and depletion | |

## Sixty Second Quiz!

**Question:** One of the most common adjustments to net income under the indirect method is adding back depreciation expense. Does this mean that depreciation represents a source of cash? Could we generate more cash flow if we depreciated assets over a shorter period?

**Answer:** No! Depreciation is added back to net income because it is an expense that does not result in a cash outflow.

**LO 6** Cash flow statements provide crucial information to users. A measure that provides further insight into the company's cash flow position is **cash flow adequacy**, which measures the cash available to meet future debt obligations after providing for taxes, interest costs, and capital expenditures. It is calculated as follows:

| Cash Flow Adequacy | = | Cash Flow from Operating Activities - Capital Expenditures |
|---|---|---|
| | | Average Amount of Debt Maturing over the Next Five Years |

**LO 7** A worksheet can also be used to derive the cash flow statement. The following is an illustration of the use of the worksheet method for the Company Z example:

| | **Balances** | | | **Cash Outflows & Inflows** | | |
|---|---|---|---|---|---|---|
| **Accounts** | **Dec. 31, Year 2** | **Jan. 1, Year 2** | **Changes*** | **Operating** | **Investing** | **Financing** |
| Cash | 100,000 | 50,000 | 50,000 | | | |
| Accounts receivable | 80,000 | 100,000 | [5] (20,000) | [5] 20,000 | | |
| Land | 400,000 | 420,000 | [2] (20,000) | | [2] 80,000 | |
| Equipment | 200,000 | 0 | [1] 200,000 | | [1] (200,000) | |
| Accounts payable | 90,000 | 70,000 | [3] (20,000) | [3] 20,000 | | |
| Common stock | 150,000 | 100,000 | [4] (50,000) | | | [4] 50,000 |
| Retained earnings | 540,000 | 400,000 | [6] 360,000 [7] (500,000) | [2] (60,000) [7] 500,000 | | [6] (360,000) |
| **Totals** | | | **0** | **480,000** | **(120,000)** | **(310,000)** |

**Comments:**

1. $200,000 cash was spent on equipment. The amount appears as a reduction in cash from investing.
2. Land with an original cost of $20,000 was sold for $80,000. The gain is deducted from the operating cash flows since it is included in net income.
3. & 5. Changes in accounts payable and accounts receivable both result in increases in the operating cash flows.
4. Stock is issued for cash. $50,000 appears in the cash flows from financing activities column.
6. Cash dividends are deducted in the financing column.
7. Net income of $500,000 appears as an inflow in the cash flows from operations column.

## Review of Key Terms

| | |
|---|---|
| **Cash equivalent** | An item readily convertible to a known amount of cash and with an original maturity to the investor of three months or less. |
| **Direct method** | The approach to preparing the operating activities section of the statement of cash flows in which cash receipts and cash payments are reported. |
| **Financing activities** | Activities concerned with the raising and repayment of funds in the form of debt and equity. |
| **Indirect method** | The approach to preparing the operating activities section of the statement of cash flows in which net income is reconciled to net cash flows from operations. |
| **Investing activities** | Activities concerned with the acquisition and disposal of long-term assets. |
| **Operating activities** | Activities concerned with the acquisition and sale of products and services. |
| **Statement of cash flows** | The financial statement that summarizes an entity's cash receipts and cash payments during the period from operating, investing, and financing activities. |

## Practice Test
## Questions and Problems

### Circle the alternative that best answers the question:

**LO 6**  1.  Which of the following is not added to net earnings to find cash flows from operations under the indirect method?
  a)  A loss on the sale of a building
  b)  Interest expense
  c)  Depreciation expense
  d)  An increase in wages payable

**LO 6**  2.  Which of the following is consistent with a firm reporting both positive cash flows from operations and a net loss?
  a)  An increase in accounts receivable
  b)  A decrease in accounts payable
  c)  An increase in inventory
  d)  A loss on the sale of machinery

*Use the following information to answer questions 3 through 6:*

The following balances appeared on Beta Company's balance sheets on December 31, Year 1, and December 31, Year 2. As reported on the income statement, sales for the year were $100,000, rent expense was $50,000, and cost of sales was $40,000. All sales and purchases were on credit.

|  | Year ended<br>Dec. 31, Year 2 | Year ended<br>Dec. 31, Year 1 |
|---|---|---|
| Accounts receivable | $20,000 | $16,000 |
| Accounts payable | 25,000 | 20,000 |
| Prepaid rent | 10,000 | 15,000 |
| Inventory | 28,000 | 25,000 |

**LO 5**   3.   Cash paid for rent during Year 2 was:
a) $40,000
b) $45,000
c) $65,000
d) $55,000

**LO 5**   4.   Cash received from customers during Year 2 was:
a) $100,000
b) $80,000
c) $96,000
d) $104,000

**LO 5**   5.   Purchases of goods for resale during Year 2 were:
a) $43,000
b) $37,000
c) $50,000
d) $40,000

**LO 5**   6.   Cash paid to creditors during Year 2 was:
a) $20,000
b) $35,000
c) $45,000
d) $38,000

**LO 5,6**   7.   Zeta Corporation reported positive net earnings for the current year, but its cash balance declined over the year. Which of the following transactions is inconsistent with this scenario?
a) Zeta retired bonds.
b) Zeta paid cash dividends to its stockholders.
c) Zeta's accounts payable balance increased.
d) Zeta bought land for cash.

**LO 2**   8.   Which of the following is not considered a cash equivalent if held on December 31, Year 1?
a) A three-month note receivable bought one month before its maturity
b) Money deposited in a 60-day certificate of deposit
c) Commercial paper with a nine-month maturity bought when it was issued on September 1, Year 1
d) Money held in the company's petty cash box

**LO 3**  9.  Which of the following statements is false?
   a)  Cash flows from operating activities include cash collections from customers and interest payments to bond holders.
   b)  Dividends declared but not yet paid should be reported as part of cash flows from financing activities.
   c)  Equipment acquired in exchange for the issue of a note payable should be reported in a separate schedule rather than directly on the statement of cash flows.
   d)  A loss on the sale of land is added back to net income to find cash flows from operating activities since the cash flows from the transaction are reported in cash flows from investing activities.

**LO 5**  10.  During Year 2, the accounts payable balance of Player Corporation increased. Which of the following statements is true?
   a)  Player Corporation's purchases were higher than the cash it paid to its creditors.
   b)  The increase in accounts payable can be ignored when preparing a statement of cash flow using the direct method.
   c)  The increase in accounts payable indicates that inventory balances must also have increased during Year 2.
   d)  An increase in accounts payable could result in net income being higher than cash flows from operations.

**LO 6**  11.  Which of the following is added to net income to find cash flows from operations under the indirect method of reporting cash flows from operations?
   a)  Increases in accounts receivable
   b)  Decreases in accounts payable
   c)  Gains on retirement of bonds
   d)  Losses on sale of long-term assets

**LO 6**  12.  If a company uses the indirect method of reporting cash flows from operations, it must separately and additionally report which of the following?
   a)  Cash received from customers and cash paid to suppliers
   b)  Cash received from the sale of fixed assets and cash paid for investments
   c)  Cash paid for purchases of inventory and cash received from customers
   d)  Income taxes paid and interest paid

**LO 6**  13.  A company has net income of $2,000,000 and cash flows from operations of $1,000,000 for the year ended December 31, 2000. All purchases and sales were on credit. Which of the following would not be consistent with these facts?
   a)  The company's cash receipts from customers were less than total sales during the year.
   b)  The company's inventory increased during the year.
   c)  The company reduced its prepayment balance during the year.
   d)  The company's accounts payable balance decreased.

*Use the following information to answer questions 14 and 15:*

The following information appears in Ventura Inc.'s financial statements for the year ended December 31, 2001:

| Year ended December 31, | 2001 | 2000 |
|---|---|---|
| Buildings and equipment | | |
| Original cost | $ 3,500 | $ 2,500 |
| Accumulated depreciation | 2,000 | 1,500 |
| Net book value | 1,500 | 1,000 |

During the year equipment with an original cost of $1,000 and a net book value of $250 was sold. All acquisitions of fixed assets during the year were for cash.

**LO 5** 14. The cash paid to acquire new buildings and equipment during 2001 was:
a) $1,000
b) $2,000
c) $1,250
d) $750

**LO 5** 15. The depreciation expense for 2001 was:
a) $1,250
b) $500
c) $750
d) $1,500

## Indicate whether each of the following statements is true or false:

**LO 6** 16. Since depreciation expense is added back to net earnings to find cash flows from operations when the indirect method is used, accelerated depreciation methods result in greater cash flows.

**LO 2** 17. Cash flow statements should report only changes to cash balances held in checking and savings accounts.

**LO 3** 18. A stock split is reported under cash flows from financing activities in the statement of cash flows.

**LO 4** 19. The only difference between the direct and indirect methods is how cash flows from operations is reported.

**LO 2** 20. A three-month note receivable with two months to maturity at the balance sheet date would not be classified as cash for the purposes of the cash flow statement.

**LO 5** 21. An increase in salaries payable would indicate that cash paid for salaries was greater than salaries expense for the period.

**LO 5** 22. An increase in inventory indicates that accounts payable have increased over the period.

**LO 6** 23. The loss on disposal of plant must be added back to net income under the indirect method.

LO 3   24.   Dividends paid are reported in the statement of cash flows as a part of the cash flows from financing activities.

LO 3   25.   The conversion of convertible bonds payable to common stock is reported as a part of cash flows from financing activities.

LO 2   26.   The purchase of a 30-day T-Bill for cash would appear as a use of cash in the investing section of the statement of cash flows.

LO 3   27.   Cash flows are categorized into three categories: investing, operating, and financing in the statement of cash flows.

LO 3   28.   Negative cash flows from investing activities indicates that the company has purchased new assets.

LO 4   29.   Although FASB prefers the direct method for reporting cash from operations, the vast majority of companies use the indirect method.

LO 6   30.   If the indirect method is used, the company need not reconcile net income and cash flows from operations.

## Complete each of the following statements:

LO 3   31.   Purchases of machinery are reported in the _____ section of the statement of cash flows.

LO 3   32.   Interest paid on bonds appears in the cash flows from the _____ section of the statement of cash flows.

LO 3   33.   _____ activities are concerned with changes in long-term liabilities and contributed capital.

LO 4   34.   The _____ method of presenting cash flows from operations requires the conversion of income statement items from an accrual basis to a cash basis.

LO 5   35.   Zeta Company's opening and closing accounts receivable balances for Year 1 were $30,000 and _____. Zeta's credit sales were $10,000 more than the cash it received from its customers in that year.

LO 2   36.   _____ include all assets that are readily convertible to a known amount of cash and have a maturity to the company of three months or less.

*Use the following information to answer questions 37 through 45.*

| Beano Corporation<br>Summary balance sheet | Year ended<br>Dec. 31, Year 2 | Year ended<br>Dec. 31, Year 1 |
|---|---|---|
| Cash | $10,000 | $ 8,000 |
| Accounts receivable | 5,000 | 6,000 |
| Inventory | 4,000 | 8,000 |
| Prepaid insurance | 3,000 | 4,000 |
| Plant and equipment | 20,000 | 17,000 |
| Accumulated depreciation | (8,000) | (6,000) |
| *Total assets* | $34,000 | $37,000 |
| Accounts payable | $11,000 | $10,000 |
| Long-term notes payable | 5,000 | 4,000 |
| Common stock | 14,000 | 14,000 |
| Retained earnings | 4,000 | 9,000 |
| *Total liabilities and stockholders' equity* | $34,000 | $37,000 |

Plant with original cost of $4,000 was sold during the year for its net book value of $2,000. Net income for Year 2 was $7,000. The company uses the indirect method to report cash flows from operations.

**LO 5** 37. Depreciation expense for Year 2 was _____.

**LO 5** 38. Dividends paid during Year 2 were _____.

**LO 5** 39. Cash flows from investing activities during Year 2 were _____.

**LO 5** 40. Cash flows from financing activities during Year 2 were _____.

**LO 6** 41. If the company uses the indirect method for reporting cash flows from operations, the change in accounts receivable balance is _____ net income to find cash flows from operations.

**LO 6** 42. If the company uses the indirect method for reporting cash flows from operations, the change in prepaid insurance balance is _____ net income to find cash flows from operations.

**LO 6** 43. If the company uses the indirect method for reporting cash flows from operations, the change in accounts payable balance is _____ net income to find cash flows from operations.

**LO 5** 44. If total sales for the year are $43,000, and the company uses the direct method for reporting cash flows from operations, cash received from customers was _____.

**LO 5** 45. If cost of sales for the year is $30,000 and the company uses the direct method for reporting cash flows from operations, cash paid to suppliers was _____.

## Answer each of the following problems:

**LO 5,6** 46. The financial statements for Zeta Corporation are presented below.

### Zeta Corporation Income Statement
### For Year Ended December 31

| *$ in millions* | 2001 | 2000 |
|---|---|---|
| Revenue | $25,000 | $22,600 |
| Cost of sales | (23,650) | (21,210) |
| Gross profit | $1,350 | $1,390 |
| Selling, general and administrative | | |
| (including depreciation) | (1,148) | (1,248) |
| Operating Income | 202 | 142 |
| Interest expense | (22) | (30) |
| Income before income taxes | 180 | 112 |
| Income tax expense | (30) | (26) |
| Net income | 150 | 86 |
| Common dividends | (60) | (55) |
| To retained earnings | 90 | 31 |
| Retained earnings January 1 | 250 | 219 |
| Retained earnings December 31 | $ 340 | $ 250 |

### Zeta Corporation Balance Sheet
### On December 31

| *$ millions* | | 2001 | | 2000 | | 1999 |
|---|---|---|---|---|---|---|
| Cash | | $ 250 | | $ 350 | | $400 |
| Accounts receivable | | 600 | | 500 | | 300 |
| Inventory | | 1,300 | | 1,000 | | 800 |
| Prepaid insurance | | 0 | | 50 | | 269 |
| Total current assets | | 2,150 | | 1,900 | | 1,769 |
| Buildings and Equipment | 2,000 | | 1,900 | | 1,800 | |
| Accumulated depreciation | (1,700) | | (1,450) | | (1,350) | |
| | | 300 | | 450 | | 450 |
| Land | | 1,660 | | 1,200 | | 1,000 |
| Total long-term assets | | 1,960 | | 1,650 | | 1,450 |
| Total assets | | $4,110 | | $3,550 | | $3,219 |
| | | | | | | |
| Accounts payable | | 800 | | 500 | | 400 |
| Notes payable | | 750 | | 500 | | 300 |
| Total current liabilities | | 1,550 | | 1,000 | | 700 |
| Bonds payable | | 220 | | 300 | | 300 |
| Total liabilities | | 1,770 | | 1,300 | | 1,000 |
| Common stock, 50 cents par value | | 2,000 | | 2,000 | | 2,000 |
| Retained earnings | | 340 | | 250 | | 219 |
| Stockholders' equity | | 2,340 | | 2,250 | | 2,219 |
| Total liabilities and stockholders' | | | | | | |
| equity | | $4,110 | | $3,550 | | $3,219 |

**Required**

Prepare the statement of cash flows for Zeta for the years ended December 31, 2001, and December 31, 2000, using both the direct and indirect methods for reporting cash flows from operating activities.

**LO 7**    47.    Refer to the information in Problem 46.

**Required**
Complete the following statement of cash flows worksheet for the year ended December 31, 2001.

| Accounts | Balances | | | Cash inflows and outflows | | |
| | Dec. 31, 2001 | Jan. 1, 2000 | Changes | Operating | Investing | Financing |
|---|---|---|---|---|---|---|
| Cash | | | | | | |
| Accounts receivable | | | | | | |
| Inventory | | | | | | |
| Prepaid insurance | | | | | | |
| Buildings & equipment | | | | | | |
| Accumulated depreciation | | | | | | |
| Land | | | | | | |
| Accounts payable | | | | | | |
| Notes payable | | | | | | |
| Bonds payable | | | | | | |
| Outstanding stock | | | | | | |
| Retained earnings | | | | | | |
| **Totals** | | | | | | |

## Critical Thinking Problem

LO 4    48.    Exhibit 1 presents the consolidated statements of cash flow for the Compaq Computer Corporation for the years ended December 31, 1996, 1995, and 1994.

## CONSOLIDATED STATEMENT OF CASH FLOWS

| Year ended December 31, In millions | 1996 | 1995 | 1994 |
|---|---|---|---|
| *Cash flows from operating activities:* | | | |
| Cash received from customers | $17,939 | $13,910 | $9,986 |
| Cash paid to suppliers and employees | -13,639 | -12,437 | -9,778 |
| Interest and dividends received | 110 | 53 | 22 |
| Interest paid | -91 | -100 | -65 |
| Income taxes paid | -911 | -543 | -319 |
| Net cash provided by (used in) operating activities | 3,408 | 883 | -154 |
| | | | |
| *Cash flows from investing activities:* | | | |
| Purchases of property, plant and equipment, net | -342 | -391 | -357 |
| Purchases of short-term investments | -1,401 | | |
| Proceeds from short-term investments | 328 | | |
| Acquisition of businesses, net of cash acquired | -22 | -318 | |
| Other, net | -26 | 6 | -51 |
| Net cash used in investing activities | -1,463 | -703 | -408 |
| | | | |
| *Cash flows from financing activities:* | | | |
| Issuance of common stock pursuant to stock option plans | 112 | 79 | 100 |
| Tax benefit associated with stock options | 91 | 60 | 53 |
| Issuance of long-term debt | 0 | 0 | 300 |
| Net cash provided by financing activities | 203 | 139 | 453 |
| | | | |
| Effect of exchange rate changes on cash | 27 | -45 | -47 |
| | | | |
| Net increase (decrease) in cash and cash equivalents | 2,175 | 274 | -156 |
| Cash and cash equivalents at beginning of year | 745 | 471 | 627 |
| | | | |
| Cash and cash equivalents at end of year | $2,920 | $745 | $471 |
| | | | |
| **Reconciliation of net income to net cash provided by (used in) operating activities:** | | | |
| Net income | $1,313 | $789 | $867 |
| Depreciation and amortization | 285 | 214 | 169 |
| Provision for bad debts | 155 | 43 | 36 |
| Purchased in-process technology | | 241 | |
| Deferred income taxes | -371 | -17 | -184 |
| Loss on disposal of assets | 5 | 2 | 2 |
| Exchange rate effect | 14 | 33 | 46 |
| Increase in accounts receivable | -210 | -863 | -926 |
| Decrease (increase) in inventories | 1,004 | -135 | -882 |
| Decrease (increase) in other current assets | 5 | -41 | -55 |
| Increase in accounts payable | 586 | 479 | 248 |
| Increase (decrease) in income taxes payable | 131 | -61 | 173 |
| Increase in other current liabilities | 491 | 199 | 352 |
| Net cash provided by (used in) operating activities | $3,408 | $883 | ($154) |

**Required**

1. Does Compaq use the direct or indirect method to present its cash flows from operations?

2. What is the main cause of the change in cash flows from operations over the three years?

3. Did Compaq raise additional capital during the three years?

4. What were Compaq's main investing activities during the three years?

5. Has income increased over the three years as much as cash flows from operations?

# Solutions

## Multiple Choice

| | | | |
|---|---|---|---|
| 1. | b | 9. | b |
| 2. | d | 10. | a |
| 3. | b | 11. | d |
| 4. | c | 12. | d |
| 5. | a | 13. | c |
| 6. | d | 14. | b |
| 7. | c | 15. | a |
| 8. | c | | |

## True/False

**COMMENT/EXPLANATION**

16. False — Under the indirect method, depreciation expense is added back to net income because it is a noncash expense. Increasing depreciation charges in any year decreases reported net income but has no impact on cash flows.

17. False — Cash flow statements should report changes in cash and cash equivalents.

18. False — Stock splits have no cash flow implications and therefore do not appear in the cash flow statement.

19. True

20. False — The note receivable would be a cash equivalent since it can be readily converted into a known amount of cash and has a maturity of three months or less.

21. False — An increase in salaries payable indicates that less cash was paid during the period than was incurred. Therefore, cash paid for salaries was less than salaries expense.

22. False — An increase in inventory indicates that goods sold or used during the period are less than goods purchased.

23. True

24. True

25. False — No cash flow takes place on conversion.

26. False — A 30-day T-Bill is a cash equivalent.

27. True

28. True

29. True

30. False — The indirect method finds cash flows from operations by making adjustments to net income.

## Fill in the Blanks

| | | | |
|---|---|---|---|
| 31. | investing | 39. | - $5,000 |
| 32. | operating | 40. | - $11,000 |
| 33. | financing | 41. | added to |
| 34. | direct | 42. | added to |
| 35. | $40,000 | 43. | added to |
| 36. | cash equivalents | 44. | $44,000 |
| 37. | $4,000 | 45. | $25,000 |
| 38. | $12,000 | | |

## Problem 46

### Zeta Corporation Statement of Cash Flows - Indirect Method
### For Year Ended December 31

| *$ in millions* | 2001 | 2000 |
|---|---|---|
| *Cash flows from operating activities* | | |
| Net income | $ 150 | $ 86 |
| Increase in accounts receivable | (100) | (200) |
| Increase in inventory | (300) | (200) |
| Decrease in prepayments | 50 | 219 |
| Increase in accounts payable | 300 | 100 |
| Increase in notes payable | 250 | 200 |
| Depreciation | 250 | 100 |
| Cash flows provided by operating activities | 600 | 305 |
| | | |
| *Cash flows from investing activities* | | |
| Purchase of land | (460) | (200) |
| Purchase of buildings and equipment | (100) | (100) |
| Cash flows used by investing activities | (560) | (300) |
| | | |
| *Cash flows from financing activities* | | |
| Redemption of bonds | (80) | - |
| Dividend payment | (60) | (55) |
| Cash flows used by financing activities | (140) | (55) |
| | | |
| Net decrease in cash | (100) | (50) |
| Cash balance, December 31, 2000 | 350 | 400 |
| Cash balance, December 31, 2001 | $250 | $350 |

## Zeta Corporation Statement of Cash Flow - Direct Method
## For Year Ended December 31

| $ in millions | 2001 | 2000 |
|---|---|---|
| **Cash flows from operating activities** | | |
| Cash receipts from customers | $ 24,900 | $ 22,400 |
| Cash from issue of notes payable | 250 | 200 |
| Cash paid to suppliers | (23,650) | (21,310) |
| Cash paid for selling and administrative expenses * | (848) | (929) |
| Interest paid | (22) | (30) |
| Income tax paid | (30) | (26) |
| Cash flows from operating activities | 600 | 305 |
| | | |
| **Cash flows from investing activities** | | |
| Purchase of land | (460) | (200) |
| Purchase of buildings and equipment | (100) | (100) |
| Cash flows used by investing activities | (560) | (300) |
| | | |
| **Cash flows from financing activities** | | |
| Redemption of bonds | (80) | - |
| Dividend payment | (60) | (55) |
| Cash flows used by financing activities | (140) | (55) |
| | | |
| Net decrease in cash | (100) | (50) |
| Cash balance, December 31, 2000 | 350 | 400 |
| Cash balance, December 31, 2001 | $250 | $350 |

Selling and administrative expenses include depreciation and a component of prepaid insurance. To find the cash flow associated with these expenses, it is necessary to exclude depreciation and adjust for the change in the prepaid balance. Thus for the year ended December 31, 2001, the cash flows from selling and administrative expenses is ($1,148 - $250 - $50) = $848.

## Problem 47

| Accounts | Balances | | | Cash inflows and outflows | | |
|---|---|---|---|---|---|---|
| | Dec. 31, 2001 | Jan. 1, 2000 | Changes (see below) | Operating | Investing | Financing |
| Cash | 250 | 350 | (100) | | | |
| Accounts receivable | 600 | 500 | [1] 100 | [1] (100) | | |
| Inventory | 1,300 | 1,000 | [2] 300 | [2] (300) | | |
| Prepaid insurance | 0 | 50 | [3] (50) | [3] 50 | | |
| Buildings & equipment | 2,000 | 1,900 | [4] 100 | | [4] (100) | |
| Accumulated depreciation | 1,700 | 1,450 | [5] (250) | [5] 250 | | |
| Land | 1,660 | 1,200 | [6] 460 | | [6] (460) | |
| Accounts payable | 800 | 500 | [7] (300) | [7] 300 | | |
| Notes payable | 750 | 500 | [8] (250) | [8] 250 | | |
| Bonds payable | 220 | 300 | [9] 80 | | | [9] (80) |
| Outstanding stock | 2,000 | 2,000 | | | | |
| Retained earnings | 340 | 250 | [10] 60 [11] (150) | | | [10] (60) [11] 150 |
| **Totals** | | | **0** | **450** | **(560)** | **10** |

**Comments:**

1. & 2.  Increases in accounts receivable and inventory appear as decreases in operating cash flows.
3.  A decrease in prepaid insurance appears as an increase in operating cash flows.
4.  $100 was spent on buildings and appears as an outflow of cash for investing activities.
5.  Depreciation for the year must be added back to operating cash flows since it is a noncash expense.
6.  $460 was spent on land and appears as a cash outflow for investing activities.
7. & 8.  The increased balances in accounts and notes payable appear as increases in operating cash flows.
9.  Bonds are redeemed for $80 and appear as a cash outflow for financing activities.
10.  Cash dividends are deducted in the financing column.
11.  Net income of $150 appears as a cash inflow in the cash flows from operations column.

## Critical Thinking Problem 48

1.  Compaq uses the direct method to present its cash flows from operations. Note however that it also provides a reconciliation of net income to cash flows from operations.

2.  The main cause of the change in cash flows from operations over the three years is the increase in cash received from customers. Clearly, Compaq's sales have increased significantly over the last year, and cash has been received for these sales, resulting in large cash inflows.

3.  Apart from issuing long-term debt in 1994, Compaq raised almost no financing during the three years, suggesting that any expansion was from internally generated funds.

4.  Compaq's main investing activities during the three years appeared to be the purchase of short-term securities in 1996. This probably indicates that the additional cash flows from operations have been invested to obtain short-term return until Compaq decides how to use the funds in the longer term. It may be planning a major expansion or acquisition and be "parking" the funds until it is ready to use them.

5.  Income has not increased over the three years as much as cash flows from operations, although net income has grown substantially, and the company has now been profitable for three consecutive years.

# Chapter 13
# Financial Statement Analysis

The chapter, dedicated to the analysis of financial statements, represents the culmination of the book. Your objective is to acquire the skills needed to analyze financial statements and to gain an understanding of how these skills can be used to help various types of decision making.

## Learning Objectives

**LO 1**  Explain the various limitations and considerations in financial statement analysis.

**LO 2**  Use comparative financial statements to analyze a company over time (horizontal analysis).

**LO 3**  Use common-size financial statements to compare various financial statement items (vertical analysis).

**LO 4**  Compute and use various ratios to assess liquidity.

**LO 5**  Compute and use various ratios to assess solvency.

**LO 6**  Compute and use various ratios to assess profitability.

## Key Textbook Exhibit

**Exhibit 13-8** provides you with a summary of key financial ratios. *Self-Test:* Which ratios use numbers from the balance sheet? Which use numbers from the income statement? Which use a combination of both? Do any ratios use numbers other than those found in the balance sheet and income statement?

## Review of Key Concepts

We use the following income statements, balance sheets, and statements of cash flows for Fife Corporation to illustrate the material in this chapter.

### Fife Corporation Income Statement
### for Year Ended December 31

| $ in millions | 2002 | 2001 |
|---|---|---|
| Revenue | $25,000 | $22,600 |
| Cost of sales | (23,650) | (21,210) |
| *Gross profit* | $1,350 | $1,390 |
| Selling, general and administrative (including depreciation) | (1,148) | (1,248) |
| *Operating Income* | 202 | 142 |
| Interest expense | (22) | (30) |
| *Earnings before income taxes* | 180 | 112 |
| Income tax expense | (30) | (26) |
| *Net earnings* | 150 | 86 |
| Common dividends | (60) | (55) |
| To retained earnings | 90 | 31 |
| Retained earnings January 1 | 250 | 219 |
| Retained earnings December 31 | $ 340 | $ 250 |

### Fife Corporation Balance Sheet
### on December 31

| $ millions | | 2002 | | 2001 | | 2000 |
|---|---|---|---|---|---|---|
| Cash | | $ 250 | | $ 350 | | $400 |
| Accounts receivable | | 600 | | 500 | | 300 |
| Inventory | | 1,300 | | 1,000 | | 800 |
| Prepaid insurance | | 0 | | 50 | | 269 |
| *Total current assets* | | 2,150 | | 1,900 | | 1,769 |
| Buildings and Equipment | 2,000 | | 1,900 | | 1,800 | |
| Accumulated depreciation | (1,700) | | (1,450) | | (1,350) | |
| | | 300 | | 450 | | 450 |
| Land | | 1,660 | | 1,200 | | 1,000 |
| *Total long-term assets* | | 1,960 | | 1,650 | | 1,450 |
| *Total assets* | | $4,110 | | $3,550 | | $3,219 |
| | | | | | | |
| Accounts payable | | 800 | | 500 | | 400 |
| Notes payable | | 750 | | 500 | | 300 |
| *Total current liabilities* | | 1,550 | | 1,000 | | 700 |
| Bonds payable | | 220 | | 300 | | 300 |
| *Total liabilities* | | 1,770 | | 1,300 | | 1,000 |
| Common stock, 50 cents par value | | 2,000 | | 2,000 | | 2,000 |
| Retained earnings | | 340 | | 250 | | 219 |
| *Stockholders' equity* | | 2,340 | | 2,250 | | 2,219 |
| *Total liabilities and stockholders' equity* | | $4,110 | | $3,550 | | $3,219 |

**Fife Corporation Statement of Cash Flows - Indirect Method**
**for Year Ended December 31**

| $ in millions | 2002 | 2001 |
|---|---|---|
| *Cash flows from operating activities* | | |
| Net income | $ 150 | $ 86 |
| Increase in accounts receivable | (100) | (200) |
| Increase in inventory | (300) | (200) |
| Decrease in prepayments | 50 | 219 |
| Increase in accounts payable | 300 | 100 |
| Increase in notes payable | 250 | 200 |
| Depreciation | 250 | 100 |
| Cash flows from operating activities | $ 600 | $ 305 |
| | | |
| *Cash flows from investing activities* | | |
| Purchase of land | (460) | (200) |
| Purchase of buildings and equipment | (100) | (100) |
| Cash flows used by investing activities | $ (560) | $ (300) |
| | | |
| *Cash flows from financing activities* | | |
| Redemption of bonds | (80) | - |
| Dividend payment | (60) | (55) |
| Cash flows used by financing activities | $ (140) | $ (55) |
| | | |
| Net cash flow | (100) | (50) |
| Opening cash balance | 350 | 400 |
| Closing cash balance | $250 | $350 |

*Note:* Fife Corporation's marginal tax rate is 40%. On December 31, 2002, its stock price was 75 cents and on December 31, 2001, it was 57 cents.

**LO 1** In analyzing financial statements, attention must be given to the assumptions on which the statements are based. In particular, the accounting principles used (for example, the depreciation method and inventory cost flow assumption) can have a significant impact on financial ratios.

•   Analysis of a set of financial statements should include comparisons both with statements from previous periods and with statements from similar companies in the same industry. Comparisons with previous periods allow us to identify trends and patterns in the company's performance. Comparisons with companies in the same industry provide insights into how the company is performing relative to companies in the same industry. For example, if an entire industry is in decline, it may be that an apparently poor performance by the company is better than that of other companies in the industry.

•   Inflation can have a significant impact on the validity of the information provided in financial statements. For example, land that was bought decades ago is reported at historic cost even though it is unlikely to bear any relationship to the current market value of the land. In analyzing companies, it is important to recognize this type of limitation of historic cost.

**LO 2** **Horizontal analysis** involves analyzing the company over time. The following table presents the horizontal analysis of Fife Corporation over years 2001 and 2002.

## Fife Corporation Income Statement
## Horizontal Analysis for Year Ended December 31

|  |  |  | Increase or Decrease | |
|---|---|---|---|---|
| $ in millions | 2002 | 2001 | $ | % |
| Revenue | $25,000 | $22,600 | $2,400 | 11% |
| Cost of sales | (23,650) | (21,210) | (2,440) | 12% |
| Gross profit | $1,350 | $1,390 | (40) | - 3% |
| Selling, general and administrative |  |  |  | - 8% |
| (including depreciation) | (1,148) | (1,248) | 100 |  |
| Operating Income | 202 | 142 | 60 | 42% |
| Interest expense | (22) | (30) | 8 | - 27% |
| Earnings before income taxes | 180 | 112 | 68 | 61% |
| Income tax expense | (30) | (26) | (4) | 15% |
| Net earnings | 150 | 86 | 64 | 74% |
| Common dividends | (60) | (55) | (5) | 9% |
| To retained earnings | 90 | 31 | $ 59 | 190% |
| Retained earnings January 1 | 250 | 219 |  |  |
| Retained earnings December 31 | $ 340 | $ 250 |  |  |

## Fife Corporation Balance Sheet
## Horizontal Analysis on December 31

|  |  |  |  | Increase or Decrease | |
|---|---|---|---|---|---|
| $ millions |  | 2002 | 2001 | $ | % |
| Cash |  | $ 250 | $ 350 | (100) | - 29% |
| Accounts receivable |  | 600 | 500 | 100 | 20% |
| Inventory |  | 1,300 | 1,000 | 300 | 30% |
| Prepaid insurance |  | 0 | 50 | (50) | - 100% |
| Total current assets |  | 2,150 | 1,900 | 250 | 13% |
| Buildings and Equipment | 2,000 |  | 1,900 | 100 | 5% |
| Accumulated depreciation | (1,700) |  | (1,450) | (250) | 17% |
|  |  | 300 | 450 | (150) | - 33% |
| Land |  | 1,660 | 1,200 | 460 | 38% |
| Total long-term assets |  | 1,960 | 1,650 | 310 | 19% |
| Total assets |  | $4,110 | $3,550 | $560 | 16% |
|  |  |  |  |  |  |
| Accounts payable |  | 800 | 500 | 300 | 60% |
| Notes payable |  | 750 | 500 | 250 | 50% |
| Total current liabilities |  | 1,550 | 1,000 | 550 | 55% |
| Bonds payable |  | 220 | 300 | (80) | - 27% |
| Total liabilities |  | 1,770 | 1,300 | 470 | 36% |
| Common stock, 50 cents par value |  | 2,000 | 2,000 |  |  |
|  |  |  |  | 0 | 0% |
| Retained earnings |  | 340 | 250 | 90 | 36% |
| Stockholders' equity |  | 2,340 | 2,250 | 90 | 4% |
| Total liabilities and stockholders' equity |  | $4,110 | $3,550 | $560 | 16% |

- **Calculation:** For each item in the balance sheet and income statement, the change from the earlier period to the later period is found; this change is then expressed as a percentage of the earlier figure. For example, for revenue, the increase from 2001 to 2002 is found from $25,000 - $22,600 = $2,400, and the percentage change is found by dividing $2,400 by 2001 revenue, $2,400/$22,600 = 11%.

- **Discussion:** The horizontal analysis of the income statement reveals that Fife Corporation's net earnings over the year have increased by 74%. This is explained by both an increase in operating income (up 42%) and a decrease in interest expense (down 27%). The operating income has increased because of the decrease in selling, administrative, and general expenses. Gross profit has in fact decreased because cost of sales increased more than revenue, but the decrease in the selling and general expenses more than compensates. When we look at the balance sheet, we see that this improvement in profitability has been accompanied by a decrease in cash, though both inventory and accounts receivable have increased. Fife's assets have increased in total, but plant and machinery has decreased while the company has increased its land holdings. Short-term liabilities have increased substantially, but the company has redeemed some of its long-term debt. This combined with the drop in cash may indicate that the company is facing a cash crunch and perhaps should consider issuing additional long-term debt. Stockholders' equity has increased by a modest 4%, even though net income increased by 74% and retained earnings increased by 36%. This is because retained earnings are small relative to the other component of stockholders' equity, contributed capital.

**LO 3** Companies of different sizes can be difficult to compare. For example, Microsoft dwarfs most other software companies, and comparing profits or losses of several billion dollars with that of a few hundred thousand dollars is difficult, unless the profit is related to other financial variables. Vertical analysis, through **common-size statements,** is used as a way of factoring out size as a variable in financial analysis. It is useful both for different companies and for the same company over different time periods. The following table presents the common-size statements for Fife. Note that in the following table, rounding may cause totals to differ from the sum of the individual percentages.

## Fife Corporation Income Statement
## Vertical Analysis for Year Ended December 31

|  | 2002 $ | 2002 % | 2001 $ | 2001 % |
|---|---|---|---|---|
| Revenue | $25,000 | 100% | $22,600 | 100% |
| Cost of sales | (23,650) | - 95% | (21,210) | - 94% |
| Gross profit | 1,350 | 5% | 1,390 | 6% |
| Selling, general, and administrative | (1,148) | - 5% | (1,248) | - 6% |
| Operating Income | 202 | 1% | 142 | 1% |
| Interest expense | (22) | 0% | (30) | 0% |
| Earnings before income taxes | 180 | 1% | 112 | 1% |
| Income tax expense | (30) | 0% | (26) | 0% |
| Net earnings | $150 | 1% | $86 | 1% |

## Fife Corporation Balance Sheet
## Vertical Analysis on December 31

| | 2002 | | | 2001 | | |
|---|---|---|---|---|---|---|
| | $ | $ | % | $ | $ | % |
| Cash | | $ 250 | 6% | | $ 350 | 10% |
| Accounts receivable | | 600 | 15% | | 500 | 14% |
| Inventory | | 1,300 | 32% | | 1,000 | 28% |
| Prepaid insurance | | 0 | 0% | | 50 | 1% |
| *Total current assets* | | 2,150 | 52% | | 1,900 | 53% |
| Buildings and Equipment | $ 2,000 | | 49% | $ 1,900 | | 54% |
| Accumulated depreciation | (1,700) | | -41% | (1,450) | | -41% |
| | | 300 | 8% | | 450 | 13% |
| Land | | 1,660 | 40% | | 1,200 | 34% |
| *Total long-term assets* | | 1,960 | 48% | | 1,650 | 47% |
| *Total assets* | | $4,110 | 100% | | $3,550 | 100% |
| | | | | | | |
| Accounts payable | | $800 | 19% | | $500 | 14% |
| Notes payable | | 750 | 18% | | 500 | 14% |
| *Total current liabilities* | | 1,550 | 38% | | 1,000 | 28% |
| Bonds payable | | 220 | 5% | | 300 | 8% |
| *Total liabilities* | | 1,770 | 43% | | 1,300 | 37% |
| Common stock, | | | | | | |
| 50 cents par value | | 2,000 | 49% | | 2,000 | 56% |
| Retained earnings | | 340 | 8% | | 250 | 7% |
| *Total stockholders' equity* | | 2,340 | 57% | | 2,250 | 63% |
| *Total liabilities and* | | | | | | |
| *Stockholders' equity* | | $4,110 | 100% | | $3,550 | 100% |

Each item in the balance sheet is calculated as a percentage of total assets, which of course is equal to total liabilities plus stockholders' equity. For example, cash in the balance sheet for December 31, 2002 is $250/$4110 = 6%. Similarly, each item in the income statement is expressed as a percentage of net sales; cost of sales in 2001 is equal to $762/$960 = 68%.

The vertical analysis of the income statement reveals two key ratios that relate the profit the company made to the level of its sales: the gross profit ratio (equal to the gross profit as a percentage of net sales) and the profit margin ratio (equal to net earnings to net sales). For Fife, the gross profit ratio decreased and the profit margin ratio stayed the same because the selling and general expenses reduced significantly. Note how large the net sales figure is relative to the operating income. In this situation, items below operating income in the income statement tend to be swamped by the large denominator, making interpretation difficult. In the balance sheets, cash as a percent of total assets has decreased substantially, though overall the total current assets percentage has only dropped slightly. The land percentage has increased and the plant and machinery percentage has decreased, resulting in a small net increase in the long-term assets percentage. The total liabilities percentage is higher, resulting from a reduction in long-term liabilities and an increase in short-term liabilities. Though the company appears profitable, it has become more reliant on short-term debt than it was previously and its cash reserves are lower. In addition, its inventory and accounts receivable have increased. Together, these would indicate that the company may face problems in meeting its short-term liabilities in future, a possibility we examine further in **LO 5** below.

**LO 4**  **Liquidity** refers to a company's ability to meet its short-term obligations. Many profitable companies have failed because of a lack of liquidity. Liquidity is therefore a critical measure when assessing financial performance. Table 13-1 summarizes the key ratios used to assess liquidity and provides the detailed calculations for Fife's 2002 statements and the ratios for both 2001 and 2002. In assessing a company's liquidity, it is critical to gain insight into the company's ability both to meet short-term liabilities and to generate short-term cash inflows.

- The **current ratio**, the **acid-test ratio**, and **working capital** all relate short-term assets to short-term liabilities. The current ratio is a measure of the cover for short-term liabilities provided by short-term assets. The acid-test ratio is a stricter test of the company's liquidity since it excludes both inventory and prepayments, which are not as readily convertible to cash as other short-term assets. Working capital is simply the difference between current assets and current liabilities. All three ratios have deteriorated over the year.

- **Cash flows from operations to current liabilities** ratio provides a measure of how the flows of cash over a period relate to the average short-term claims on that cash. For Fife, this ratio has improved over the year.

The turnover ratios for both accounts receivable and inventory provide insight into how well these two short-term assets are being managed.

- The **accounts receivable turnover ratio** gives the average number of times that accounts were turned over (or collected) during the year. This ratio can also be used to find the **number of days' sales in receivables**, or the average number of days that accounts remain outstanding. For Fife, there has been a slight drop in both ratios, indicating that collections from customers have slowed slightly.

- The **inventory turnover ratio** gives the number of times the inventory was replaced during the year, and **the number of days' sales in inventory ratio** provides the number of days on average that goods spent in inventory. These ratios have again declined slightly for Fife.

- The **cash-to-cash operating cycle** gives the number of days on average it takes between goods being bought and the cash being received for the sale of the goods. Fife had an increase in this cycle of about four days.

Overall, Fife's short-term liquidity has deteriorated, with the most significant deterioration being in the coverage of short-term liabilities.

**LO 5**  **Solvency** refers to a company's ability to remain in business in the long term. Solvency is determined mainly by the ability of a company to service its debts and pay for its investments. Measures of solvency are therefore based on the relationship between long-term debt and equity, and on the ability to cover financing costs and investment. Table 13-2 summarizes the key ratios used to assess solvency, and provides the detailed calculations for Fife's 2002 statements and the ratios for both 2001 and 2002.

- A critical measure of a company's solvency is its **debt-to-equity ratio**. This ratio measures the extent to which the company is reliant on debt to finance its activities, or its **capital structure**. Since debt is less risky than equity and the required return on debt is lower than that required on equity, and since interest is tax deductible, debt provides the company with a relatively cheap source of financing. However, very high levels of debt can threaten the company's existence, since failure to meet principal and interest payments can result in the debt holders liquidating the company to ensure repayment of what they are owed. The debt-to-equity ratio provides a measure of the company's reliance on debt. Fife's ratio has increased over the year, indicating that Fife is becoming more reliant on debt. Whether or not this is likely to cause problems in turn depends on how easily the company can meet its interest payments.

- The **times interest earned ratio** indicates the company's ability to meet its current year's interest payments out of current year's earnings. Because Fife's earnings increased and its interest expense decreased over the year, the times interest earned ratio increased. This indicates that Fife's ability to meet its interest payments had improved.

- Since net income and cash flows from operations often differ substantially, the times interest earned ratio does not necessarily measure the company's ability to meet the cash obligations associated with debt, but the **debt service coverage ratio** does. For Fife, this ratio has decreased over the period largely as a result of the redemption of debt in 2002.

- In order to survive, companies must invest. The majority of investment by companies is funded internally and the **cash flows from operations to capital expenditure ratio** provides a measure of the company's ability to fund its capital expenditure from internally generated funds. Though Fife's ratio has increased over the year, it is still unable to generate internally all of the cash it needs for investment.

**LO 6**   Ultimately, the company's ability to survive depends on how effectively the resources of the company are used. **Profitability** measures indicate the return that is earned on the resources of the company as a whole and on the investment in the company of different classes of investors. Table 13-3 summarizes the key ratios used to assess profitability and provides the detailed calculations for Fife's 2002 statements and the ratios for both 2001 and 2002. We have already discussed both the gross profit ratio and the profit margin ratio. We now consider the rate of return ratios, which measure the relationship between income earned and investment made.

The **return on assets ratio** is the income earned on all assets used by the company. In the numerator of the ratio, the return to the equity holders (net income) is added to the return to debt holders (interest expense). However, since net income is measured after tax, interest expense is also measured after tax. Fife's return on assets has increased in 2002 and we can break this ratio down further to understand it better. Return on assets can be broken down into **return on sales** and **asset turnover**.

$$\text{Return on assets} = \frac{\text{Net income} + \text{Interest expense, net of tax}}{\text{Average total assets}}$$

$$= \frac{\text{Net income} + \text{Interest expense, net of tax}}{\text{Net sales}} \times \frac{\text{Net sales}}{\text{Average total assets}}$$

| Return on assets | = | Return on sales | x | Asset turnover |
|---|---|---|---|---|

We can see that Fife's return on sales has increased over the year, but its assets turnover has decreased slightly. We conclude that the increased return on assets is due to a higher return on sales.

A further group of profitability ratios consider the various components of returns to stockholders.

- **Return on stockholders' equity** is the rate of return paid on the average funds provided by common stockholders. For Fife, this has increased substantially over the year.

- **Earnings per share** is the earnings after interest and taxes attributable to each share of common stock. Again for Fife, this has increased over the year.

- The **dividend payout ratio** measures the proportion of earnings per share that are paid out as dividends. For Fife, this ratio has decreased, indicating that a higher proportion of Fife's earnings have been retained than in the previous year.

Two further ratios are of importance when assessing the return to common stockholders.

- The **price-earnings ratio** compares the current market price with current earnings per share. This ratio is often regarded as an indication of the stock market's confidence in the company, but it must be interpreted with caution since factors such as choice of accounting method and the firm's discount rate can also impact the price-earnings ratio. It would appear that in Fife's case, in spite of higher earnings, the market now has less confidence in the company.

- A further ratio that is related to the company's market price is the **dividend yield**, which expresses dividend per share as a percentage of market price per share. Dividend yield must again be interpreted with caution since the dividend is only one component of the return that stockholders receive, the other being the change in the stock's market price. For Fife, the dividend yield has decreased over the period.

### Table 13-1  Liquidity analysis

| Measure/Ratio | Formula | Calculation 2002 | 2002 | 2001 |
|---|---|---|---|---|
| Working capital | Current assets - Current liabilities | 2150 - 1550 | 600 | 900 |
| Current ratio | $\dfrac{\text{Current assets}}{\text{Current liabilities}}$ | $\dfrac{2150}{1550}$ | 1.39 | 1.9 |
| Acid-test ratio (quick ratio) | $\dfrac{\text{Cash + Marketable securities + Short-term receivables}}{\text{Current liabilities}}$ | $\dfrac{850}{1550}$ | 0.55 | 0.85 |
| Cash flows from operations to current liabilities ratio | $\dfrac{\text{Net cash from operations}}{\text{Average current liabilities}}$ | $\dfrac{600}{0.5 \times (1550 + 1000)}$ | 0.47 | 0.36 |
| Accounts receivable turnover ratio | $\dfrac{\text{Net credit sales}}{\text{Average accounts receivable}}$ | $\dfrac{2500}{0.5 \times (600 + 500)}$ | 45.5 times | 56.5 times |
| Number of days' sales in receivables ratio | $\dfrac{\text{Number of days in period}}{\text{Accounts receivable turnover}}$ | $\dfrac{360}{45.5}$ | 7.9 days | 6.4 days |
| Inventory turnover ratio | $\dfrac{\text{Cost of goods sold}}{\text{Average inventory}}$ | $\dfrac{23650}{0.5 \times (1300 + 1000)}$ | 20.6 times | 23.6 times |
| Number of days' sales in inventory ratio | $\dfrac{\text{Number of days in period}}{\text{Inventory turnover}}$ | $\dfrac{360}{20.6}$ | 17.5 days | 15.3 days |
| Cash to cash operating cycle ratio | Number days' sales in inventory + Number days' sales in receivables | 7.9 + 17.5 | 25.4 days | 21.7 days |

### Table 13-2 Solvency analysis

| Measure/Ratio | Formula | Calculation 2002 | 2002 | 2001 |
|---|---|---|---|---|
| Debt-to-equity ratio | $\dfrac{\text{Total liabilities}}{\text{Total stockholders' equity}}$ | $\dfrac{1770}{2340}$ | 0.75 | 0.58 |
| Times interest earned ratio | $\dfrac{\text{Net Income + Interest expense + Income tax expense}}{\text{Interest expense}}$ | $\dfrac{150 + 22 + 30}{22}$ | 9.18 | 4.73 |
| Debt service coverage ratio | $\dfrac{\text{Cash flows from operations, before interest and tax}}{\text{Interest and principal payments}}$ | $\dfrac{600 + 22 + 30}{22 + 80}$ | 6.39 | 12.03 |
| Cash flows from operations to capital expenditure ratio | $\dfrac{\text{Cash flows from operations-Total dividends paid}}{\text{Cash paid for acquisitions}}$ | $\dfrac{600 - 60}{560}$ | 0.96 | 0.83 |

### Table 13-3 Profitability analysis

| Measure/Ratio | Formula | Calculation 2002 | 2002 | 2001 |
|---|---|---|---|---|
| Gross profit ratio | $\dfrac{\text{Gross profit}}{\text{Net sales}}$ | $\dfrac{1350}{25000}$ | 5.4% | 6.2% |
| Profit margin ratio | $\dfrac{\text{Net income}}{\text{Net sales}}$ | $\dfrac{150}{25000}$ | 0.6% | 0.4% |
| Return on assets | $\dfrac{\text{Net income + Interest expense, net of tax}}{\text{Average total assets}}$ | $\dfrac{150 + 20 \times (1 - 0.4)}{0.5 \times (4110 + 3550)}$ | 4.2% | 3,1% |
| Return on sales | $\dfrac{\text{Net income + Interest expense, net of tax}}{\text{Net sales}}$ | $\dfrac{150 + 20 \times (1 - 0.4)}{25000}$ | 0.6% | 0.4% |
| Asset turnover ratio | $\dfrac{\text{Net sales}}{\text{Average total assets}}$ | $\dfrac{25000}{0.5 \times (4110 + 3550)}$ | 6.53 | 6.58 |
| Return on common stockholders' equity | $\dfrac{\text{Net income - Preferred dividends}}{\text{Average common stockholders' equity}}$ | $\dfrac{150}{0.5 \times (2340 + 2250)}$ | 6.53% | 3.7% |
| Earnings per share | $\dfrac{\text{Net income - Preferred dividends}}{\text{Weighted average no. of common shares outstanding}}$ | $\dfrac{150}{4000}$ | 3.75 cents | 2.1 cents |
| Price-earnings ratio | $\dfrac{\text{Current market price}}{\text{Earnings per share}}$ | $\dfrac{75 \text{ cents}}{3.75 \text{ cents}}$ | 20 times | 27 times |
| Dividend payout ratio | $\dfrac{\text{Common dividends per share}}{\text{Earnings per share}}$ | $\dfrac{1.5 \text{ cents}}{3.75 \text{ cents}}$ | 0.4 | 0.6 |
| Dividend yield ratio | $\dfrac{\text{Common dividends per share}}{\text{Market price per share}}$ | $\dfrac{1.5 \text{ cents}}{75 \text{ cents}}$ | 2.0% | 2.4% |

# Review of Key Terms

| | |
|---|---|
| **Accounts receivable turnover ratio** | A measure of the number of times accounts receivable are collected in a period. |
| **Acid-test or quick ratio** | A stricter test of liquidity than the current ratio that excludes inventory and prepayments from the numerator. |
| **Asset turnover ratio** | The relationship between net sales and average total assets. |
| **Cash flows from operations to capital expenditures ratio** | A measure of the ability of a company to finance long-term asset acquisitions from cash from operations. |
| **Cash flows from operations to current liabilities ratio** | A measure of the ability to pay current debts from operating cash flows. |
| **Cash-to-cash operating cycle** | The length of time from the purchase of inventory to the collection of any receivable from the sale. |
| **Current ratio** | The ratio of current assets to current liabilities. |
| **Debt service coverage ratio** | A statement of cash flows measure of the ability of a company to meet its interest and principal payments. |
| **Debt-to-equity ratio** | The ratio of total liabilities to total stockholders' equity. |
| **Dividend payout ratio** | The percentage of earnings paid out as dividends. |
| **Dividend yield ratio** | The relationship between dividends and market price of a company's stock. |
| **Earnings per share** | A company's bottom line stated on a per-share basis. |
| **Gross profit ratio** | Gross profit to net sales. |
| **Horizontal analysis** | A comparison of financial statement items over a period of time. |
| **Inventory turnover ratio** | A measure of the number of times inventory is sold during a period. |
| **Leverage** | The use of borrowed funds and amounts contributed by preferred stockholders to earn an overall return higher than the cost of these funds. |
| **Liquidity** | The nearness to cash of the assets and liabilities. |
| **Number of days' sales in inventory** | A measure of how long it takes to sell inventory. |
| **Number of days' sales in receivables** | A measure of the average age of accounts receivable. |
| **Price-earnings ratio** | The relationship between a company's performance in the income statement compared with its performance in the stock market. |
| **Profit margin ratio** | Net income to net sales. |
| **Profitability** | How well management is using company resources to earn a return on the funds invested by various groups. |
| **Return on assets ratio** | A measure of a company's success in earning a return for all providers of capital. |
| **Return on sales ratio** | A variation of the profit margin ratio; it measures earnings before payments to creditors. |
| **Return on common stockholders' equity ratio** | A measure of a company's success in earning a return for the common stockholders. |
| **Solvency** | The ability of a company to remain in business over the long term. |

| Times interest earned ratio | An income statement measure of the ability of a company to meet its interest payments. |
| Vertical analysis | A comparison of various financial statement items within a single period with the use of common-size statements. |
| Working capital | Current assets minus current liabilities. |

## Practice Test
## Questions and Problems

### Circle the alternative that best answers the question:

**LO 4**  1.  Which of the following ratios is most likely to be specified in a debt covenant requiring adequate liquidity to be maintained?
   a)  Debt-to-equity ratio
   b)  Quick ratio
   c)  Asset turnover ratio
   d)  Earnings per share

**LO 4,5** 2.  Which of the following ratios is immediately affected by a stock repurchase?
   a)  Dividend payout ratio
   b)  Debt-to-equity ratio
   c)  Gross profit ratio
   d)  Inventory turnover ratio

**LO 6**  3.  Corporation A and Company B have price-earnings ratios of 18 and 35 respectively. Which of the following cannot be concluded from the companies having different price-earnings ratios?
   a)  A's stock price is lower than B's and its earnings are higher.
   b)  B's stock price is expected to grow faster than A's, though their earnings are currently identical.
   c)  A and B's stock prices are identical, but B has low earnings in the current year because of an extraordinary loss.
   d)  A is a better bargain than B since both companies' earnings are identical but A's stock price is cheaper.

**LO 2**  4.  Which of the following types of analysis is most useful in comparing the accounts of two companies of very different sizes?
   a)  Horizontal analysis
   b)  Vertical analysis
   c)  Comparisons with industry norms
   d)  Comparisons with data for the economy as a whole

**LO 3**  5.  Which of the following calculations would be carried out in a vertical analysis?
   a)  Accounts receivable is calculated as a percentage of total assets.
   b)  The difference over two years between the net book value of fixed assets is calculated as a percentage of the first year's fixed assets book value.
   c)  Current assets are expressed as a percentage of current liabilities.
   d)  Net credit sales are expressed as a percentage of average accounts receivable.

*Use the following summary information from Beta Company's financial statements for its first and second years of operations to answer questions 6 through 8.*

| Beta Company ($000's) | Year ended Dec. 31, Year 2 | Year ended Dec. 31, Year 1 |
|---|---|---|
| Sales | $1,400 | $1,000 |
| Cost of sales | 1,200 | 800 |
| Net income | 50 | 40 |
| Current assets | 800 | 650 |
| Current liabilities | 700 | 500 |
| Inventories | 500 | 400 |
| Cash and marketable securities | 100 | 130 |

**LO 4,6** 6. Which of the following statements is false?
   a) Although sales increased, both the gross profit ratio and the profit margin ratio declined during Year 2.
   b) Sales, gross margin, and net income either were unchanged or increased in Year 2.
   c) Working capital increased in Year 2.
   d) Inventories were a smaller percentage of current assets in Year 1 than in Year 2.

**LO 4** 7. The current ratio for Year 2 is:
   a) 1.143
   b) 0.625
   c) 0.143
   d) 0.714

**LO 4** 8. The inventory turnover ratio in Year 2 is:
   a) 2.4
   b) 2.67
   c) 3.0
   d) 3.11

**LO 5** 9. The company announces a stock dividend. The effect on the debt-to-equity ratio is:
   a) an increase.
   b) a decrease.
   c) no change.

**LO 4** 10. Beta Company increased the credit period allowed to customers. The increase in the credit period would:
   a) increase working capital.
   b) decrease accounts receivable turnover.
   c) increase cost of sales.
   d) increase debt-to-equity ratio.

**LO 5** 11. Alpha and Beta are identical companies except that Alpha's debt-to-equity ratio is 4:1, and Beta's debt-to-equity ratio is 1:1. Which of the following statements is true?
   a) Alpha's return on stockholders' equity can be expected to be lower than Beta's.
   b) Alpha is less risky than Beta.
   c) Alpha's inventory turnover can be expected to be higher than Beta's.
   d) Alpha's times interest earned ratio will be expected to be lower than Beta's.

**LO 5** 12. Jalama Jugs Inc. have a debt-to-equity ratio of 3:1 on December 31, 2002, and a debt-to-equity ratio of 2:1 on December 31, 2001. Which of the following transactions, taken alone, could result in that change in the debt-to-equity ratio?

 a) Jalama repaid bonds during 2002.

 b) Jalama paid a large cash dividend during 2002.

 c) Jalama issued common stock during 2002.

 d) Jalama paid interest on bonds during 2002, but overall had positive net income.

**LO 4** 13. Jalama Jugs Inc. have a quick ratio of 1:1 on December 31, 2002, and a quick ratio of 0.5:1 on December 31, 2001. Which of the following could result in that change in the quick ratio?

 a) Jalama's cash balance increased over the year.

 b) Jalama's accounts payable decreases.

 c) Jalama's accounts receivable increases.

 d) All of the above.

**LO 6** 14. On March 31, 1999, Field Flowers Corporation has a year-to-date return on assets of 8% and a return on sales of 2%. Field's asset turnover is:

 a) 16 times.

 b) 8 times.

 c) 0.25 times.

 d) 4 times.

**LO 6** 15. For the years ended December 31, 2002 and 2001, Solvang Danish Corporation has gross profit margins of 15% and 10%, and profit margin ratios of 3% and 5% respectively. Total revenues in each year were identical. Which of the following is consistent with this scenario?

 a) Cost of sales was higher in 2002 than in 2001, and selling, general, and administrative costs were lower in 2002 than in 2001.

 b) Cost of sales was lower in 2002 than in 2001, and selling, general, and administrative costs were higher in 2002 than in 2001.

 c) Cost of sales was higher in 2002 than in 2001, and selling, general, and administrative costs were identical in 2002 and in 2001.

 d) Cost of sales was identical in 2002 than in 2001, and selling, general, and administrative costs were higher in 2002 and in 2001.

## Indicate whether each of the following statements is true or false:

**LO 2** 16. Horizontal analysis allows significant changes across time to be identified.

**LO 1** 17. Changes in the accounting principles of a company can be ignored when performance is being analyzed over time.

**LO 3** 18. Inflation can result in performance appearing better than it actually is.

**LO 4** 19. Common size statements are most useful if the companies being compared are of similar size.

**LO 4** 20. The quick assets ratio and the current ratio both indicate ability to stay in business in the long term.

LO 4   21. Turnover ratios indicate the level of activity in a particular area, the higher the ratio, the higher the level of activity.

LO 4   22. If the current ratio increases over a period, then working capital also increases.

LO 5   23. Return on assets can be analyzed into return on sales and asset turnover.

LO 5   24. Even though debt is a cheaper form of financing than equity, a company that has high levels of debt may be jeopardizing its ability to stay in business in the long term.

LO 3   25. Vertical analysis involves relating balances in the balance sheet to their related income statement item.

LO 5   26. When a company issues stock for cash, its debt-to-equity ratio decreases.

LO 4   27. When a company issues stock for cash, its quick ratio increases.

LO 6   28. When a company issues debt for cash, its gross profit increases.

LO 4   29. When a company has a stock split, its current ratio is unaffected.

LO 6   30. When a company pays interest on its bonds, its profit margin ratio decreases.

## Complete each of the following statements:

LO 6   31. The net income attributable to each share of common stock is known as the

_____.

*Use the following information to answer questions 32 through 36:*

| Beezo Corporation Selected financial information | Year ended Dec. 31, Year 2 | Year ended Dec. 31, Year 1 |
|---|---|---|
| Net income | $ 300,000 | $ 200,000 |
| Interest expense | 50,000 | 40,000 |
| Total liabilities | 1,000,000 | 700,000 |
| Total stockholders' equity | 1,300,000 | 1,000,000 |
| Net sales | 1,000,000 | 800,000 |

Beezo's marginal tax rate is 40%.

LO 5   32. Beezo's interest expense net of tax for Year 2 is _____.

LO 5   33. Beezo's average assets over Year 2 is _____.

LO 5   34. Beezo's return on sales for Year 2 is _____.

LO 5   35. Beezo's asset turnover for Year 2 is _____.

LO 5   36. Beezo's return on assets for Year 2 is _____.

**LO 5**  37. The ratio that indicates a company's ability to meet current year's interest payments out of current year's earnings is _____.

**LO 4**  38. For a retailer or wholesaler, the average length of time between the purchase of merchandise for sale and the eventual collection of cash from the sale is called the _____.

**LO 5**  39. A company can reduce its _____ ratio by retiring debt and issuing additional stock.

**LO 4**  40. _____ turnover can be improved by adopting more stringent credit policies for customers.

**LO 3**  41. _____ is a comparison of various financial statement items within a single period with the use of common-size statements.

**LO 4**  42. _____ is a measure of the ability of a company to finance long-term asset acquisitions from cash from operations.

**LO 4**  43. _____ is a measure of the ability to pay current debts from operating cash flows.

**LO 5**  44. The ability of a company to remain in business over the long term is called _____.

**LO 6**  45. _____ indicates how well management is using company resources to earn a return on the funds invested by the various groups.

## Answer each of the following problems:

LO 2,3   46. The income statement of Little Green Inc., a computer manufacturer, for the three years 2000 through 2002 is given below.

**Little Green Inc.**
**Statement of earnings**

| $ in millions                Year ended | December 31, 2002 | December 31, 2001 | December 31, 2000 |
|---|---|---|---|
| Revenue | $  64,523 | $  64,766 | $  68,931 |
| Cost of sales | 35,069 | 32,073 | 30,715 |
| **Gross profit** | 29,454 | 32,693 | 38,216 |
| Operating expenses | | | |
| Selling, general, and administrative | - 19,526 | - 21,375 | - 20,709 |
| Research, development, and engineering | - 6,522 | - 6,644 | - 6,554 |
| Restructuring charges | - 11,645 | - 3,735 | -0- |
| | - 37,693 | - 31,754 | - 27,263 |
| **Operating income** | - 8,239 | 939 | 10,953 |
| Other income, principally interest | 573 | 602 | 495 |
| Interest expense | - 1,360 | - 1,423 | - 1,324 |
| **Earnings before income taxes** | - 9,026 | 118 | 10,124 |
| Provision for income taxes | 2,161 | - 716 | - 4,157 |
| **Net earnings before changes in accounting principles** | - 6,865 | - 598 | - 5,967 |
| Effect of changes in accounting principles | 1,900 | - 2,263 | -0- |
| **Net earnings** | $ - 4,965 | $ - 2,861 | $  5,967 |

**Required**

1.      Prepare a horizontal analysis of Little Green for the three years.

2.      Prepare a vertical analysis of Little Green for the three years.

3.      On the basis of your analysis, comment on Little Green's profitability for the three years.

4.      When Little Green announced its results for 2002, the stock price of Little Green increased. Can you think of an explanation of why such a massive loss should result in an increase in stock price?

**LO 4,5** 47. For each of the transactions listed below, indicate the immediate effect on each of the following: debt-to-equity ratio, current ratio, and profit margin. Use + to indicate an increase, - to indicate a decrease, ? to indicate an indeterminate effect, and 0 to indicate no effect. Assume an initial current ratio of more than 1-to-1.

| | | Debt-to-equity ratio | Current ratio | Profit margin ratio |
|---|---|---|---|---|
| 1. | Cash is acquired through issue of additional common stock. | | | |
| 2. | Federal income tax due for the previous year is paid. | | | |
| 3. | A fixed asset is sold for cash at less than book value. | | | |
| 4. | Merchandise is sold on credit at a loss. | | | |
| 5. | Payment is made to trade creditors for previous purchases. | | | |
| 6 | A cash dividend is declared and paid. | | | |
| 7. | Short-term notes receivable are sold at a discount. | | | |
| 8. | A profitable firm increases its fixed assets depreciation allowance account. | | | |
| 9. | Trading securities are sold below the fair value shown in the balance sheet. | | | |
| 10. | Ten-year notes are issued to pay off accounts payable. | | | |
| 11. | A wholly depreciated asset is retired. | | | |
| 12. | Accounts receivable are collected. | | | |
| 13. | A stock dividend is declared and paid. | | | |
| 14. | Equipment is purchased with short-term notes. | | | |
| 15. | 35% of the common stock of another firm is acquired by the issue of additional common stock and accounted for by the equity method. | | | |

## Critical Thinking Problem

**LO 4,5** 48.  The Goleta Fruit Company was established on January 1, Year 1, and the
following information is available for its first year of operations:

| | |
|---|---|
| Net income | $60,000 |
| Accounts payable | $30,000 |
| Short-term notes payable | $70,000 |
| Return on sales | 20% |
| Gross profit ratio | 60% |
| Quick ratio | 100% |
| Receivables turnover | 10 |
| Inventory turnover | 6 |

All sales and purchases were on credit. Accounts payable and short-term notes payable are the
only current liabilities at year-end. Cash and cash equivalents, inventory and accounts receivable
are the only current assets at year-end.

**Required**
Find the following for Year 1.
1.  Sales revenue

2.  Gross margin

3.  Cost of sales

4. Year-end inventory

5. Purchases

6. Cash paid to creditors

7.   Year-end receivables

8.   Cash received from customers

9.   Year-end cash balance

10.  Year-end current ratio

## Solutions

### Multiple Choice

| | | | |
|----|---|-----|---|
| 1. | b | 9. | c |
| 2. | b | 10. | b |
| 3. | d | 11. | d |
| 4. | b | 12. | b |
| 5. | a | 13. | d |
| 6. | c | 14. | d |
| 7. | a | 15. | b |
| 8. | b | | |

### True/False

**COMMENT/EXPLANATION**

16. True

17. False — Changes in accounting principles can have a significant impact on both the income statement and the balance sheet. These changes should be considered when analyzing a period in which a change in accounting principle took place.

18. True

19. False — Common-size statements allow companies of different sizes to be meaningfully compared since each income statement figure is expressed as a percentage of sales and each balance sheet figure is expressed as a percentage of total assets.

20. False — Both the quick assets ratio and the current ratio are measures of liquidity, which indicates the ability of the company to meet short-term obligations.

21. True

22. True — If the current ratio increased over a period, then current assets increased more than current liabilities. Working capital, which is the difference between current assets and current liabilities, therefore must also have increased over the period.

23. True

24. True

25. False — In a vertical analysis, each income statement figure is expressed as a percentage of sales and each balance sheet figure is expressed as a percentage of total assets.

26. True

27. True

28. False — Issuing debt has no immediate impact on profitability.

29. True

30. True

## Fill in the Blanks

31. earnings per share
32. $30,000
33. $2,000,000
34. 33%

35. 0.5
36. 16.5%
37. times interest earned ratio
38. cash-to-cash operating cycle

39. debt-to-equity
40. receivables
41. vertical analysis
42. cash flows from operations to capital expenditure ratio
43. cash flows from operations to current liabilities
44. solvency
45. profitability

## Problem 46

1. **Horizontal analysis**
**% Change from previous year**

| Year ended | Dec. 31, 2002 | Dec. 31, 2001 |
|---|---|---|
| Revenue | -0.38% | -6.04% |
| Cost of sales | 9.34% | 4.42% |
| **Gross profit** | -9.91% | -14.45% |
| Operating expenses | | |
| Selling, general and administrative | -8.65% | 3.22% |
| Research, development and engineering | -1.84% | 1.37% |
| Restructuring charges | 211.78% | ∞ |
| | | |
| **Operating income** | -977.42% | -91.43% |
| Other income, principally interest | -4.82% | 21.62% |
| Interest expense | -4.43% | 7.48% |
| **Earnings before income taxes** | -7749.15% | -98.83% |
| Provision for income taxes | 401.82% | -82.78% |
| **Net earnings before changes in accounting principles** | -1047.99% | -89.98% |
| Effect of changes in accounting principles | -183.96% | ∞ |
| **Net earnings** | -73.54% | -147.75% |

2.      **Vertical analysis**

| Year ended | Dec. 31, 2002 | Dec. 31, 2001 | Dec. 31, 2000 |
|---|---|---|---|
| Revenue | 100% | 100% | 100% |
| Cost of sales | 54.35% | 49.52% | 44.56% |
| **Gross profit** | 45.65% | 50.48% | 55.44% |
| Operating expenses | | | |
| Selling, general and administrative | -30.26% | -33% | -30.04% |
| Research, development and engineering | -10.11% | -10.26% | -9.51% |
| Restructuring charges | -18.05% | -5.77% | 0 |
| | -58.42% | -49.03% | -39.55% |
| **Operating income** | -12.77% | 1.45% | 15.89% |
| Other income, principally interest | 0.89% | 0.93% | 0.72% |
| Interest expense | -2.11% | -2.2% | -1.92% |
| **Earnings before income taxes** | -13.99% | 0.18% | 14.69% |
| Provision for income taxes | 3.35% | -1.11% | -6.03% |
| **Net earnings before changes in accounting principles** | -10.64% | -0.92% | 8.66% |
| Effect of changes in accounting principles | 2.94% | -3.49% | 0 |
| **Net earnings** | -7.69% | -4.42% | 8.66% |

3.      Little Green's results over the three years are dominated by the massive restructuring charges for 2002 and 2001. These charges include the costs of both divesting Little Green of unprofitable divisions and downsizing staff numbers. From the vertical analysis, we can see that the gross profit margin declined over the three years but that selling and research and development costs stayed relatively stable. From the horizontal analysis we can see that revenues declined and that costs rose, resulting in the drop in gross margins observed above. Overall, however, the restructuring charges are the dominant feature of these three years' results.

4.      Stock prices reflect expectations about the future. The fact that the stock price rose on the announcement of 2002's results suggests that expectations about the company improved. One possible explanation is that the large restructuring charges were a signal to investors that Little Green's management was addressing some of the problems that the company had been experiencing over a number of years. Although in the short term the large restructuring costs led to losses, in the long run they would result in a more streamlined, efficient, and profitable company.

## Problem 47

| | | Debt-to-equity ratio | Current ratio | Profit margin ratio |
|---|---|---|---|---|
| 1. | Cash is acquired through issue of additional common stock. | – | + | 0 |
| 2. | Federal income tax due for the previous year is paid. | – | – | 0 |
| 3. | A fixed asset is sold for less than book value. | + | + | – |
| 4. | Merchandise is sold on credit at a loss. | + | – | – |
| 5. | Payment is made to trade creditors for previous purchases. | – | – | 0 |
| 6 | A cash dividend is declared and paid. | + | – | 0 |
| 7. | Short-term notes receivable are sold at a discount. | + | – | – |
| 8. | A profitable firm increases its fixed assets depreciation allowance account. | + | 0 | – |
| 9. | Trading securities are sold below the fair value shown in the balance sheet. | + | – | – |
| 10. | Ten-year notes are issued to pay off accounts payable. | 0 | + | 0 |
| 11. | A wholly depreciated asset is retired. | 0 | 0 | 0 |
| 12. | Accounts receivable are collected. | 0 | 0 | 0 |
| 13. | A stock dividend is declared and paid. | 0 | 0 | 0 |
| 14. | Equipment is purchased with short-term notes. | + | – | 0 |
| 15. | 35% of the common stock of another firm is acquired by the issue of additional common stock and accounted for by the equity method. | – | 0 | 0 |

## Critical Thinking Problem 48

1.  Return on sales  $=$  $\dfrac{\text{Net income}}{\text{Sales}}$

    20%  $=$  $\dfrac{\$60,000}{\text{Sales}}$

    Sales  $=$  $\dfrac{\$60,000}{20\%}$

    Sales  $=$  $\$300,000$

2.  Gross margin = 60% x Sales

    = 60% x $300,000

    = $180,000

3.  Gross margin = Sales - Cost of sales

    Cost of sales = Sales - Gross margin

    = $300,000 - $180,000

    = $120,000

4.  Inventory turnover = $\dfrac{\text{Cost of sales}}{\text{Average inventory}}$

    Average inventory = $\dfrac{\text{Cost of sales}}{\text{Inventory turnover}}$

    Average inventory = $\dfrac{\$120,000}{6}$

    = $20,000

    = 0.5 x (Opening inventory + Closing inventory)

    and Opening inventory = $0

    so Closing inventory = $40,000

5.

| Inventory | | | |
|---|---|---|---|
| Jan. 1 | 0 | | |
| **Purchases** | **160,000** | 120,000 | Cost of sales |
| Dec. 31 | 40,000 | | |

6.

| Accounts payable | | | |
|---|---|---|---|
| | | 0 | Jan. 1 |
| **Cash to creditors 130,000** | | 160,000 | Purchases |
| | | 30,000 | Dec. 31 |

7.  Receivables turnover = $\dfrac{\text{Sales}}{\text{Average accounts receivable}}$

    Average accounts receivable = $\dfrac{\text{Sales}}{\text{Receivables turnover}}$

    = $\dfrac{\$300,000}{10}$

    = $30,000

    Ending accounts receivable = $60,000

8.

| Accounts receivable | | | |
|---|---|---|---|
| Jan. 1 | 0 | | |
| Sales | 300,000 | **240,000** | **Cash received from customers** |
| Dec. 31 | 60,000 | | |

9. Quick ratio $=$ $\dfrac{\text{Cash + Accounts receivable}}{\text{Current liabilities}}$

Cash + Accounts receivable $=$ Quick ratio x Current liabilities

$=$ Quick ratio x (Accounts payable + Notes payable)

$=$ 100% x ($30,000 + $70,000)

$=$ $100,000

Cash $=$ $100,000 - Accounts receivable

$=$ $100,000 - $60,000

$=$ $40,000

10. Current ratio $=$ $\dfrac{\text{Current assets}}{\text{Current liabilities}}$

$=$ $\dfrac{\text{Cash + Inventory + Accounts receivable}}{\text{Current liabilities}}$

$=$ $\dfrac{\$40,000 + \$40,000 + \$60,000}{\$30,000 + \$70,000}$

$=$ 1.4:1